Database Law

Anirban Mazumder

Database Law

Perspectives from India

Springer

Anirban Mazumder
West Bengal National University of Juridical
Sciences
Kolkata
India

ISBN 978-981-10-2199-2 ISBN 978-981-10-2200-5 (eBook)
DOI 10.1007/978-981-10-2200-5

Library of Congress Control Number: 2016947025

Printed on acid-free paper

This Springer imprint is published by Springer Nature
The registered company is Springer Science+Business Media Singapore Pte Ltd.

Foreword

Database industry is a new entrant to the knowledge society driven by the information and communication revolution, breaking down traditional knowledge systems, territorial barriers and regulatory arrangements. Who owns it and how it is controlled are not clear except to those who are involved in production and distribution of databases. With developments in technology, the database industry is undergoing phenomenal growth, the implications of which cannot be predicted even by experts in the field. There is certainly a need to protect rights over information products; at the same time there is greater need to provide access to electronic databases if the industry were to serve the public interest in the knowledge-driven developmental processes. Nations are looking for an appropriate legal framework which on the one hand, will encourage the industry to grow and compete, while on the other serve public interest in improved access and quality. In this mission, Dr. Anirban Mazumder's work is a pioneering one and is likely to influence policy making in several jurisdictions.

In six chapters lucidly written in a manner that laymen can also understand, the author examines information as property in the changing socio-economic concept of property itself. He goes on to analyse the application of copyright law as an appropriate instrument for protection of databases, keeping in mind the public versus private controversy and the requirement of originality as a key element in copyright law. The question is raised on how much of regulation is appropriate to create a balance between access and abuse. Giving monopoly rights on information and information products will certainly inhibit societal interests. Can the balance between proprietary interests on information products and public interests on access and quality be achieved by market forces or technology itself? Can the principles of copyright law respond adequately to the challenges involved? This is the question the author tries to answer in Chap. 3 under the heading 'Copyright Law, Databases and its Protection'. According to the author, courts have tried out various standards with no certainty on whether the originality test can serve the purpose. It is felt that competition law, contract law and technological tools can to some extent achieve desirable protection of databases.

Chapters 4 and 5 are devoted to critical analysis of the European experience in database protection and the several legislative attempts in this regard made in the USA. According to the learned writer 'the European Union Directive is not clear in its scope and do not have an established interpretation in the copyright law'. A similar uncertainty in securing an effective balance between protection and access of databases remains in the US system as well.

The major contribution of the work is in looking at Indian aspirations, its present legal regime on database rights and the suggestions for a new legal framework advanced by the author to meet the aspirations. The author admits the key role of state interventions in India including the Traditional Knowledge Digital Library and Information Technology Act of 2000. However, the challenge for a right balance remains for which the author proposes ten guidelines for policy planners to consider. It includes incorporation in the new law a *sui generis* right to non-original databases and copyright on original databases. Government oversight is necessary to ensure fair use and public interest protection. For this mandatory registration before commercial exploitation of database right is desirable. The emphasis in the new law should be more on progress of commerce rather than expression of ideas. The new legislation according to the proposed guidelines must differentiate between different types of databases and offer protection only for those created for commercial markets. The privacy law is considered enough to address wrongs committed against private databases.

For commercial databases, the guidelines suggest provision for fair use and compulsory licensing for protecting public interest. The creators of commercial databases, the author contends, should be allowed to commercially exploit their product and prevent unauthorized access and utilization. They should be allowed to use both contractual and technological measures to achieve the desired goal. Time limit to be prescribed under the new legislation can be based on the time, effort and cost invested in creating the database provided it gives a short period of protection to the creator by offering commercial head start over competitors.

The research that has gone into the writing of this book is impressive going by the extensive bibliography cited and the exhaustive analysis done on different models of regulation now in place in different countries. Having given the detailed guidelines for the new legislation, one would normally expect the author, who is an experienced law teacher, to have given the draft legislation itself as an appendix to this book. The government now will be well advised to invite the author to collaborate with the draftsmen in shaping the new legislation for database protection while promoting its fair use and commercial exploitation. India can give a head start to the database industry given the leadership it commands over information technology applications and innovations.

I congratulate Prof. Anirban Mazumder for writing this book on a difficult theme of wide contemporary interest, perhaps the first of its kind in the subject. I wish him many more years of scholarly achievements in his academic journey.

May 2016

Prof. (Dr.) N.R. Madhava Menon
Chancellor, Gum Ghazidas Central University
Chattisgarh;
Chairman, Menon Institute of Legal Advocacy Training
Trivandrum;
Former VC, National Law School of India University
Bangalore;
National University of Juridical Sciences
Kolkata;
Former Director, National Judicial Academy
Bhopal;
Chancellor, NUEPA
New Delhi

Preface

India enjoys the unique combination of a knowledge society and phenomenal growth in information technology which results in generating massive informational products. In such a situation, a state's law is expected to offer minimum incentive in generating such products, keeping robustness of public domain intact. This manuscript is a step towards this direction.

Chapter 1 analyses information as property and examines its features. Information has become a very valuable resource in today's society. It has an impact on the economic, social and cultural spheres of a nation because of its great utility. However, if this information is regulated strictly and access is restricted to only certain groups of consumers, there will be a divide in the information market.

Information that is of public interest and in the public domain is of immense value to people and therefore sensitive to monopolization. This has especially been felt with the use of intellectual property right in protecting databases. It was anticipated that IPR in databases would effectively restrict free flow of information and become an obstacle to the advancement of science, research and society. Thus Chap. 2 displays the interaction between information and intellectual property.

Chapter 3 critically examines pros and cons of copyright law in offering protection to databases. The protection of databases by copyright law is an issue under great debate. Protecting information as property has proved to be extremely difficult due to the lack of exclusivity of possession and enjoyment. Copyright law has, however, maintained a balance between rewarding an author's efforts and making information accessible to the society for its advancement.

The European Union adopted a Directive on Legal Protection of Databases to protect non-original databases, both in electronic and paper form. Protection under the Directive can be renewed in case of a substantial change in the existing database. The Directive also allows creators to prevent extraction and reutilization of full or substantial part of the database. In both Europe and USA, the general concern of securing effective balance between protection and access to databases, however, remains. The comparative analysis of European and American model of protection of databases have been the focus of Chaps. 4 and 5.

The focus of Chap. 6 is to develop a road map for India. The growth of digital technology has contributed to an exponential growth in the information industry, which has positively influenced not only compilation of information but also its dissemination. Legislations like the Information Technology Act 2000 have come up as an added protection for electronic databases in India. The new legislation must balance between private interest and public right while ensuring commercial need of database producers, access to information and prevention of unfair competition.

This book, being one of the pioneering publications on database law in India, will help bridge the gap in existing literature on database and intellectual property law and will hopefully pave the way for many more such books in future.

I especially acknowledge the support of the Max Planck Institute for Intellectual Property, Munich, in offering me a scholarship to conduct this study. I am extremely grateful to my teacher, Prof. Dr. N.S. Gopalkrishnan, for guiding me to do this research. I take this opportunity to express my gratitude to Prof. Dr. N.R. Madhava Menon for his constant support and for writing the foreword of this book. This work would not have been possible without the support and encouragement of my three Vice Chancellors, Prof. Dr. B.S. Chimni, Prof. Dr. M.P. Singh and Prof. Dr. P. Ishwara Bhat. I have no words to express my indebtedness to my mother and my wife for continuously encouraging me to complete this work. My son Apratim is the source of my energy and the guiding star in my life. I am thankful to my students Mr. Tapabrata Mukherjee and Ms. Arpita Sengupta for the formatting work they have done. I am equally thankful to Ms. Sneha Singh for proof reading the manuscript. I need to record my thanks to Ms. Sagarika Ghosh and Ms. Nupoor Singh of Springer for taking me through the journey of publication.

I dedicate this book to my father, Late Pijush Kanti Mazumder, who himself was a judge and who introduced me to the legal education—*'Pita swarga, Pita dharma, Pita hi Paramang Tapo: Pitori pritima pannay. Priyantay sarva devata'*.

Kolkata Anirban Mazumder
Buddha Purnima 2016

Contents

1 Information, Property and Protection 1
1.1 Role of Information in Today's World 1
1.2 Justification for Protection 2
1.3 Changing Features of Property 3
1.4 Information as Property 6
1.5 Tangibility and Intangibility 10
1.6 Private and Public Interest 11

2 Copyright, Access and Information Society 15
2.1 Copyright Protection and Public/Private Interest 15
2.2 Copyright and Access to Information 18
2.3 Copyright and Free Speech 23
2.4 Copyright and Incentive for Investment 25
2.5 Requirement of Originality in Copyright Law 36

3 Copyright Law, Databases and Its Protection 41
3.1 Analysis of Copyright Law 41
3.1.1 Objectives of Copyright 41
3.1.2 Interpreting Originality in Copyright 43
3.1.3 Originality—Traditional Approach 44
3.1.4 Changing Notion of Originality 44
3.1.5 Traditional V. Modern Approach 45
3.1.6 Sweat of the Brow Doctrine 46
3.1.7 Rationale for Sweat Doctrine 47
3.1.8 Origin of Sweat Doctrine 48
3.1.9 Implication of Sweat Doctrine 49
3.1.10 Fall of Sweat Doctrine 50
3.1.11 Is Sweat Doctrine Still Valid? 50
3.1.12 Fallacies of Sweat Doctrine 53
3.1.13 Application of the Sweat Doctrine in India 56

3.2 Impact on Copyright Law . . . 57
3.3 Impact of the Feist Judgment on Copyright Law . . . 59
3.4 Impact on Databases . . . 59
3.5 Importance of Copyright in Protecting Databases . . . 69
3.6 Position of Database v. Protection . . . 74
3.7 Role of Competition Law in Maintaining Balance . . . 86

4 Database Protection: European Experience . . . 99
4.1 Role of Database Directive in Protecting Database . . . 99
4.1.1 Definition of Database . . . 101
4.1.2 Substantial Investment . . . 102
4.1.3 Creation, Extraction and Reutilization . . . 104
4.1.4 Exceptions . . . 107
4.1.5 Term of Protection . . . 107
4.2 Role of Database Directive in Limiting Monopoly . . . 108
4.3 Evaluation of Database Directive . . . 113
4.4 BHB Factor . . . 124

5 Aborted American Attempts . . . 129
5.1 Definition of Database . . . 130
5.2 Unauthorised Use . . . 130
5.3 Investment . . . 131
5.4 Infringement . . . 131
5.5 Permitted Use . . . 132
5.6 Penalty . . . 133
5.7 Duration . . . 133
5.8 Review . . . 134
5.9 Comparison . . . 134
5.10 Comments . . . 135
5.11 Effects . . . 136
5.12 Concluding Remarks . . . 137

6 Indian Database Industry and Its Aspirations and Existing Legal Regime . . . 139
6.1 Indian Database Industry . . . 139
6.2 Response of Indian Database Industry . . . 141
6.3 Existing Legal Regime in India . . . 142
6.3.1 Nineteenth Century . . . 143
6.3.2 Twentieth Century . . . 144
6.3.3 Twenty First Century . . . 148
6.4 Principles for New Legislation . . . 149

Conclusion . . . 151

Bibliography . . . 157

About the Author

Dr. Anirban Mazumder a graduate of Calcutta University, received his LL.B. from The University of Burdwan, West Bengal, India. He went on to complete his masters in Law from the National Law School of India University, Bangalore, and his M. Phil from the National University of Juridical Sciences, Kolkata, India, from where he also obtained his Ph.D.

He specializes in Intellectual Property Law and Information Technology Law, teaching both subjects at the undergraduate and graduate levels. Dr. Mazumder, a Fellow of the Max Plank Institute for Intellectual Property, Munich, has been a Visiting Scholar at the Touro Law School, New York University, USA, and Cardiff University, Wales, UK. He has also been a Cegla Scholar at Tel Aviv University, Israel.

He is the Principal Investigator in both a UGC Major Research Project and a Judicial Academy Project, and is a Visiting Professor at the Maulana Abul Kalam Azad University of Technology, West Bengal, and International Management Institute-Kolkata.

Dr. Mazumder is one of the members of the Expert Committee on Utility Model, constituted by the Department of Industrial Policy and Promotion, Ministry of Commerce, Govt. of India. He is also a member of the Copyright Enforcement Advisory Council, constituted by the Ministry of Human Resource Development, Govt. of India.

Introduction

Information is considered as power in the digital age. Creation, manipulation and use of information are major activities of developed societies. Information has always played a very important role in developing economy of a country. Information has its own value but once it is collected, organized, assessed, preserved and presented in a methodical way, its value gets multiplied and this is precisely the function of a database. Database is defined as a collection of works or materials arranged, stored and assessed methodically. The business of database is a voluminous one as it involves information which is important, voluminous and easily accessible.

In the agricultural age, law facilitated the use and ownership of land. In the industrial age, law influenced ownership of industry. Likewise in information age, law is expected to facilitate use and ownership of information. Law being an instrument which regulates market has a vital role in shaping up the database industry. The investment of time and energy in selection, collection, arrangement and presentation of information justifies the protection of the outcome.[1] Along with its business perspective, information and database contribute to development of sciences and legal system. Information being a tool to be used regularly in the day-to-day life, any attempt to regulate the access and use of information may be counterproductive.[2] As different aspects of life is influenced by databases, so law must step forward in governing social, economical and political issues relating to databases.

The history has witnessed significant changes in copyright laws. The shift from the traditional concept of originality, requiring merely an independent creation, to a higher standard, requiring at least a minimal degree of creativity, is not without

[1]Rees C, Chalton S (1998) Database Law. Jordans, p 1.

[2]Biotechnology companies are locking and withholding access to much of their information as they believe that law does not protect their investment. This obstacle to academic usage of these databases will shrink the public domain. Shulman S (1999) Owning the Future, Houghton Mifflin p 240. In: Greenbaum D S (2003) The Database Debate: In Support of an Inequitable Solution. Alb L J of Sci and Tech. 13:431.

its implication. The negation of the sweat of the brow doctrine, through which copyright would subsist in works created by the mere application of labour, has greatly influenced the database industry. Since most countries including India are realizing the impact of this doctrine, it becomes important to study its rise and fall and its impact on the database industry. The application of the doctrine, however, is dependent on the interpretation of the objectives of copyright law and the treatment of originality, and therefore it becomes important to investigate these facets of the law as well.

Growth of Database Industry and Need for a Fresh Look

Database is a huge source of information which can give business a competitive advantage. It provides ready-made information about product, market, customer, supplier, etc. It is no doubt an important asset for the business. There is no doubt why this valuable asset will not be target of copy. Databases are expensive to produce but cheap to reproduce. Technical protective measures to prevent unauthorized copying have been proved to be ineffective. Databases are non-excludable (one person cannot exclude another person from consuming), and the combination of high fixed cost (in producing) and low or negligible marginal cost (in reproducing) makes it inherently non-rival (consumption possibility of one individual does not depend on quantity consumed by others).[3] Database industry is a thriving information industry, which makes knowledge accessible to public.

According to the Directive, a database is a 'collection of works, data or other independent materials arranged in a systematic or methodical way and capable of being individually accessed by electronic or other means'.[4]

The reference to 'other means' is intended to include database, which can be accessed by the human eye. For instance, the EC Directive would cover non-electronic encyclopaedias within its ambit. Further, the phrase 'systematic and methodical' seems to establish a low threshold, although haphazard collection of facts will still not be considered to constitute a database.

The combined effect of 'collection' and 'independent' is that, to qualify as a database, the author must bring together a number of separate items, which are meaningful in absence of other items. There may be works in which copyright already subsists such as films, photographs, text, sound recording, or even items of mere data like share prices, telephone numbers or other factual or statistical data. Thus, although a collection of films may qualify as a database, an individual film would not. While an individual film consists of a number of constituent underlying works, namely the film itself, sound recordings and musical compositions,

---

[3]Belleflamme P (2003) Pricing Information Goods in the Presence of Copying. In: Gordon W J, Watt R (ed) The Economics of Copyright, Edward Elgar, U.K., p 26.

[4]EU Directive (96/9/EC) Article 1.1.

those works are not 'independent' from one another in as much as they are only meaningful when viewed as a series of moving images.[5] A final requirement for a collection of independent materials to form a database is that the items must be capable of being 'individually accessed'.

India is blessed with knowledge economy and booming software industry. As a cumulative effect of both, it is expected that India will have a strong database industry. To support this fast-growing database industry, the legal regime in India with reference to databases should encourage investors to invest in this sector. There can be a serious doubt about possible legal protection available in India for database in the context that India does not have something similar to database right and also India's position on originality is not clear in the backdrop of recent Eastern Book Company litigation. This typical situation existing in database industry necessitates offering a fresh look at the possible legal protection to databases in India.

---

[5]*See* Epstein M A (1999) Epstein on Intellectual Property, Aspen Law & Business, Section 10.01 [D].

Chapter 1
Information, Property and Protection

1.1 Role of Information in Today's World

The world is undergoing a transition to 'new economy'—the economy which is knowledge based and where knowledge is the key input of competition in the market as well as the main factor for the growth of the market. This economy has brought significant structural change and influenced corporate strategy, organization of market and pattern of consumption.[1]

Information plays the role of a building block in the Information Age. Human beings have eternal desire for information. Proprietary right over the use of information is a vital issue. If it is believed that information of the world should be freely available to the inhabitants and if it is also believed that it is impossible to own information truly, then any restriction in subsequent use of information has to be strongly justified. The issue will become further complicated if it is argued that investment of time and effort in collecting, selecting, arranging and presenting information is to be rewarded by creating a new property right.

> But the question clearly goes beyond economics in the strict sense, as information increasingly becomes not just a key input for competition in the market but also a factor of social and cultural progress. In this scenario, the problem is how to achieve the difficult balance between the needs to stimulate the generation and availability of information, with clear social and economic benefit that it brings and at the same time guarantee that the information brings the greatest possible number of external benefits (or spin-offs) which entails encouraging its spread and use.[2]

---

[1]Shapiro C, Varian H (1999) Information Rules: Strategic Guide to the Network Economy. Harvard Business School Press, Boston. In: WIPO Standing Committee on Copyright and Related Rights (2002) The Impact of Protection of Non-Original Databases on the Countries of Latin America and the Caribbean, Eights Sessions, Geneva, p 5.
[2]WIPO Standing Committee on Copyright and Related Rights (2002) The Impact of Protection of Non-Original Databases on the Countries of Latin America and the Caribbean, Eights Sessions, Geneva, p 2.

A. Mazumder, *Database Law*, DOI 10.1007/978-981-10-2200-5_1

As the developing countries are at present more consumers than producers of information products, the argument also sometimes depends on the socio-economic condition of the country. Information is a 'good thing' and the attitude towards information is 'the more the merrier'.[3] The value stored in information can be protected to some extent through contract but the limitation of this system is that any disclosure agreement cannot offer full proof arrangement where the value of information will not be leaked. Information once shared with anyone becomes a part of his knowledge and thus the said information cannot be returned and it is very difficult to prevent any subsequent use of this information. Overt use of the information can be attempted to be controlled through terms of disclosure agreement but covert use of the information is beyond regulation.

The exclusivity of use or enjoyment is an essential feature of property right and information per se lacks it.[4] In *Faccenda Chicken Ltd. v. Fowler,*[5] Lord Justice Kerr held that the ex-employee might use confidential information acquired in the course of previous employment and sales of information, which fell short of trade secret, could not be protected. Justice Cross observed in *Printers & Finishers Ltd. v. Holloway,*[6] if knowledge in question could not be readily separated from his general knowledge then subsequent use of the knowledge in question could not be restrained.

1.2 Justification for Protection

Commodification of information has become an established fact in today's world. Information can be sold and bought like any other commodity. The demand of information is based on its utility and the value of information can be calculated by considering the cost involved in retrieving and presenting information. But these will never reflect the intrinsic value of information. Are we assessing the value of information or the value of the medium through which information is conveyed?

This takes us to the definitional issue. How do we define information? Is it synonymous with knowledge or information has to go through a transformation to be matured into knowledge. If information has independent existence from the medium then information can be described as subset of knowledge.[7] The value of information is determined by the users while the cost of information is determined by the producers. The uncertainty of value of information depends on the users as different users perceive information in different ways depending on time, place and context.

---

[3]Rees, Chalton, supra note 1, at 3.

[4]Rees, Chalton, supra note 1, at 6.

[5](1986) 1 All E.R. 617.

[6](1964) 3 All E.R. 731.

[7]Feather J (2004) The Information Society. Facet Publishing, p 112.

It may be difficult to assign any absolute value to any information which may be considered as intrinsic to it.

Apart from its economic value, there may be social and cultural value of information. Sometimes the value of information depends on its suitability and availability. How much money the end user of information is ready to pay to acquire that information can be an indicator to its value. Some information is available for free and some information is sold and purchased like private goods.[8] The uninformed or under-informed person or organization assumes the role of information buyer in the information market place and they buy information from information suppliers and that is how information market operates. If this information market is regulated with stringent rules or if the access to information is controlled then the situation will lead to the creation of two groups—information rich and information poor.[9]

1.3 Changing Features of Property

Property is a complex legal concept. Today the concept of property is de-physicalised. Property does not consist of things but it consists of rights in things or right to things. 'The very meaning of the word property in its legal sense is that which is peculiar or proper to any person that which belongs exclusively to one. The first meaning of the word from which it is derived—proprius—is one's own'.[10]

W.N. Hohfeld describes property as legal interest that exists only between persons in respect of things.[11] As property consists of legal relation between people, so there is no need for a tangible object to constitute property. Property can be described as a bundle of divisible rights. Property often assumes exclusive interest but Blackstone's observation that property assumes absolute dominion of owner is obsolete.[12]

> There is nothing which may more properly called property than the creation of the individual brain. For the word property means, a man's very own and there is nothing more his own than the thought, created, made out of no material thing….The best proof of ownership is that, if this individual man or woman had not thought, realized in writing or in music or in marble, it would not exist……If Farmer Jones does not raise potatoes from a land, Farmer Smith can but Shakespeare cannot write Paradise Lost nor Milton Much Ado.[13]

[8]Id., p 114.

[9]Id., p 115.

[10]Warren, Brandeis (1890) The Right to Privacy. HarvLR 4:193.

[11]Hohfeld (1913) Some Fundamental Legal Conceptions as Applied in Judicial Reasoning. YaleLJ23:16.

[12]Vandervelde (1980) The New Property of the Nineteenth Century: The Development of the Modern Concept of Property. BuffL R 29:325.

[13]Bowker R (1886) Copyright: Its Law and its Literature. In:Warren, Brandeis, supra note 15, at 153.

Property can well be described as complex bundle of rights, duties, powers, immunities as it is not a self explanatory term. The legal interest represented by property often takes their form from the context. Labour theory of property acquisition views the property as an element of political liberty.[14] From the economist's point of view, property right is an incentive to encourage conduct which is desirable by regulating action of others in relation to that protected interest. Similarly property rights may be withdrawn to discourage undesirable conducts.[15]

Knowledge has its existence in two possible ways—as goods which are developed from knowledge and then those goods are marketed where dissemination of knowledge can take place through patent information, reverse engineering and the raw knowledge itself—whose dissemination has to be controlled by IPRs.[16]

Intellectual property cannot be compared with wine as the comparison will lead to anomalous results. The production cost of knowledge is very high and the reproduction cost of knowledge is very low. Intangible properties like information create a new situation as they do not exist like land or chattel.

In *Millar v. Taylor*[17] Judge Yates observed 'nothing can be object of property which has not a corporeal substance'. This concept has become obsolete now. Common law has already extended concept of property to include good will and trade mark. The importance of these case laws has been reduced by enacting legislation on patent and trade mark. It was observed in *International News Service v. Associated Press*[18] that news must be regarded as quasi property, considering the fact that one should not reap where he has not sown which lead to the doctrine of misappropriation, though Court carefully avoided that it was granting property rights to news.

When historical facts are subject matter of news, no copyright subsists on them, though the author is responsible for discovering and gathering the facts. But the question remains that after publication, with reference to the news, whether any rights or privileges originate and if it is to what extent? The court however pointed out that communication of news gathered by the plaintiff for commercial purpose was prohibited. In other words, an exclusive right to commercially exploit news was created by the court which was nothing but property right. This creation of property right was to prevent free riding as it could have undesirable consequences in the given circumstances.

The concept of free riding suggests that we have the right to reap only when we sow the crop. But the information and crop are fundamentally different in nature.

---

[14]Weinrib A S (1988) Information and Property. Toronto L. J. 38:121.

[15]Id., p 121.

[16]Supra note 7, at 8.

[17](1769) 98 E.R. 201.

[18]248 US 215 (1918). The defendant copied news items from the early edition of plaintiff's paper and distributed to its members. Court granted injunction preventing from copying and selling of news gathered by plaintiff until its commercial value passed.

Crops are tangible property and possession of it by one precludes possession by anyone else. Whereas many people can posses same piece of information at one time.[19]

If intangibles are to be protected as property then exclusive possession has to be created by legal restriction. This will lead to a situation where those who put their labour in creating the intangible will reap the fruits of their labour. It has the negative consequence as well. If the intangible is a kind of 'public good' then the benefit of it should be available to many even at the cost of the creator losing the exclusive possession. Here society gets the benefit from free riding and it contributes to the progress of the society.

> In most important fields of human activity it is not usually considered wrong to imitate valuable things, ideas and methods. The more acceptable to the society the thing is, the more others are encouraged to imitate it. Education is founded upon this premise, as it progresses in science, art, literature, music and government. We have but to look around us to see that our dynamic economy is one which thrives upon and requires rapid imitation of innovated trade values.[20]

In *Krouse v. Chrysler Canada Ltd.,*[21] the trial judge Haines observed that Krouse possessed a commercially valuable advertising ability which ought to be protected as 'there is a direct relationship between the quality of his professional work and his ability to command advertiser's money'. This advertising power was not an accident but a result of hard and superlative work. To preserve the incentive for such work, free riding should not be encouraged. But on appeal this decision was reversed as it was observed that there was no actual appropriation. However there could be an action for invasion of right to exploit Krouse's personality.

The concept of property right in intellectual property originates from Lockean Labour Theory. 'Though the Earth, and all inferior Creatures be common to all Men, yet every Man has a Property in his own Person. The labour of this Body, and the Work of his Hands, we may say, are properly his. Whatsoever he then removes out of the State that Nature hath provided, and left it in, he hath mixed his Labour with and joined to it something that is his, and thereby makes it his Property…'.[22]

Expenditure in the information technology indicates that digital property or digitized information is gathering huge wealth. The global marketplace for information and communications technology (ICT) will tap $3 trillion this year and will reach almost $4 trillion by 2009, according to *Digital Planet 2006*, new study released by the World Information Technology and Services Alliance (WITSA). The marketplace posted an 8.9 % average annual growth rate between 2001 and

---

[19]Libling (1978) The Concept of Property: Property in Intangibles. LQR 94:103.

[20]Chafee (1940) Unfair Competition, Harv LR 53:1289.

[21](1972) 25 D.L.R. (3d) 49. The defendant, automobile manufacturer had used an action photograph of the plaintiff , a professional football player to advertise its cars. No consent was taken to use the picture. Plaintiff alleges that by associating him with the product, defendant misappropriated something of commercial value and thus injured his property right.

[22]Locke J (1690) Two Treaties of Government, Book II, Chap. V.

2005 and added $1 trillion in new spending between 2001 and 2006. ICT spending volumes represent 6.8 % of global Gross Domestic Product between 2001 and 2005.[23]

1.4 Information as Property

Information enjoys a unique feature as it exists as such as intangible property and also as recorded tangible property. Know-how is a type of information but it has its own characteristics as it serves as asset of an organization and it does not lose its value with repetitive use but it loses it essence when it is disclosed to unauthorized parties.[24] Information which involves personal significance possesses a different quality as misappropriation of them will call for special damages to compensate the stress caused by disclosure.[25]

In *Herbert Morris Ltd. v. Saxelby,*[26] Lord Shaw opined that trade secrets may not be taken away by a servant as they are master's property. Lord Sterndale held in *Re Keene,*[27] formula for manufacture of products known only to members of a

---

[23]World Information Technology and Services Alliance, The Global Information Economy.www.witsa.org/press/degitalplanetpressrelease_rev.doc. Accessed 16 Nov 2006. Among other key findings of this year's *Digital Planet* report:

- Communications products and services represent the largest single category of ICT spending in 2006 with $1.57 trillion, but software is the fastest growing category, up year to year by 9.9 %;
- Consumers spend one out of every four ICT dollars worldwide. Per capita ICT spending increased almost $29 between 2005 and 2006, from $537.91 to $566.89. Per capita ICT spending has increased every year since 2001;
- ICT spending per employee is up almost 40 % between 2001 and 2006. Global ICT spending per employee reached $1,277 in 2006 and is expected to top $1,500 by the end of the decade;
- In spending by country, the top ten ICT spending countries remain fixed in rank between 2001 and 2005. In descending order, these are: the United States, Japan, Germany, United Kingdom, France, China, Italy, Canada, Brazil and Korea. In 2006, China catches France in the total ICT spending race, with outlays of $142.3 billion. In 2007, China is expected to jump ahead of France and ahead of the United Kingdom in 2008. By 2009, China will be the third largest ICT spending country. Also of interest, India will replace Korea as a member of the top ten in 2007 with $65.5 billion;
- China is also a powerhouse in rates of spending, with a 20.9 % annual increase in 2006 for outpacing any other member of the top ten. In fact, China ICT annual growth rates exceed 20 % every year between 2001 and 2006. This trend is expected to continue through the decade, growing to almost 26 % by 2009;
- The Americas will grow the slowest of the three broad regions charted in Digital Planet, at 4.4 % between 2005 and 2009. The Americas' share of ICT spending will shrink from 44 % last year to 39 % in 2009. Asia-Pacific will grow at 11.1 % from 2005 through 2009.

[24]Rolls-Royce Ltd. v. Jeffrey (1962) 1 All E.R. 801.

[25]Ichard v. Frangoulis (1971) 2 All E.R. 461.

[26](1916) 1 A.C. 688.

[27](1922) 2 Chap. 475.

partnership, constituted partnership property. These decisions treat confidential information as a species of property.[28] But the question still remains that what is the position of information which is not confidential information? In *Boardman v. Phipps,*[29] Lord Upjohn dissented that information is not property in normal sense but Equity will restrain transmission to another in breach of confidence. Chief Justice Latham in *Federal Commissioner of Taxation v. United Aircraft Corporation*[30] observed that transfer of information cannot be treated as transfer of property as transfer or still has everything he had before and transferee will continue to have what he received even after the contractual time is over.

> Knowledge is valuable but knowledge is neither real nor personal property. A man with a richly stored mind is not for that reason a man of property. It is only in a loose metaphorical sense that any knowledge as such can be said to be property.[31] Information per se was not regarded as property for the purpose of Theft Act 1968.[32] Justice Buckley observed in *Exchange Telegraph v. Howard*[33] the knowledge of a fact which is unknown to many people may be the property of a person in that others will pay the person who knows it for information as to that fact. In unpublished matter there is at common law a right of property.

Law Commission did not support the attempt to bring common law principles or principles governing transfer of property into the field of law of confidence.[34] Cornish has offered three prong test to identify the proprietary quality of information which are 1. whether possession of information generates rights against those who misappropriate it, 2. does assignee of information acquires assignor's right to sue against those who acquire it directly or indirectly, breaching confidence, 3. in case of more than one licensees, does one attain priority over the other and on what principle.[35]

The most problematic issue in creating proprietary right over information is the classification of information as all information cannot be termed as property and there is no guideline so as to which information should be treated as property and which should not. Justice Fullagar observed in *Deta Nominees Pct. Ltd. v. Viscount Plastics Pvt. Ltd.*[36] that whether information is property depends on the expectation of a reasonable person. If a reasonable person, considering all circumstances, nature of information, relationship of parties, recognizes information to be property of another person and not his own, then information assumes the shape of property.

---

[28]Clarke L(1990) Confidentiality and the Law. Lloyd's of London Press Ltd., p 88.

[29](1967) 2 A.C. 46.

[30]68 C.L.R. 525. In: Clarke, supra note 33, at 90.

[31]68 C.L.R. 525. In: Clarke, supra note 33, at 91.

[32]Oxford v. Moss (1978) 68 Crim. App. Rep. 183. The case involved student gaining unauthorized access to examination paper and was which was not considered as theft.

[33](1906) 22 T.L.R. 375.

[34]Report No. 110, (1981), p 9. In: Clarke, supra note 33, at 99.

[35]Cornish, Llewelyn (2003) Intellectual Property. Sweet & Maxwell, p. 240. In: Clarke, supra note 33, at 104.

[36](1979) V.R. 167.

The proprietary right over information also includes issues of conflicting interest having impact on social policy. Policy to encourage non disclosure of information breaching confidence has to counter-weigh against policy of free speech and free flow of information.[37] Professor Gareth Jones observed[38] that the basis of the restitution claim is no longer implied contract or property but a broad equitable duty of good faith, namely, that he who has received information in confidence shall not take unfair advantage of it and this principle is wide enough to protect the plaintiff who imparts, in confidence, any confidential information whatever be its substance. The later part strongly indicates that the obligation does not vary with the substance of information. English Law Commission[39] felt that the courts do not confine themselves to purely equitable principles in solving the problems which arise in breach of confidence cases and it would seem more realistic to regard the modern action as being *sui generis*.

In *Saltman Engineering Co. Ltd. v. Campbell Engineering Co. Ltd.*[40] Lord Greene M.R. indicated this obligation in terms of rights as he pointed out, 'If a defendant is proved to have used confidential information, directly or indirectly obtained from a plaintiff, without the consent, express or implied, of the plaintiff, he will be guilty of an infringement of the plaintiff's right.' Stuckey[41] took a contrasting position by deciding that action for breach of confidence, when not based upon implied or express contractual obligation, enforces purely equitable obligation arising out of a proven relationship of trust and not property rights in information.

Some judicial action protects certain information which may be regarded as species of property and some judicial action protects all information which may be regarded as confidential per se. Differentiating from Prof. Gareth Jones, G. Forrai observes that all that can be safely stated therefore is that the degree of secrecy required by the courts in these cases will depend on the nature of the information, circumstances of the case.[42] Stuckey observes that so called property in information is merely a benefit, enforced in equity and a benefit, conferred by right in personam and not a proprietary interest enforceable against the whole world and thus confidential information should not be equated with a species of equitable property.[43] But it can be compared with property so far as the remedy is concerned.

---

[37]Clarke, supra note 33, at 106.

[38]Jones G (1970) Restitution of Benefits Obtained in Breach of Author's Confidence. LQR86:463.

[39]English Law Commission Working Paper on Breach of Confidence (1974), No. 58. In: Stuckey J E (1981) The Equitable Action For Breach of Confidence: Is Information Ever Property? Syd L R 9:402.

[40](1948) 65 R.P.C. 203.

[41]Stuckey, supra note 44, at 404.

[42]Forrai G (1971) Confidential Information—A General Survey. Syd LR 6:382.

[43]Stuckey, supra note 44, at 405.

In *Macmillan v. Dent,*[44] Justice Buckley observed that there exists a right to property in literary composition of an author but it is in abstract sense and in concrete sense it is words written on paper. Cases on letter and manuscripts that have got copyright under common law evolved the notion regarding information as property. Some information as personal information or confidential information have commercial values and have attributes of property. To introduce action of breach of confidence as means to protect the proprietary right over information was an equitable remedy. The common law requirements for such action are to prove duty, breach of duty and damages but in equity, the requirement is to prove breach of a duty and then an action in personam will follow. As Lord Denning puts it 'he who has received information shall not take unfair advantage of it. He must not use it to the prejudice of him who gave it without obtaining his consent'.[45] But Justice Holmes observed in *E.I. Du Pont de Nemours v. Masland*[46] that irrespective of secret information; defendant must know that there is a special confidence. The property may be denied but not the confidence. So the important issue is the special relation and not the property.

Trade secrets are characterized as property in three different ways—1. through employment contract prohibiting sharing of information, 2. through taxation principles, whether it constitutes fixed capital asset, 3. through fiduciary duty. The first type originates from the question who owns the professional expertise—does it belong to the employer or employee. In *Herbert Morris Ltd. v. Saxelby,*[47] Lord Shaw observed 'trade secrets …may not be taken away by a servant, they are his master's property…..On the other hand, a man's aptitude, his skill, his dexterity, his manual or mental ability……they may and they ought not to be relinquished by a servant, they are not his master's property, they are his own property'. In the second type, status of information is discussed only for the purpose of tax. In *Jeffrey v. Rolls-Royce Ltd.,*[48] agreement to impart know-how were held to be a method of trading and thus money received through it was considered as taxable income. Here the discussion of information as property was only to categorize use of information for tax purposes. The third type comes up in case of conflict of business and interest. In *Bell House Ltd. v. City Wall Properties Ltd.,*[49] the company chairman acquired the knowledge regarding source of finance for property development, during transacting business of the company. The Court of Appeal held that as the knowledge was acquired in the course of transacting company's business, so the knowledge was asset of the company and belonged to the company.

---

[44](1907) 1 Chap. 107. In: Stuckey, supra note 44, at 406.

[45]Seager v. Copydex (1967) 1 W.L.R. 923.

[46](1917) 244 U.S. 100.

[47](1916) 1 A.C. 688.

[48](1960) 40 Tax Cas 443.

[49](1966) 2 W.L.R. 1323.

1.5 Tangibility and Intangibility

In general sense information is not property at all. It is open to all who have eyes to read and ears to hear. The true test is to determine in what circumstances information has been acquired.[50] The unique feature of intangible property is that they can be taken by others without depriving the owner's possession of it. But the loss due to taking away intangible property without permission is just like tangible property. In *Oxford v. Moss,*[51] a student found out question set in examination before the examination was held. Section 60(1) of the Theft Act provides that 'a person is guilty of theft if he dishonestly appropriates property belonging to another with the intention of permanently depriving the other of it'. The question paper itself was the property of the University. The Court of Appeal held that there was no property in the information capable of being the subject of a charge of theft under Theft Act 1968. So it appears that if a paper is permanently removed from the University, it would be theft but if the paper is removed with the intent to memorize it and return it, then it would not be a theft. This creates an odd situation as there is no value of the paper itself, the values is due to the information stored in that paper and it is this information which makes it worthy to be taken. The decision of *Oxford v. Moss* makes the information stored in question paper worthless and does not appear to be logical.

> The University's property interest in the paper was injured in a very real sense. It is true that they retained unimpaired ownership in the piece of paper throughout, but as a question paper it was rendered quite useless. It is unrealistic to consider the proprietary interest as consisting solely in the piece of paper without regard to what is imbued on it. A blank piece of paper is of negligible value. An examination paper, the preparation of which can involve hours of work by several skilled persons, is a relatively valuable thing. To equate it with the piece of paper would be no more sensible than to equate a banknote with the piece of paper on which it is printed.[52]

> The information is not visible, tangible property, but there is a valuable right of property in it which the court ought to protect, in every reasonable way, against those seeking to obtain it from the owner without right, to his damage....If the defendant can obtain it from the owner of the same kind of property and the two may become competitors....But if the defendant surreptitiously and against the plaintiff's will takes from the plaintiff and appropriates the from of expression which is the symbol of the plaintiff's possession and thus by direct attack, as it were, divides the plaintiff's possession and shares it, this conduct is a violation of the plaintiff's right to property.[53]

---

[50]Stuckey, supra note 44, at 414.

[51](1979) Fed. Crim. L.R. 119.

[52]Comment on Oxford v. Moss (1979) Crim. L. R. 119.

[53]F.W. Dodge Co. v. Construction Information Co. 66 N.E. 204 (1903).

1.6 Private and Public Interest

Information can possess many characteristics of other form of property. Information can be sold, licensed, can be a subject of trust and can be bequeathed. To deny free ride of information by using it without payment would affect the foundation of human progress. At the same time there would be little incentive to invest if it is not readily protected. Thus free riding may affect productive effort which should be encouraged.

In Canada, two cases namely, R v. Stewart[54] and R v. Offley[55] observed two conflicting opinions between the judges on an issue of huge importance in the information age, i.e. whether information can be treated as property and thus can be stolen. Action for breach of confidence enforces a broad duty of good faith and relationship of trust or confidence inbuilt in it and it does not protect property right in information.

[54](1983) 149 D.L.R. (3d) 583. The accused was hired to obtain name and telephone number of six hundred employees of a hotel for the purpose of organizing union. The information was kept in a file was protected through security arrangement as was considered confidential. The accused approached an employee to get that information and offered to pay for it. He was charged with commission of theft. Section 283(1) of Criminal Code defines theft as 'everyone commits theft who fraudulently and without colour of right takes or fraudulently and without colour of right converts to his use or the use of another person, anything whether animate or inanimate with the intent…..to deal with it in such a manner that it can not be restored in the condition in which it was at the time it was taken or converted'. At trial the accused was acquitted as Judge Krever observed 'if this interpretation should be thought inadequate to meet the needs of modern Canadian society, particularly because of its implication for the computer age, the remedy must be a change in the law by Parliament. It is not for a court to stretch the language used in a statute dealing with the criminal law to solve problems outside the contemplation of the statute'. On appeal it was reversed as Judge Houlden observed 'the last half of the twentieth century has seen as exponential growth in the development and improvement of methods of storing and distributing information. I believe that Section 283(1) of the Code is wide enough to protect the interest of those who compile and store such information and to restrain the activities of those who wrongfully seek to misappropriate it. While clearly not all information is property, I see no reason why confidential information that has been gathered through the expenditure of time, effort and money by a commercial enterprise for the purpose of its business should not be regarded as property and hence entitled to the protection of the criminal law'.

[55](1986) 45 Alta.L.R. (2d) 23. The accused was hired by employer to do security check on job applications. He approached police department officials, seeking access to a pool of computer stored information in order to determine if any applicant had criminal records. When told that the information was available to law enforcement agencies, he befriended a police officer to do this for a fee. The officer reported this and the accused was arrested while exchanging money and information. He was charged with theft. The trial judge convicted him but on appeal it was unanimously held that confidential information was incapable of being stolen.

In Prince Albert v. Strange[56] the court observed that the plaintiff had common law right of property in the etching which was extended to the information describing the work as it was wholly for their private use and to withhold altogether from knowledge of others. There are few other cases where similar situation occurs; like property right in trade mark evaporates if it is used widely generically, adverse possession of land for a long time negates title holder's property rights, copyright and patent protection comes to an end after limited period.

Judge Buckley observed in one of the Exchange Telegraph cases[57] (Exchange Telegraph Co. Ltd. v. Howard and Manchester Press Agency Ltd.) 'The plaintiff carries on the business of collecting and distributing information. The knowledge of a fact which is unknown to many people may be the property of a person in that others will pay the person who knows it for the information as to that fact. In unpublished information there is a right to property. The plaintiffs here sue, not for copying at all, but in respect of that common law right to property in information which they had collected and were in a position to sell. Their case is that the defendant stole their property which the defendant has surreptitiously obtained and used it in rivalry with them.'[58]

In Seager v. Copydex,[59] the plaintiff had invented an improved carpet grip and while negotiating with the defendant voluntarily disclosed details of it. The negotiation broke down and the defendant started producing similar carpet grip. Lord Denning observed the principle of equity—he who has received information in confidence shall not take unfair advantage of it and hold the defendant liable although there was no express finding of bad faith and it was observed that it was a case of unconscious plagiarism.

In Franklin v. Giddins,[60] the defendant stole budwood twigs from the plaintiff's orchard and started breeding the plaintiff's unique nectarine in competition with him. Judge Dunn observed 'when the defendant stole budwood from the plaintiff's orchard, what he got is trade secret—the information which the genetic structure of

[56](1849) 2 DeG & Sm. 643. A set of etchings made by Queen Victoria and her husband were sent to the printer to be engraved. Copies of engraving came to the hands of defendant who prepared a catalogue describing works for a public exhibition. The Court prohibited both the exhibition and distribution of catalogue.

[57]Exchange Telegraph Co. Ltd. v. Gregory & Co. (1896) 1 QB 147, Exchange Telegraph Co. Ltd. v. Central News Ltd. (1897) 2 Chap. 48, Exchange Telegraph Co. Ltd. v. Howard and Manchester Press Agency Ltd. (1906) 22 T.L.R. 375. In these cases, plaintiff firm was engaged in business of collecting information about stock prices, horse races, sporting news, respectively, brought an action against the defendant who was surreptitiously obtaining the information, from one of the subscriber of the plaintiff, contrary to the terms of agreement between plaintiff and subscribers, and using in course of its own business. In all the three cases, plaintiff obtained injunction against defendant restraining it from copying the information on the basis of property right in the information.

[58]Exchange Telegraph Co. Ltd. v. Howard and Manchester Press Agency Ltd. (1906) 22 T.L.R. 375.

[59](1967) 2 All. E. R. 415.

[60](1978) Qd. R. 72.

the wood represented was of substantial commercial value and much time and effort was spent by the plaintiff while developing it and could not be duplicated by anybody whatsoever and other people are expected to respect the plaintiff's right to property. These rights which are given to plaintiffs in these cases are nothing but property rights and that is why the court prevents others from using it.

In R. v. Mc Ewen,[61] the accused had broken into another person's premises and taken some bottles of intoxicating liquors. He was charged with theft. But Section 88 of Prohibition Act 1937 provides that 'no property rights of any kind existed in intoxicating liquors'. The court observed that since theft was interference with property right and intoxicating liquor could not be subject of property so there could not be theft in the present situation and the charge was dismissed. It is unlikely that the objective of Prohibition Act was to offer immunity to those who steal other's liquor. It shows that a more contextual analysis of concept of property is required. If property is considered as a complex bundle of right, then the situation will be clearer. Due to the Prohibition Act, those who possess intoxicating liquor would enjoy less extensive aggregate of legal relations than that for other properties. For example contract to sell liquor could not be enforced and could not claim compensation if liquors were confiscated. But it did not mean that due to the Prohibition Act, all attributes of property would be evaporated and so he would be able to resist if someone takes those liquors by force. The bottom line is what is not property under civil law, can be very will a property under criminal law to constitute theft.

In U.S. v. Bottone[62] documents dealing with secret manufacturing process were photocopied and then restored to the files. The court held that the copies were goods and it was stolen as it was converted and taken by fraud. The court observed 'in such a case where the physical form of the stolen goods is secondary in every respect to the matter recorded in them, the transformation of the information in the stolen papers into a tangible object never possessed by the original owner should be deemed immaterial. It would offend common sense to hold that these defendants fall outside the statute simply because, in efforts to avoid detection, their confederates were at pains to restore the original paper and to transport only copies or notes, although an oversight would have brought them within it.'[63]

Taking anything of value without consent should be treated to be within the statute and should be treated as theft. In R v. Stewart[64] Judge Houldern observed that all information is not property. But confidential information is definitely property. Information is confidential if the release of it would be injurious to the owner and of advantage to his rivals, if it is already not in public domain and if it is reasonable to treat it as such considering usage and practice of the industry. If R v. Stewart decision is considered as unwarranted judicial activism then it may be

---

[61](1947) 2 D.L.R. 62.

[62]365 F. 2d 389 (1966).

[63]365 F. 2d 389 (1966).

[64](1983) 149 D.L.R. (3d) 583.

pointed out that the word 'anything' in Criminal Code definition of theft hardly requires any stretching to include confidential information within it. Confidential information is a natural and desirable adaptation to the modern concept of property. In comparison with patent law, all valuable information may not be patented and it is also expensive to obtain, so confidential information protection is complimentary to the patent protection.

Collection and arrangement of information is vital to any commercial enterprise. Compilation of information may be sometimes so important that it can be marked as confidential. This compilation may cover wide variety of topics. For a commercial enterprise, it may include computer programs regarding all aspect of business, list of suppliers, and note on efficiency of suppliers, reliability, and time taken for delivery, list of customers, and need of customers, directions for manufacturing and list of employees. This compilation can be very well the most important asset of the company. It may be argued that it is difficult to consider information as property as it evaporates once it reaches public domain or someone else independently comes out with the same compilation.

Chapter 2
Copyright, Access and Information Society

2.1 Copyright Protection and Public/Private Interest

Information is an invaluable social resource. Before information is given a strenuous legal protection, it must be made sure that protection is warranted and carefully delineated. The mechanism to stimulate dissemination and use of new knowledge is an important incentive for generating knowledge. Access to information is an issue which concerns various categories of users. Information which is in public domain, information where database constitutes the only source of that information, information relating the academic and scientific research and other information of public interest are always sensitive to monopolization and consequent restriction in use. There are databases like databases on remote sensing activities, which are by their nature unique and cannot be reproduced independently by third parties and in these cases possibility of monopoly becomes greater.[1] By introducing intellectual property rights in non-original databases, private rights will be created in the information contained in the databases which would seriously damage the content of public domain in the domain of scientific, educational and legal information.[2]

[1]The Association of Research Libraries have noted that prices of such journals rose by 115 % between 1986–1994 which was the result of a market which was monopolistic and controlled by a small group of publishers. Maurer M (1999) Raw Knowledge: Protecting Technical Databases for Science and Industry. Workshop on Promoting Access to Scientific and Technical Data for the Public Interest: An Assessment of Policy Options, National Academy of Sciences, January 1999.
[2]Maurer SM, Scotchmer S (1999) Intellectual Property Rights: Database Protection: Is It Broken and Should We Fix It? Sci 284:789.

A. Mazumder, *Database Law*, DOI 10.1007/978-981-10-2200-5_2

National Research Council, National Academy of Sciences, National Academy of Medicine, National Academy of Engineering, National Sciences Foundation and National Institute of Health objected to any legislation in the United States that might restrict data or information as they feared that IPR in databases would put an obstacle to free circulation of information through price rise and private appropriation.[3] It is observed that social benefit increases when knowledge is more disseminated. All information related to law are in public domain but today a lawyer or researcher who has to purchase law books and CD-ROMs, subscribes to online databases. So when access to databases is restricted, for example by pay per use system, it becomes an obstacle to advancement of sciences as the researchers tend to compromise with the quality of research because of the additional cost for having access to databases. Heller observed it as tragedy of anti-commons.[4]

Any increase in the cost of accessing databases will have a chain reaction in the society as the research is likely to compensate the higher cost with another source of revenue based on the result of the research either through patenting or other means of exclusion of research output. This has been indicated by the increase of private involvement in collection and generation of data. This can also lead to a strategy of scientific collaboration in the model of 'open science'.[5] There is an increasing demand for consumer's access to information like weather data, maps, and statutory registers.

Copyright protection for a compilation is confined to selection and arrangement of information and reproducing selection and arrangement will infringe either copyright in compilation or database. Information recorded in a work qualifying for copyright protection may be used and re-expressed till reuse does not amount to reproduction of substantial part of it and to this extent underlying information in a copyrighted work remains in public domain.[6]

Digital technology has created considerable tension for traditional concepts of copyright law. Digital Millennium Copyright Act in the United States and

[3]When commercialization of images from Landsat satellite in the USA was privatized, price raised from $400 to $4400 per images. Reichman, Samuelson (2001) Intellectual Property Rights in Data? http://www.eon.law.harvard.edu/h2o/property/alternatives/reichman.html. In: Colston C (2001) Sui Generis Database Right: Ripe for Review JILT3. http:// www.elj.warwick.ac.uk/jilt/01-3/colston.html. Accessed 17 Nov 2006.

[4]When many individuals have right to exclude in a scare resources, acting separately they can cause collective squandering by under utilizing it. Heller M (1998) The Tragedy of Anti Commons. Harv L Rev 111(3):621–688.

[5]Baron P (2001) Back to Future: Learning from the Past in the Database Debate. Ohio State L J 62:880.

[6]In Elanco Product Ltd v. Mandops Ltd 1980 RPC 213. Patent on herbicide expired. The defendant marketed it with an accompanying leaflet with detailed instruction as to use the herbicide. Much of the information was in public domain. The plaintiff—the original inventor alleged that the leaflet infringed their copyright in the leaflet they provided with the tin. The court granted injunction and held that defendant could not use plaintiff's skill and judgment to save themselves the trouble and cost of assembling literature.

Information Society Directive in the European Union have affected freedom of expression as it does not recognize the right of private copying.[7] The apprehension is that information published in copy protected form, without having any other source shall be effectively monopolized. ALLEA (All European Academics) expressed concern that scientific research would be affected because of the Directive as the Directive limits the access to data for research and scientific purposes.[8]

Christophe Geiger feels that the over protection offered to the copyright owner is detrimental to public interest. Due to this overprotection, the balance existing within copyright law has disappeared. According to him copyright's internal limits cannot restore this balance and it requires external solution, that is, to him human rights.[9] Copyright addresses a conflict between different interests and different fundamental freedoms. These conflicts are between interest of the copyright owner and that of the public. The conflict is about the owner's copyright and public's right to information. Christophe Geiger observes that existing copyright regime is so tilted towards publishers (originality level is brought down, term of protection has been extended, exceptions have been narrowed down) that traditional justifications are not enough to maintain the balance.[10] According to him, considering that human right is a part of the national and international constitutional law can provide better justification.

Christophe Geiger thinks that *sui generis* protection for database has the potential for monopolization of information and creating multiple intellectual property rights over same subject matter, affecting access to information.[11] This possibility arises only in cases where database is the only source of particular information. Compulsory licensing and broad exceptions will be better balancing factors. The lengthy process of litigation in case of competition law does not make a certain remedy for denial of access.[12] The possibility of perpetual protection for database right can also jeopardize the human rights in general and public's right to information in particular.

---

[7]Arrest of Russian programmer on criminal charges for developing software to circumvent Adobe's copy-protection technology for digital book. http://www.epccentral.org/dmca.html. Colston, supra note 72.

[8]First Evaluation of Directive 96/9/EC on Legal Protection of Databases, Commission of The European Communities, Brussels, 12 Dec 2005, p 21.

[9]Book Review of Christophe Geiger, (2006) E.I.P.R. 357.

[10]Id.

[11]Id.

[12]Apart from high degree of litigiousness due to a legislation on competition, it only solves the problem of undue appropriation by competitors and not by users, recourse to unfair competition is available only ex post, it does not solve the problem of information Samaritan who for non-economic reason extracts data and then make it available to public for free, the legislation does not give any exclusive or transferable right and the concept of unfair competition varies from country to country. Supra note 7, at 15.

2.2 Copyright and Access to Information

Does copyright prevent free access to information? The Library of Alexandria felt that money or a lack of infrastructure was not the main problem of information in society; rather the greatest problem was copyright.[13] OECD also emphasized on reconciliation between effective IPR protection and the need for access to information.[14] The increasing perception among the academic community is that copyright hinders access to knowledge.[15] Considering the negative impacts of copyright, it is important to ensure free access to information.[16] This issue becomes more pertinent in case of developing countries. Intellectual property is justified to preserve for the authors the fruits of their work as well as to disseminate ideas. Authors are encouraged to create new works and there by contribute in disseminating new ideas. Copyright law should be drafted in such a way so as to maintain balance between protection of the author and interest of the society.[17]

'The Framers of the U.S. Constitution intend copyright itself to be the engine of free expression. By establishing a marketable right to the use of one's expression, copyright supplies the economic incentive to create and disseminate ideas.'[18] Principles of natural law, constitutional principles and norms of international law have influenced principles of copyright law to emerge.[19] Two conflicting but important issues are to be carefully balanced through copyright legislation—on author's side, property right and right of personality and on the user's side, freedom of expression and freedom of information.[20]

The exclusive right created by copyright works under different limitations to ensure free access to information. These are like, ideas themselves are not protected, but expressions which have originality are protected. Protection is for a limited period, protected expressions can be used if it is required in public interest, protected expressions can also be used for private purpose, teaching and research.

[13]Geiger C (2006) Copyright and Free Access to Information: For a Fair Balance of Interest in a Globalize World. E.I.P.R. 366.

[14]OECD Report on the Scientific Publishing Industry, Digital Broadband Content: Scientific Publishing, Sept 2005.

[15]Geiger, supra note 82, at 366.

[16]Hugenholtz P (1996) Adapting Copyright to the Information Superhighway: The Future of Copyright in a Digital Era. Kluwer. In: Geiger, supra note 82, at 366.

[17]'The Congress shall have the power securing for limited times to Authors and Inventors the exclusive right to their respective writings and discoveries'. Article 1, Section 8, American Constitution.

[18]Griffiths J, Suthersanan U (2005) Copyright and Free Speech. Oxford University Press. In: Geiger, supra note 82, at 367.

[19]Fundamental Rights, Universal Declaration of Human Rights, European Convention on Human Rights.

[20]Geiger, supra note 82, at 368.

These principles are recognized by international instruments like Berne Convention, TRIPS and WCT.[21]

In information society, knowledge has become a contributing factor in economy and thus attempts have been made to reserve the use of information through intellectual property right and as a result the difference between idea and expression is becoming blurred. This situation is reflected in cases of sole source database and business method patent.[22] The technical development in copying and distributing attained a new height through digital technology and it affected investors negatively as it allowed users to copy and share documents quite easily. To challenge these threats investors took resort to technical device that prevents copying and circumventing measures were considered as illegal.[23] These technical devices would not be in a position to appreciate the legitimacy of purpose and decide accordingly. Thus investors would like to regulate access through technology instead of through law.

Technology will always have effects—positive and negative. Internet being a huge source of information can play a pivotal role in education and research and at the same time Internet poses threat for fundamentals of copyright. Public domain should be defined in clear terms to include matters like essential public information, official documents and texts. States are given discretion to decide the ambit of public domain; so states should make full use of it like patentable subject matter.[24] While defining, public domain should have space to accommodate technical and social changes. The definition can also include works of social, cultural and economic importance to keep them outside the purview of exclusive right.[25] These can be sports, cultural and other events as well.

Anything corollary to the exception can also be enforced against the right holder and thus if a technical measure hinders the user from enjoying the use permitted by law, then the user can enforce that hindrance.[26] But this right is made available to only limited situations and it does not cover rights like digital private copy or quotation right. The Directive[27] provides that appropriate measure can be taken to

[21]Articles 7 and 10 of Berne Convention, Article 9 of TRIPS, Article 2 of WCT.

[22]Geiger, supra note 82, at 368.

[23]WCT 1996.

[24]Article 27, TRIPS.

[25]Following Article 3(a)(1) European Directive 97/36 (on television)—'Member States may take measures … to ensure that broadcasters under its jurisdiction do not broadcast on an exclusive basis events which are regarded by the Member States as being of major importance for society in such a way as to deprive a substantial proportion of public … of possibility of following such event via live coverage or deferred coverage on free television'

Article 9, Convention of Council of Europe on Transfrontier Television, 1989, '…to examine and where necessary, take legal measure …… to avoid right of public to information being undermined due to exercise of exclusive right'.

[26]Section 95b(2) German Copyright Act, user is entitled to demand from the right holder support required for exercise of certain legitimate uses. In: Geiger, supra note 82, at 370.

[27]Article 6.4.

enforce functioning of limitations but no explanation has been given to describe what constitutes appropriate measure. If Articles 8[28] and 9[29] are considered to ensure access to information, it may be found that they do not constitute sufficient means to reach the objective as it all depends on the interpretation of the term 'lawful user'.[30] A careful observation indicates that the exception to *sui generis* right in Article 9 for private purpose and teaching and research allows only extraction and not re-utilization.

Reichman and Samuelson has described this as fool's gold. The condition attached to 'lawful user' is not to perform acts which conflict with normal exploitation of the database or unreasonably prejudice the legitimate interests of the maker of the database.[31] This results in affecting access to information.[32] Information which is already in public domain can be expressed in a different language as it does not put the database into public domain. Reproduction for the purpose of analyzing the design or evaluating the embodied concept, processor system has not been included in case of databases with the objective of limiting commercial uses than non commercial uses. Law can be made to prohibit technical measure which prevents any privilege authorized by law as the solution of problem in copyright lies in the copyright itself.[33]

Principles of copyright must ensure that rights of the users are balanced with rights of authors. In digital environment, private copying has not been recognized but exception has been made to allow copy for scientific purpose to ensure access to information.[34] This should be coupled with enforceable right to overcome technical barrier. Every author is a researcher and user at the first place. The author takes note of the existing literature at the time of creating work. Thus denying private copy would negatively affect the creative process of the author. Here the purpose of copy becomes important. Copy for consuming music may not be allowed but copy for producing a literary work may be allowed, knowing very well the practical difficulty of cross checking it one might require to copy a piece of music in order to get information about it and it may not be necessary that one plays the music every time to enjoy it. User's right management is more desirable than digital right

[28]The maker of a database which is made available to the public in whatever manner my not prevent a lawful user of the database from extracting and/or reutilizing insubstantial part of the contents evaluated qualitatively or quantitatively for any purpose whatsoever.

[29]Lawful user of a database which is made available to public in whatever manner may without authorization of the maker of the database, extract or reutilize a substantial part of its content in case of extraction for private purpose of the content of a non-electronic database, in case of extraction for teaching and scientific research for non commercial purpose, in case of extraction for administrative or judicial purpose.

[30]Thakur (2001) Database Protection in the European Union and the United States. IPQ 100.

[31]Article 8, Database Directive.

[32]Reichman, Samuelson, supra note 72.

[33]Geiger, supra note 82, at 371.

[34]Section 53(2)(1) German Copyright Act.

management.[35] To balance both sides private copying should be continued along with equitable remuneration which will satisfy both the author and user.

Statutory licenses can create a situation where users will not be prohibited and right holder will also get financial compensation. So every time the use of an existing work makes it possible to create a new work, a remuneration right will take birth and it will work as replacement of exclusive right.[36] It is doubted whether this arrangement will satisfy the three-step test provided by international instruments.[37] A fair user can always re-gather data and re-compile database without infringing or seeking license. This does not affect competition. The competition is not from the regular fair user but from the efficient second comer who has access to information in public domain and can offer a price competition to the first maker. This creates an incentive for the first maker to provide license at a reasonable rate. This competition will bring more efficiency to data collection and remove the fear of monopolistic behaviour from the database maker. This logic has been criticized as it does not consider the fact that recreation of database will be inefficient and uneconomic and thus there will be de facto monopoly of the database maker.[38] Moreover most of the data originate from only one source and most of the data are out of public domain which leads to a situation where there will be more restriction than access to free information.

Copyright should not hinder access to information but rather promote it and it has to be achieved by balancing different interests. Instead of increasing sanction, law should be made acceptable which is possible in case of copyright only when it does not deviate from its objective. As books are build on preceding books, creation of new information rely on preceding collections. Database protection should treat this development as priority, particularly within the context of scientific and educational research.

International Council of Science prepared principles for addressing restrictions in using scientific databases.[39] Technological changes can always influence collection of information. Sometime technology can make competition very easy by creating a state of inadequate protection and sometime it can create over protection,

---

[35]Geiger, supra note 82, at 371.

[36]Geiger, supra note 82, at 371.

[37]Article 9 Berne Convention, Article 13 TRIPS, Article 10 WCT, the limitation to exclusive right—1. must qualify as special case, 2. should not conflict with normal exploitation and 3. should not unreasonably prejudice the interest of the right holder.

[38]Thakur, supranote 99, at 100.

[39]Celera Genomics database of the Human Genome published in Science magazine at the HUGO Satellite Meeting 'Intellectual Property and Related Socio-legal Aspects of the Human Genome Project', University of Edinburgh, 23 Apr 2001. Licenses must be secured for the extraction of sufficient data to perform any of the named and necessary computations, evaluations or enhancements of the data that would be considered the norm in computational genome biology. Though this relates to contractual protection for a database, in an environment where free access to full information was expected for the benefit of all, the effect of such guarding of a database may be seen to illustrate the fears of researchers and scientists. http://www.codata.org/codata/data_access/principles.htm. In: Colston, supra note 72.

especially in case of sole source data provider. It cannot only raise the prices but also can prevent access to information completely. The State can intervene in these cases to offer access to these databases which have become building blocks of knowledge.[40]

The future of access to information is threatened as de facto monopoly over data becomes increasingly realistic. It has been observed that result of cases like Feist[41] and Tele-Direct,[42] which can prevent others from appropriating information in a compilation of facts would limit the ability of later authors to build upon earlier works. This would affect the progress in both arts and sciences.[43] As IPRs can consolidate monopoly and can affect efficiency and welfare, intellectual property regime must have adequate space for public policy arrangements like protection of competition, which can limit the abuse of monopoly and promote dissemination of knowledge. It has been apprehended that sooner or later all commercially valuable information will end up being protected as part of databases.[44]

Any attempt to incorporate a regime in the line of the Database Directive should be carefully studied so that its influence on access to information which is a key component for social and economic development in the new global scenario is not affected. It has to be remembered that public sector supplies information for free of charge or with little consideration and sometime this information may be related to metrology, agriculture, hydrography, demography, health, cartography, geology, environment etc. Sometime local users consumes localized databases and local users consume information in foreign databases.

Creation of new IPR in databases can create a danger in disturbing the balance between protection and dissemination and it will lean towards protection. Over-protected database regime would not create new ideas or goods but rather it would protect investment in collation and arrangement which is against the traditional objectives of IPRs, indirectly suggesting that IPRs are to encourage economic activity. Prof. Hugenholtz observed that in most of the European countries, database right had been categorized as a neighbouring right but from an economic perspective it was an understatement as he believed that potential anti competitive effect of the database right on the information market was much more than that of copyright or neighbouring right.

The monopoly created by copyright leaves unlimited alternative forms of expression to unlimited number of authors but the database right creates monopoly that is difficult or even impossible to invent around and thus confers significant market power. Cases where databases are the only source of information, it might

---

[40]Reichman, Samuelson, supra note 72.

[41]499 US 340 (1999).

[42](1997) 154 DLR 4th 328.

[43]Denicola R C (1981) Copyright in Collection of Facts: A Theory for the Protection of Non Fiction Literary Work. Colum L Rev 81:516.

[44]Maurer, Scotchmer, supra note 71, at 789.

result in a near—absolute downstream information monopoly.[45] On the other hand creating private property rights in intangible assets will not inevitably create commercial and social problem. Private property coupled with monitoring and supervision can create a balance between commercial market and public domain.

If it is socially desirable to encourage database protection, it is also socially desirable that information and ideas remain in the public domain. If facts and ideas remain accessible to consumers and competitors then more informational goods will be produced and eventually that will increase knowledge. It is an established principle in copyright law that protection of private interest should not block access to information.

Copyright protects expression and not idea, so ideas will not be monopolized. The *sui generis* law for protection of databases concentrates more on competition policy rather than promotion of culture. Thus it does not give more emphasis on public access. Digital technology influences databases in two ways—1. technology makes piracy of databases relatively easier and justifies a stronger protection, 2. technology helps the database maker to control access of user, track unauthorized access and charge for every sort of use of database and thus makes access to databases more difficult.

Kreiss observed that accessibility required two important features—users of work must be able to obtain a physical copy of the work and ideas and expressions must be available in human understandable terms.[46] Copyright protects original work of authorship and idea becomes work when it is reduced into writing in any medium through any material form. Ideas are so incorporeal that it does not take the shape of property but expressions are very well stand as property.[47] Idea-expression concept offers consumers a number of expressions of one ideas and that increases access to knowledge. Digital dilemma has created a combination of promise and peril as it improved access to information through technology but the same technology has created a hurdle to get access to information and thus the gap between information rich and information poor has further increased.[48]

2.3 Copyright and Free Speech

Copyright does not restrict free speech as it offers the author the exclusive right to specific expression and it does not protect the idea and also it permits fair use of the expression.[49] The Copyright Term Extension Act 1998 extended duration of

[45]Hugenholtz B (2004) Abuse of Database Right—Sole Source Information Bank under the EU Database Directive, Conference on Antitrust, Patent and Copyright, Paris, 2004.

[46]Kreiss R A (1995) Accessibility and Commercialization in Copyright Theory UCLA L Rev 43:1.

[47]Yen A C (1990) Restoring the Natural Law: Copyright as Labour and Possession. Ohio State LJ 51:517.

[48]Cohen J E (1998) Copyright and Jurisprudence of Self Help. Berk. Tech LJ 13:1089.

[49]Eldred v. Ashcroft 537 US 186.

copyrighted works by 20 years period. The United States Supreme Court held that the Copyright Term Extension Act 1998 was not unconstitutional as it did not restrict free speech.[50] The copyright patent clause of the US constitution provides,' Congress shall have power to promote Progress of Science and Useful Arts by securing to Authors for limited times the exclusive right to their writing'.[51]

US Supreme Court in Eldred v. Ashcroft[52] did not find anything in the text and history of the constitution which prevents limited term of copyright being extended by another limited term. The word 'limited time' in copyright clause does not mean inalterable but rather it means confined within certain limits. So extension of copyright term by 20 years which was confined within certain limits did not violate constitutional mandate. The benefit of the extension of copyright term was given to existing and future work, so that all of them could be governed even-handedly.

In 1993 European Union extended copyright term to life plus 70 years and made a provision not to allow this extended protection to the works of non-EU countries who did not offer similar extended term. So for the interest of reciprocity, the copyright term extension was justified. The extended term of protection would encourage more investment in creating more copyrightable works. Copyright Term Extension Act 1998 did not change the contours of copyright. The First Amendment secures freedom to make or decline to make one's speech. Thus the First Amendment of Copyright Term Extension Act 1998 is unwarranted.

Justice Breyer in his dissenting judgment in Eldred v. Ashcroft[53] quoted from Walterscheid[54] 'the economic effect of this 20 year extension—the longest blanket extension since the Nation's founding—is to make the copyright term not limited but virtually perpetual. Its primary legal effect is to grant the extended term not to authors, but to their heirs, estates or corporate successors. And most importantly, its practical effect is not to promote but to inhibit, the progress of 'Science'—by which word the Framers meant learning or knowledge'.

Even the personality approach can justify extension of copyright protection by inclusion of adaptation works but it may suffer difficulty in including work of information as personality in low authorial information works is less than apparent and thus does not qualify for copyright protection. The personality approach also expanded the scope of copyright protection by liberating it from any particular form and thereby allowing work irrespective of form to come under copyright protection.

But the question still remains whether copyright at all should protect functional, commercial works as the Court denied copyright protection to price catalogue of bathroom fixtures in J.L. Mott Iron Works v. Clow[55] and observed 'We discover

---

[50]Id.

[51]Article 1, Section 8 cl 8, US Constitution.

[52]Supra note 118.

[53]537 US 186.

[54]Walterscheid E (2000) The Nature of the Intellectual Property Clause: A Study in Historical Perspective. William S Hein & Co., p 125.

[55]82 F. 316 (7th Cir. 1897).

nothing original in the treatment of the subject, it is merely the picture of the bath tub in ordinary use…The question, therefore which confront us is, were such things intended to be protected by the constitutional provision in question? The object of that provision was to promote the dissemination of learning, by inducing intellectual labour in works which would promote the general knowledge in science and the useful arts. It is not designed as a protection to traders in the particular manner in which they might shot their wares. It sought to stimulate original investigation, whether in literature, science, or arts, for the betterment of the people, that they might be instructed and improved with respect to those subjects'.

2.4 Copyright and Incentive for Investment

The value of information in the commercial world is well understood and the informational works well fit into the principles of copyright law as it protects works like directories, calendars and statistical reports. If these works are valuable enough to be the target of piracy, they should be important enough to be protected. Commercial value of low authorial works can support justification for copyright protection. In Bleistein v. Donaldson Lithographing Co,[56] Justice Holmes observed 'if they command the interest of any public, they have a commercial value—it would be bold to say that they have not an aesthetic and educational value and the taste of any public is not to be treated with contempt'.

According to Justice Holmes, copyright can be awarded to both works with creative value and with commercial value. There can be two complimentary rationales for copyright protection—copyright protects against appropriation of both authorial personality present in a work and the labour and resource invested in it. When right in derivative work borrows justification from personality theory, the same cannot support low authorial work and the labour theory can support the hard work of second comer who adds his own labour to existing information to claim copyright. 'The doctrine of new and different use which permit copying of information in illustration of new and original proposition or for any other purpose not substantially the same as the plaintiff's use. There is no recognized principle which will prevent a subsequent compiler from copying common material from an existing compilation and combining them in a new form or using them for a different purpose'.[57]

In high authorship work, right to control adapted versions flow from personality right of self determination, that is to control manifestation of himself in various forms. Statutory expansion does not any more support a similar claim of hard work by a second comer in case of dramatization or translation works. The continuing

[56]188 U.S 239 (1903).

[57]Drone E S (1879) A Treatise on The Law of Property in Intellectual Productions in Great Britain and The United States. Little Brown & Co., Boston, p 424.

emphasis on protection of author's labour and investment in the making of informational works reflect the influence of expanded scope of high authorship copyright and along with that diminishing effect of new toil defense by the second comer in case of low authorial work is also reflected. This is closely linked with the existing standard of technology as when mere copying is costly and time consuming, addition of independent material to existing material can justify as significant contribution but the same may not be true if technology makes copying more simple and an easy job. As reproduction and dissemination of information became cheaper and faster, ability of the second comer to compete with the initial compiler increased.

The new technology helped the second comer to save time and money by copying the previously compiled information and thus pressure increased to protect information. With this faster and better means of copying, the quantum of copying leading towards infringement has been reduced. The new copying and distributing technology may force the Court to stretch copyright protection for low authorial work even to non-competing appropriation.

The modern view regarding copyright principle supports more the personality concept of original authorship rather than labour theory. The Courts may like to extend copyright protection to low authorial works depending on uniqueness of selection and arrangement. The reluctance of the court in this regard is mainly due to threat of monopolizing the facts and thus copyright protection often emphasizes on the need for keeping data free. Two other factors which influence the decision in these cases are economic harm of the first compiler and opportunity to reprimand the free rider. The new technology helps copying and developing derivative works in such a way that scope of copyright protection for low authorial works becomes very limited and can offer very little protection in a meaningful manner.

The United States Copyright Act 1909 mentioned directories, gazetteers and other compilations as categories of works register-able for copyright.[58] But 1976 Act removed specific mention of directories and gazetteers and added 'copyright protection subsists in original work of authorship'. Compilation was defined as works formed by the collection and assembling of pre-existing materials or of data that are selected, coordinated, or arranged in such a way that the resulting work as a whole constitutes an original work of authorship.[59]

It turned out to be original work of authorship included compilations if compilations as a whole constituted an original work of authorship. The emphasis was on original authorship which was not defined by statute but discussed through judicial decisions which created more controversy than clarifying it. As a result original authorship could cover a wide range of low authorial works—those whose investment of labour justified protection and those whose selection and arrangement justified protection.

---

[58]17 U.S.C. Section 5(a).

[59]17 U.S.C. Section 101.

The Second Circuit Court denied copyright protection to index card reporting daily bond information where the gathering of information for the card was a simple clerical work and required no exercise of judgment.[60] The Court rejected the grant of copyright on the basis of sweat of the brow doctrine as it felt that it would threaten public's access to information as it would guard a large amount of factual research materials. The logic of the Court's argument here (threatening public's access to information) indicated the effect of copyright or scope of copyright protection whereas the issue involved was copyright-ability of index card. Here if the index card was protected from verbatim copying, that would not prevent others from acquiring the same information elsewhere or using this information in different works.

The Court indicated that had they copied the volume in which daily bond cards were bound and infringement might have been found. Thus it appeared that without wholesome appropriation, sweat would not merit copyright protection. In other words it became that copyright ability of sweat would depend on extensiveness of copying. But copyright-ability and infringement should be dealt with separately as a work should be either copyrightable or not but it should not depend on the wholesale copying.

Professor Goreman observed 'Court should resolve the problem of full copyright protection under the rubric of infringement and fair use rather than of copyright-ability. This in turn will offer greater flexibility, enabling the court to label as infringement those works which interfere with the monopoly of the copyright holder without bringing a commensurate benefit to the public…'.[61]

Sweat is a strong argument for original authorship but should the personality concept be considered exclusively for the purpose of authorship? It is possible that considering the technological development sweat for informational work has in fact become a very little endeavour and hence loses the justification for copyright protection. This argument does not in any way affect labour intensive work of authorship. This technological superior position has not only challenged copyright-ability of low authorial work but also raised doubts about the maker of compilation. Who should be the author of computer assisted database—maker of the software who assists the database or the person who takes initiative to make the database?[62]

The problem of substantial labour pre-requisite for copyrightability is the assessment of quantum of labour that justifies copyright protection. How much of labour is required? And whether all labour is to be treated alike or there are some efforts which generate more sweat than others. A work by work analysis will require the court to differentiate between works which genuinely generates more

[60]Financial Information Inc. v. Moody's Investors Serv. Inc. 808 F 2d. 204 (2nd Cir. 1986).

[61]Gorman (1963) Copyright Protection for the Collection and Representation of Facts. Harv L Rev 76:1569.

[62]Samuelson (1986) Allocating Ownership Right in Computer-Generated Works. Univ Pitt L Rev 47:1185.

sweat and socially useful work like map created from original survey, for which copyright incentive is presumed to be essential and works which are collected rather easily such as maps created from data collected from variety of published sources, for which copyright would arguably be superfluous.

The social benefit theory justifies copyright protection by noting that social benefits will not follow in the absence of copyright. Address list, law reports, maps remains to be as useful as it was in the last century and as they are socially beneficial even today, copyright in these works should continue as it was in the last century. Even if court could indicate criteria to decide on social value, the standard cannot be predictable. No doubt the question will still remain whether copyright is the most appropriate means to ensure production of these works.

In case of compilations, there shall be many subjective choices regarding selection and arrangement. Like selection of stocks which will be representative of market trends, is completely a subjective choice. This selection and arrangement is a reflection of personality. The arrangement of materials can point out the selector's idea about a theme and his treatment of the theme. Like several law schools have their case books on different subjects, these case book may contain similar cases but the detailed table of contents of case books will be different and will represent the characteristics of the respective compiler. The structuring of chapters will reflect the perception of the editor of the case book. In case of database there is one more problem which is the nature and utility of database.

For a database, comprehensiveness is more important than selection and arrangement and thus the attention of the database maker is on making the database exhaustive and not goes for any unique style of selection. Moreover each researcher wants to exploit the data of a database in different fashion depending on their research focus, which makes it more logical to make the database more exhaustive rather than based on any particular selection criteria. With so much of subjective element in the preparation of informational work, the authorship of it becomes very evident and can call for personality concept in support of justification along with labour and social benefit theory.

Copyright protects against copying. There may be three types of copying so far as low authorial informational works are concerned—1. Close copying of all or substantial portions of the work in preparation of a competing work, 2. Use of work as a starting point to save a competitor time, money and effort, 3. Reproduction of substantial element of information in the creating of a different but not directly competing work.[63]

The 1976 Act precludes certain work of authorship from copyright protection like idea, procedure, process, and system, method of operation, concept, principle, and discovery, regardless of their form of expression.[64] Considering this exclusion, the first type of copying (full or substantial work) will cause infringement but the

[63]Ginsburg (1990) Creation and Commercial Value: Copyright Protection of Works of Information. Colum L Rev 90:1903.

[64]Section 102(b).

second type of copying (using as starting point) will be considered as consultation of the work and will not be considered as infringement and the third type of infringement (reproducing information only) will be considered as re-manipulation of data and will not be considered as infringement.

The issue of infringement is decided after considering the originality of copied portion in such a way that more original the copied material, the more protection it will deserve. But in case of facts, as it falls within the excluded group, so it will never be protected however original it may be. In low authorial work, form of original is so minimal that there shall not be infringement unless the whole work is virtually copied. The labour approach to originality may change the perception. If the second comer uses the work only as starting point and second work is not a copy of the first one, even then it can be a case of infringement on the ground that the first work is a product of labour of the first author.

The situation of the third type of copying is placed in a better position as it adds a lot of its own material along with material taken from the first comer and it does not create a competing work. This also gets support from social benefit theory as the society gets new combinations of information and thus it contributes to the promotion of knowledge indirectly. In determining infringement thus, both high labour work of the first author and low or negligible labour work of second author become important criteria.

The Court will keep it in mind that although the defendant has invested his labour but the fact that he copied portions of plaintiff's work, the defendant has spared him from putting the labour to that extent. 'Directory Services Co. tells us that it did not infringe because its agent too was industrious. This is irrelevant. The infringement comes from the fact that Directory Services copied Rockford Map's output, not from the fact that it ended with a different plot map.

The second map at issue contained all the same information as the plaintiff including planted errors and did not add any new information'.[65] Re-manipulation of data is discouraged to secure the investment of the first compiler, though it may go away from the conceptual framework of the copyright law. 'If the compiler's protection is limited solely to the form of expression, the economic incentives underlying the copyright laws are largely swept away….Moreover given the manner in which information is stored in automated electronic compilations, an emphasis upon arrangement and form in compilation protection becomes even more meaningless than in the past'.[66] The danger of this argument is that it does not consider copyright protection in forms and arrangement and recognizes commercial value of gathered facts and thereby it rejects the personality based approach of authorship.

In case of high authorship works like biographies and news reports Court observes goal of copyright law in a different manner. 'The protection accorded to the copyright holder has never extended to history, to be documented facts or

[65]Rockford Map Publishers Inc. v. Directory Services Co. 768 F2d. 145 (7th Cir. 1985).

[66]National Business Lists Inc. v. Dun & Bradstreet Inc. 552 F.Supp. 89.

explanatory hypothesis….The scope of copyright in historical account is narrowed indeed, embracing no more than the author's original expression of particular fact and theories already in public domain…There can be no copyright in the order of presentation of the facts, nor indeed in their selection'.[67] The strength of protection grows in inverse proportion to the amount of personal authorship.[68] Thus more the history books exposition of fact looks like telephone book, the more protection the information receives. In case of high authorship information work like historical document, it has literary value independent of the information contained in it but in case of low authorial information work like telephone book, the basic value is a source of information.

Copyright should not only be concerned about authorial personality but also investment protection in case of information of commercial value. The principles need to be re-examined on the basis of existing technology. If computer can copy and reorganize information, failure to protect information will deprive meaningful incentive to the compiler.

Incentive model presumes that copyright is needed to prompt authors to take up creative labour.[69] Personal authorship becomes irrelevant in an inquiry into incentives.[70] If copyright's role to create incentive then copyright should be given only when incentive is required and the burden of proof is on the author to demonstrate that he needs incentive and thus should be given copyright and protection may be created. 'Glory is the reward of science and those who deserve it scorn all meaner views, I speak not of the scribblers for bread, who teases the press with their wretched productions. …It was not for gain that Bacon, Newton, Milton, Locke instructed and delighted the world, it would be unworthy of such men to traffic with dirty book sellers for so much as a sheet of letter press. When the book seller offered Milton five pound for his Paradise Lost, he did not reject it and commit his poem to the flames, nor did he accept the miserable pittance as a reward for his labour, he knew that real price for his work was immortality and that posterity would pay it'.[71]

Landes and Judge Posner felt that some protection was appropriate but inquired how much protection would wield the greatest production of works from the first and second author.[72] This maximizing author's return is not necessarily creating a monopoly over the work. 'The economic philosophy behind the clause (Constitution's copyright clause) empowering Congress to grant patent and

[67]Hoehling v. Universal City Studios Inc. 618 F.2d 972 (2nd Cir. 1980).

[68]Gorman (1982) Fact or Fancy? The Implication for Copyright. J Copy Soc 560.

[69]Gordon (1989) An Inquiry into the Merit of Copyright: The Challenges of Consistency, Consent and Encouragement Theory. Stan L Rev 41:1343.

[70]Yen, supra note 116, at 517.

[71]Lord Camden (1774). In: Ginsburg, supra note 132, at 1908.

[72]Landes, Posner (1989) An Economic Analysis of Copyright Law. J Legal Stud 18:325.

copyright is the conviction that encouragement of individual effort by personal gain is the best way to advance public welfare'.[73]

Landes and Posner while addressing the author's economic interest in control over derivative works observed that scope of copyright monopoly extends beyond mere reproduction to comprehend the various ways in which a work may be recast or transformed.[74] Hardcover sales of a book may not generate enough revenue to recoup its advance but subsidiary right may prove to be real source of income. This economic analysis of derivative work is not only applicable for high authorship work but it can also be for low authorship work of informational product. Investment for creating directory may be discouraged if the scope of protection does not cover the full value of work. The value of directory can be extended to rearranging or creating sub directories. As re-manipulated compilation may be a copyrightable work, so if control over copyright is awarded to the author of the derivative work rather than to the first author, the exploitation of the derivative work can interfere with exploitation of the first work.

A directory arranged by address may not affect the sale of a directory arranged by address if they operate in two different works. But if they operate in same market each can pose potential to undermine other's market as a third party can reverse engineer directory arranged by address to create another competing directory arranged by name. This cannot be termed as infringement, although copying a name directory to produce another name directory may affect reproduction right. Copying a derivative work (address directory) to create another name directory is like acquiring information from public domain and which cannot be objected. Copyright in re-manipulation does not make sense if a third party can revise a name directory and create address directory to compete with the original address directory.

This economic argument can be made to protect low authorship informational work against re-manipulation but the possible impact is that it can affect the other copyright principle of not protecting data itself.[75] 'By limiting potential rewards in the copyright market....by refusing to extend copyright to new uses...the entrepreneurial calculus which precedes risk taking in authorship and publishing is shifted in the direction of not taking a chance, i.e., not writing or publishing a risky work whether ideologically or economically risky'.[76]

It will be interesting to find out whether fact-expression dichotomy has the same role in the copyright law as idea-expression. Protection of idea depletes the universe of themes and subjects about which people are expected to write, compose and design. If idea-expression dichotomy is applied strictly, it restricts the scope of protection of computer program as it denies effective coverage and thus calls for a

[73]Mazer v. Stein, 347 US 201 (1954).

[74]Landes, Posner, supra note 141, at 353.

[75]Hurt, Schuman (1966) The Economic Rationale of the Copyright. AMEco Rev 56:435.

[76]Ladd (1983) The Harm of the Concept of Harm in Copyright. J Copy Soc 30:421.

sui generis protection for computer program where some amount of idea can be protected.[77]

Copyright's goal of encouraging and enabling both first and second author to create and disseminate useful works depends on how the first author presents the fact and how the second author uses them. Facts contained in works of high authorship can be treated as part of public domain as they become inseparable from the second author's worldview and becomes necessary building blocks for second comer's subsequent creations. 'It would be unlikely for an author to make inadvertent use of directory listing because we do not normally learn the contents of directories…Protection of the facts in plaintiff's directories…did not prohibit defendants from consulting the same pre-existing sources that plaintiff had consulted. As a result plaintiff's copyright did not remove facts from the public domain, it simply prohibited a single albeit more efficient route to unearthing them'.[78]

It is difficult to substitute idea-expression concept with economic value criteria. Thus it becomes extremely important what is characterized as expression, so that the remaining portion can be termed as 'idea'. Fact-expression concept makes sense in case of a work like narrative history. Here limiting extent of copyright to the first author's subjective contribution allows the second author to account for all sources and also offers the first author extensive protectable material through selection, arrangement, description and evaluation of facts. In case of low authorial work, if the first and second work operates in the same market, the second comer's free reuse of the first compilation, does not advance public access but discourages the production of these works. If the second comer competes with the first one, the public will not make any gain of knowledge but the incentive of first compiler will be compromised. Even if the second comer exploits different markets, if there is a possibility that the first compiler may exploit that market by repackaging the product, then also the interest of the first compiler is weakened.

Reliance to incentive alone may turn out to be counterproductive. Maximum incentive can be offered only by creating exclusive control over any recombination made out of information contained in a compilation. The effect of this is to cut-off public access to new informational works if there is no mechanism to force the first author to grant licenses. The term of copyright is such a long period that if an informational work is blocked for such a long time, that itself can cause serious injury to the content of public domain. Balancing between commercial value of low authorial compilation and promoting creation of and access to wide variety of informational works is a challenge to the copyright law.

The scope of copyright protection has grown from mere reproduction to public performance and derivative right as copyright accommodated not only print media but also photograph, motion pictures, sound recording and computer program.

[77]Menell (1989) An Analysis of the Scope of Copyright Protection for Application Programs. Stan L Rev 41:1045.

[78]Litman J (1990) The Public Domain. Emory L Rev 39:965.

Copyright protection in factual compilation can be extended to include re-manipulation of information by extending derivative work to low authorial information work and by creating a different kind of copyright for low authorial informational work which will necessarily combine authorial presence, labour and investment as justification. Along with this if the scope of infringement is limited to selection and arrangement in a factual compilation, considering the high level of technology; it will compromise the interest of the compiler.

In the absence of copyright protection, copying can be prevented to some extent by protective contract. In case of online services, keeping track of copying is possible but otherwise it is a difficult proposition. It is more difficult for the information provider to make out whether the copy of information is for private use or for resale or repackaging of information. It is possible for service provider to charge a high price to cover uncompensated resale of information. If the information is provided through free standing mode like CD ROM, then securing payment for copying becomes all the more difficult. Copying from print media is virtually impossible to keep track of as no professional photocopying establishment, office, libraries keep track of what is being copied and hardly people take permission from publishers to photocopy informational works.[79] So it can be observed that individual supervision of the fact of copying on behalf of proprietors is difficult.

In this situation, collective administration (like Copyright Clearance Center) of right can offer some benefit to the proprietor. But generally the right licensed is the right to reproduce and not the derivative work right. The information provider may try to secure control even after the delivery by obtaining acquirer's consent not to reuse the information without the permission of the provider or without paying royalty. Even without copyright, the information can reach to the hands of the third party through unauthorized access or hacking. To address a solution, anti-copying device is not an alternative as private users need to copy databases. If resale of information is considered to be a problem then in some cases due to nature of information, such as stock exchange information, old information which do not have much market. Thus for such information, resale is not a problem. It has been observed that privatizing information through contract, encryption and similar devices may carry greater individual and social costs than would a copyright system.[80] If the author expends more in protecting information than in gathering information, it will compromise with the quality of collection. The greater protection cost will deter the author from entering the market.

Landes and Posner have argued with respect to copyright law that beyond some level copyright protection may actually be counterproductive by raising the cost of expression and thereby cutting off the production of new and different works. Full copyright protection for compilation of data which allows the author to prevent any kind of copying, may turn to be counterproductive, as subsequent compilers under

[79]Liebowitz (1985) Copying and Indirect Appropriability: Photocopying of Journals. J Pol Econ 93:945.

[80]Kitch (1980) The Law and Economics of Rights in Valuable Information. J Legal Stud 9:683.

this protection can start from the scratch by going to the source and then get full copyright over their compilation. If the second comer is not willing to start from scratch, he is free to negotiate with the first compiler for a license to copy and re arrange. This may give an opportunity to the first compiler to charge a prohibitively high price for recombining data. Even the first compiler may refuse to grant license as he has no obligation to grant license. Sometimes the first compiler refuses to grant license as he wants to come out with a derivative work in future. The first compiler may refuse the license if the second comer wants an exclusive licensee.

Collective licensing may prove to be effective in such situations as it assists both copyright owners and users and it has been proved to be effective in case of performing rights and to some extent in cases of photocopying. Collective licensing tries to balance between transaction cost and greed of licensors and it offers equal access to data. Collective licensing tries to reduce the transaction cost and thereby facilitates access to data by deciding the fee on the basis of the capacity of the user and not on the nature and quantity of material copied. It is true that the justification for compulsory licensing is transaction cost but it does not mean that if this transaction cost does not exist, owner of copyright will be willing to license his work to all who like to use his work as copyright is based on the right to exclude others from exploiting the work protected by copyright.

The more important purpose of compulsory licensing is to nullify the effect of monopoly created by owner of copyright, by compelling the owner to make the work accessible to interested people. It is also true that through fair use defences, work may be accessible to people but the difficulty is that it does not allow anyone to determine ex ante what can be copied and to what extent, as fair use is a very fact specific defence.[81] If in a given legal regime, no protection is available for informational works; compulsory license will help to make the information available for exploitation. Thus compulsory licensing will be effective both for under protection of informational work (where the work is held to be not original or protection is available only for selection and arrangement) overprotection of informational work (where re-manipulation of information is inducted). Compulsory license can be effective tool in balancing between protection and dissemination.

If a compulsory license regime is proposed for informational work, it can even absorb the effect of reintroducing the sweat or investment concept, i.e., protection for gathering information and the effect of introducing that copyright extend to protection of information also. This proposed change should come with the criteria that protection should be available only if informational work has been publicly disseminated, considering the objective of copyright law is to disseminate works among public. It is equally true that incentive to produce is not necessarily incentive to disseminate as copyright law not only protects published work but also unpublished work.[82]

[81]Fisher W (1988) Reconstructing the Fair Use Doctrine. Harv L Rev 101: 1661.

[82]Swanson (1988) The Role of Disclosure in Modern Copyright Law. J Pat & Tra Off Soc 70:217.

The compulsory license can replace contractual protection in cases where other means of protection are too costly and the owner is willing to disseminate the work among the public. The compulsory license is effective for promoting public dissemination of new compilation based on prior information and thus it is not only offering compensation but also removing control over derivative work. It has to be remembered that in case of confidential information, compulsory license does not work as it goes against the purpose of confidential information.

Compilations which are not yet disseminated into public or which are still in gestation period, compulsory license is not effective as it undermines the goal of encouraging creation of new informational work by discouraging the compiler to take advantage of releasing the work first into the market. The compulsory licensing can be effective in creating opportunity for third parties for coming out with competing compilations. It has to be remembered that the compulsory licensing can operate for right to create derivative work but not for right of reproduction. But in this process the producer is deprived of the right to prevent copying and reshuffling of data in creation of different databases.

The compulsory licensing does not offer right to sell, lease, and transfer or reproduce the original copy. Here it can be mentioned 'slipping' is different from reproducing as 'slipping' refers to copying by reference where the second comer contacts all whose name is found in the first compilation and takes permission to include them in the second compilation.[83] Although in essence, it creates a competing compilation but the process involves something more than copying. It can be observed that 'slipping' stands in between derivative work and reproduced work. Often the social benefit arising out of open production of identical work gets overshadowed by disincentive which follows from that. If it is found that policing of right of reproduction is so expensive that lower return from compulsory license is more than the negotiated price minus enforcement cost, then compulsory license can stand as superior incentive.[84]

In Blestein v. Donaldson,[85] Justice Holmes paired personality and commercial value concept together and declared that 'individuals are not free to copy the copy of an original work' and as argument he placed 'even a copy is the personal reaction of an individual upon nature'. Although the earlier view condemned copying the copy as it compromised first author's laboriously earned property but Justice Holmes argued 'copying also misappropriated some aspect of author's personality'. According to Justice Holmes, under copyright, a work can be protected because it embodies the author's personality and also it represents a commercial value.

Copyright respects both—original personal imprint of the author on the work and investment of labour and resources. The high and low authorship work does not much differentiate on the issue of copyright status but on the scope of protection. The copyright owner of high authorship work is entitled for compensation for

---

[83]Ginsburg, supra note 132, at 1931.

[84]Ginsburg, supra note 132, at 1932.

[85]188 US 239 (1903).

derivative work and at the same time can have control over the work as it reflects the personality of the work. But in case of low authorship work which does not reflect personality of the author, there is no justification to have control over the derivative work.

The availability of compensation through licensing can prove to be more attractive to the producer of the compilation than insecurity of litigation but license can offer only compensation but no control of the derivative work. The compulsory license creates an opportunity to get reward for the initial producer's investment of labour and capital and also allows subsequent compiler to exploit information without incurring the cost of independent generation of the same data.

2.5 Requirement of Originality in Copyright Law

Intellectual property rights are seen as system of incentives intended to promote the creation of new objects, knowledge and ideas, so as to grant monopoly to its creators to allow them to secure income from commercial exploitation of their creations as Jeremy Bentham observed the usefulness of the limited monopolies to encourage production of things. Thomas Jefferson emphasized on the social benefits of free dissemination of ideas—'If nature has made any one thing less susceptible than all others of exclusive property, it is the action of the thinking power called an idea, which an individual may exclusively possess as long as he keeps it to himself, but the moment it is divulged, it forces itself into the possession of everyone, and the receiver cannot dispossess himself of it. Its peculiar character, too, is that no one possesses the less, because every other possesses whole of it……That ideas should freely spread from one to another over the globe, for the moral and mutual instruction of man and improvement of his condition, seems to have been peculiarly and benevolently designed by nature, when she made them like fire, expansible over all space, without lessening their density in any point and like the air in which we breathe….incapable of confinement or exclusive appropriation'.[86]

The main points on this issue remains—1. Knowledgeis 'non-rival' goods, means consumption of which by a person does not limit access or use by other consumers, 2. Once knowledge has been disseminated, it becomes difficult or impossible to prevent in absence of a legal barrier, others from using it who does not wish to pay, 3. Free dissemination of knowledge is beneficial to society as it contributes in creation of new knowledge, 4. Intellectual property rights are temporary monopolies that are granted in exchange for creation of new things.

Copyright or so called right to print and publish was developed in mediaeval England. With the advent of printing press, the art of publishing became very

[86]Devid P A (2002) Does the New Economy Need all the Old IPR Institutions? Digital Information Goods and Access to Knowledge for Economic Development, WIDER Conference for the New Economy in Development, Helsinki, 2002. In: supra note 7, at 7.

popular. The King asserted control over publishing to control formation of dissent and influencing public opinion. By royal charters and letters patent, authors or printers were granted the privilege to publish and import. This was followed by establishment of Stationers' Company and book seller's monopoly was continued with it. Statute of Anne was enacted in 1709 to secure the rights of authors as its preamble suggested 'An Act for the Encouragement of Learning, by vesting the Copies of printed Books in the Authors or Purchaser of such Copies, during the Times therein mentioned'. The preamble also echoed the objective of preventing printers and book sellers from publishing 'Books and other Writings without Consent of the Authors and Proprietors .... to their very great Detriment and too often to the Ruin of them and their Families and for encouragement of learned Men to compose and write useful Books'.

The creation of a statutory copyright raised the issue whether copyright under common law still existed after the enactment of the statute. In Donaldson v. Beckett[87] it was held that with the passing of Statute of Anne, common law right and remedies of the author no longer existed and were governed solely by the statute. The nature of copyright is such that there must be as embodiment of the work. It is not sufficient that the work be in the mind of the creator. Some early statute of copyright described the subject of copyright as new and original.[88] The Copyright Act 1911 confirmed that work in respect of which copyright is claimed must be original.

The question that remains is that in what sense must the work be original? Work will lack originality if it is copied from another. This does not mean that the subject matter should be new as required in patents. It is essential that the work is created by the author. Is it necessary that the author must expend some intellectual effort to get protection? Is it sufficient for copyright that the author exerts labour and incur expenses? Whether industrious gathering and listing of data qualify a work to be original or it requires some additional elements like selection or arrangement. It is an elementary principle of copyright law that there can be no copyright in fact as the author may record a fact but does not create the fact.

From the beginning, the purpose of copyright is public welfare. It recognizes need of Enlightenment—'the encouragement of learning'.[89] Hugh Laddie observed, 'The whole human development is derivative. We stand on the shoulders of the scientists, artists and craftsmen who preceded us. We borrow and develop what they have done, not necessarily as parasites but simply as the next generation. It is at the heart of what simply we know as progress. When we are asked to remember the Eighth Commandment, 'thou shalt not steal', bear in mind that borrowing and developing have always been acceptable'.[90]

---

[87](1774) 1 ER 837.

[88]Telstra Corporation Ltd. v. Desktop Marketing Systems Pvt. Ltd 2001 FCA 612.

[89]Patterson L R (1968) Copyright In Historical Perspective, p 147.

[90]Laddie H (1996) Copyright: Over-strength, Over-regulated, Over-rated? EIPR 5:253.

The US constitution mandate is based on this principle.[91] TRIPS[92] and WCT[93] also recognize this principle. The concept of copyright is based on the premise that to protect public interest, private enjoyment of work should be considered as privilege and to be continued with, considering it as social obligation of copyright.[94] Copyright is designed to protect originality or in other way skill, labour and judgment involved in a work. Access to copyrighted work is recognized as permitted work and idea-expression dichotomy is treated as integral part of the issue.[95]

In Bleistein v. Donaldson Lithographing Co[96] Court rejected the argument that copyrightable work must rise to some level of aesthetic merit and observed 'The work is the personal reaction of an individual upon nature. Personality always contains something unique. It expresses its singularity even in the hand writing and a very modest grade of art has in it something irreducible which is one man's alone. That something he may copyright unless there is a restriction in the word of the act.' Locke observed that every man has a property in his own person. So anything created by labour of his body or work of his hands, belong to him as one owns the fruit of one's effort.[97] The right to one's personality both transcends property and perhaps somewhat contradictorily is embraced within the right of property in its widest sense.[98]

> The principle which protects personal writings all other personal productions not against theft and physical appropriation but against publication in any form is not the principle of private property but that of an inviolate personality. The right of property in its widest sense, including all possession, including all rights and privileges and hence embracing the right to an inviolate personality, affords alone that broad basis upon which the protection which the individual demands can be rested.[99]

Let us find out if there is difference in scope of protection between personality based concept and labour based concept of copyright law. Both the approaches would not consider laboriously prepared variation of existing work as infringement.

---

[91]U.S. Constitution, Article 1, Section 8, cl. 8.

[92]Article 7—'The protection and enforcement of intellectual property rights should contribute to the promotion of technological innovation and to the transfer and dissemination of technology, to the mutual advantage of producers and users of technological knowledge and in a manner conducive to social and economic welfare and to a balance of rights and obligations'.

[93]Preamble—'Recognizing the need to maintain a balance between the rights of authors and the larger public interest, particularly education, research and access to information as reflected in the Berne Convention'.

[94]Zimmerman D L (1994) Copyright in Cyberspace: Don't Throw Out the Public Interest with the Bath Water. Ann Surv Am L 403.

[95]Section 29, Copyright, Designs and Patents Act 1988, Article 10, TRIPS.

[96]188 US 239 (1903).

[97]Locke J (1955) Second Treatise of Civil Government, Gateway, Chap. V, Section 27. In: Hughes (1989) The Philosophy of Intellectual Property. Geo L J 77:287.

[98]Warren, Brandeis, supra note 15, at 193.

[99]Warren, Brandeis, supra note 15, at 193.

The variations need not be extensive to capture the personality of the second comer and in that case the personality approach will recognize more works with little variations from earlier works. Justice Kaplan observed 'the changing status of authors in the nineteenth century, from imitative craftsman to professionals conscious of their unique individuality, led in the nineteenth century both to increasing intolerance of copying and to disapproval composition of heavily dependent on predecessor's work'.[100]

The expansion of scope of author's right, from reproduction right to adaptation right, has been influenced both by labour approach and personality approach. Labour approach may not satisfactorily answer why the fruits through translation and dramatization should be reaped by the original author when they are the product of labour from translator and dramatist. The personality approach can offer the missing link to the question. In Holmes v. Hurst,[101] the United States Supreme Court determined that it was not infringement to reprint portions of a magazine in which chapters of Holmes' book The Autocrat of the Breakfast Table had been published serially when the magazine in which the material first appeared had not been copyrighted.

The Court rejected Holmes's argument that the copyright attached only to the form in which his work ultimately appeared. Had the Court held that the serial publication of the work in magazine form was not a copyrightable book then magazine publication would have had to bearing on the copyright status of the book. Because the Court held the serial publication to constitute publication of the book, the magazine's non-compliance with copyright formalities cast Holmes' literary work into public domain. Subsequent publication in the book form could not revive the copyright. The Court observed 'It is the intellectual production of the author which the copyright protects and not the particular form which such production ultimately takes and the word book is not to be understood in its technical sense of a bound volume but any species of publication which the author selects to embody his literary product'.

This concept of copyright in authorial creation which is nothing but an intellectual production will allow copyright to subsist on any work irrespective of its form and this will allow copyright to enlarge its scope and embrace many more new types of works in modern times which are yet to form its distinct character. The literary products thus can be well interpreted to go beyond the realm of literature and can cover works like film and software.

The greatest benefit of the digital economy is the universal access which allows any information to be made available to anyone, anywhere and at any time but this advantage challenges the basic premise of intellectual property law and makes it difficult to protect the rights of the owner. Exclusivity means the ability of the owner to control access to the product as the seller will have absolute control over the product so far as access and distribution is concerned and here free riding

---

[100]Kaplan B (2005) An Unhurried View Of Copyright. Lexis Nexis, p 17.

[101]174 US 82 (1899).

becomes impossible. The concept of rivalry denotes that consumption of a product by one will affect the supply from others as it happens in case of retail goods where one product cannot be enjoyed by two persons at one time.

Most forms of intellectual properties are by nature non exclusive and non rival as ideas; concepts are readily accessible to many at one time without any control of the seller. Naturally the sufficient incentive to take risk to develop and market new products is missing. In such a situation government tries to create artificial exclusivity so that the required incentive can be created through legislation.[102] The guiding principle of copyright law is to allow exclusivity as much necessary to provide incentives to creativity but otherwise to protect public domain. The exclusivity created by the Govt. is artificial and arbitrary and it requires to be constantly watched so that discouragement of free riding should not discourage the social process of incremental development.[103]

This exclusivity problem has affected digital property as well as digital goods, which can be consumed by consumers and competitors without compromising its quality or quantity. This always prompts for free riding without compensation. Digital property can be accessed, copied, modified and transferred so easily that intellectual property law is finding it very difficult to create the artificial exclusivity. When the digital property is a database then it becomes further difficult proposition for law to create the same exclusivity.[104] Computers can archive, compare and manipulate in such a way that collection and arrangement of data has become a very easy job and it has created more problems for maintaining the exclusivity as a balance has to be made between incentives to promote creation of useful compilation and free access to information.

[102]Landes, Posner, supra note 141, at 328.

[103]Breyer S (1970) The Uneasy Case for Copyright: A Study of Copyright in Books, Photocopies and Computer Programs. Harv LRev 84:281.

[104]Plotkin M (1999) The times they are changin'. Vend J Int'l L Prac 1:46.

Chapter 3
Copyright Law, Databases and Its Protection

3.1 Analysis of Copyright Law

3.1.1 Objectives of Copyright

Today if the knowledge is shared with someone then it may create competitor (the person with whom the information is shared) and diminishes the value of the person who has shared the knowledge and even the person who has shared the knowledge may lose the market.[1] Stronger and rigorously policed international standard of intellectual property will facilitate creation of more intellectual property rights which in turn will fetch more innovation and investment. The reverse has also been argued[2] that intellectual property makes information costlier and adversely affects progress. Knowledge is not only power but also source of profit in modern economy as rightly described by Peter Drucker that the basic economic resource 'is and will be knowledge'.[3] As the management of knowledge is and has been the main game, the protection of intellectual property rights has become so important.

When information is valuable, people will not be interested in divulging it unless it is backed by disclosure agreement, knowing very well that disclosure agreement will not be able to avoid leaking out some of the information in the process of handling it. Once the information is shared with, it becomes knowledge in the mind of the person with whom it has been shared and it becomes extremely difficult to control further use of the information. The difficulty in treating information as property is the notion that information of the world should be freely accessible to

[1]Stasik E (2003) Patent Or Perish. Althos Publishing, p 7–8.
[2]Copying and imitating is a tool to be used in the process of learning and acquisition of skill. Creator of innovation also borrows ideas from others and intellectual property right will make information costlier which in turn will make borrowing difficult and progressively choke innovation. Drahos P, Braitwaite J (2002) Information Feudalism. Earthscan Publications, London, p 2.
[3]Drucker P (1993) Post Capitalist Society. Harper Business, New York, p 8. In: Drahos, Braitwaite, id., p 39.

A. Mazumder, *Database Law*, DOI 10.1007/978-981-10-2200-5_3

the people of the world and information once acquired cannot be forgotten.[4] The exclusivity of possession and enjoyment which are considered to be important feature of property right are lacking in case of information and making it difficult to be considered it as property.

Man has always strived for progress. A few of such attempts may be recognized as the most important in human development until now. The discovery of fire, the invention of the wheel and learning the art of cultivation are some examples. The invention of the printing press cannot be far behind. Without the protection afforded by copyright, the invention of the printing press would not be of such relevance as it is today.

The aim of copyright laws in the U.S., derived from the copyright-patent clause in the Constitution, is to 'promote the progress of Science and useful Arts'. It does so by protecting investment of skill, time, labour and money towards the production of abundant information[5] by creating a useful and effective mechanism, which allows the author to exploit his work for economic benefits.[6] In turn, such information may be relied on by others to create more information thus leading to greater knowledge and progress in an umpteen number of fields.

Copyright, therefore, provides an incentive to authors to make information publicly available. Copyright utilizes sound economic principles of rewarding an author's effort to advance a much broader social cause.

In some cases though, it becomes important to discern which one of the two is the ultimate goal that copyright law seeks to advance. In the seminal case of *Feist Publications v. Rural Telephone*,[7] the United States Supreme Court made it abundantly clear that the primary objective of copyright law in the country was not to reward the labour of authors but to promote the 'progress of Science and useful Arts'. In fact, this was recognized much earlier in *Baker v. Selden*,[8] wherein it was held that "The very objective of publishing a book on Science and Arts is to communicate the useful knowledge which it contains. But this objective would be frustrated if the knowledge could not be used without incurring the guilt of piracy". Thus, it seems evident that in applying copyright law, courts in the United States must give precedence to the social objective of copyright at the expense of the reward theory.

In the civil law systems, only a work of personal, intellectual creation is worthy of protection. In other words copyright laws have been framed with the objective to protect works of authorship, which are regarded as an extension of the personality of the authors. This approach is reflected in the broader framework of protection granted to authors in civil law countries. Here the author's rights are not limited to

[4]Rees, Chalton, supra note 1, at 5.

[5]Goldstein P (2000) Copyright. Aspen Law & Business, Section 2.2.1.

[6]Bainbridge D (2002) Intellectual Property. Pearson Education Ltd., p 33.

[7]499 US 340 (1991).

[8](1880) 101 US 99.

economic rights of exploitation alone, but have traditionally extended to moral rights.[9]

The common law system in the United Kingdom has taken a more commercial approach to copyright, the rationale being to reward those who spend time, skill and effort in creating intangible property of the kind which can be exploited by being reproduced, performed, etc. In this system, copyright law fundamentally exists to prevent others from taking unfair advantage of an author's skill and efforts.[10] This treatment of copyright is best summed up in the words of Justice Peterson in *University of London Press Ltd. V. University Tutorial press Ltd.*[11] where he stated 'There remains the rough practical test that what is worth copying is *prima facie* worth protecting."

The Berne Convention came up with two fold objectives—to deal with challenges like unauthorized performance of protected works, particularly in the fields of literary and musical work and unauthorized manufacturing and disseminating of copies of protected works, particularly based upon the reprinting of books.[12]

Such an identification of the objective of copyright law is especially important involving factual works or compilations, which essentially is the subject matter of this research. If the reward theory were the basis of copyright then the subsistence of copyright in such works would be justified by the application of the sweat of the brow doctrine, but if its real objective is the advancement of science and useful arts, or the protection of the personality of an author, then such a claim, and the sweat of the brow doctrine itself, must be rejected.

3.1.2 Interpreting Originality in Copyright

As a rule copyright subsists only in *original* works and thus *originality* assumes a significant position in copyright laws.[13] The need for originality arises from the fact that rights for economic exploitation of the work should not be granted if it is a mere copy of an existing work or any other material already in the public domain. The requirement of originality, as stated earlier, is closely related to the objective of copyright law and therefore it must be interpreted accordingly. According to

---

[9]Moral rights include (a) The right to be identified as the author of the work i.e. the 'paternity right' (b) The right of an author of a work to object to derogatory treatment of that work i.e. 'integrity right' (c) A general right, that every person has, not to have a work falsely attributed to him.

[10]Bainbridge, supra note 179, at 62.

[11][1916] 2 Chap. 601.

[12]Ricketson S (1886–1986) The Berne Convention For The Protection Of Literary And Artistic Works, p 17–19. In: Hilty R M (2006) Five Lessons About Copyright In The Information Society. J Copy Soc USA, 53:103.

[13]It may however be noted that prior the Copyright Act (1909) (UK) originality was not a statutory pre-requisite to copyright protection.

Goldstein, "The aim of copyright law is to direct investment towards the production of abundant information, while the aim of patent law is to direct investment towards the production of efficient information. The relatively lax originality standard aims at the first object while patent law's novelty and non-obviousness requirements aim at the second."[14]

3.1.3 Originality—Traditional Approach

Originality is a necessary pre-requisite to copyright in UK and is mandated by S.1 (1)(a) of the Copyright Act 1988. However in the absence of originality being defined in the statute the issue has once again been left open for the courts to decide. In this regard the House of Lords has decided in *University of London Press v. University Tutorial Press Ltd*[15] that originality merely requires "only that a work should not be copied but should originate from the author." In other words, a work is original and may command copyright protection, even it is similar to a prior work, provided it was not copied from such prior work, but is rather a product of the independent skill and labour of the author. Moreover in order to qualify for protection, a sufficient amount of 'skill, labour and judgement' should be expended in the creation of a work.

Creativity has never been a *sine qua non* for the subsistence of copyright in a work[16] and the courts have shown no explicit departure from this interpretation of originality. However in the absence of any guiding principles as to the quantum of skill and judgment required,[17] the question of subsistence of copyright in a work has to be determined on the facts of a particular case.

3.1.4 Changing Notion of Originality

Originality is a constitutional requirement in the United States.[18] It is an established principle that the requirement of originality is fixed at a low threshold and may easily be satisfied as long as it has not been copied from another source.[19] The sole requirement of independent creationto satisfy originality standards was highlighted by Judge Learned Hand in *Sheldon v. Metro-Goldwyn Pictures Corp.*,[20] in which

[14]Goldstein, supra note 178, at Section 2.2.1.

[15][1916] 2 Chap. 601.

[16]Bentley, Sherman (2001) Intellectual Property Law. Oxford University Press, p 93.

[17]As was pointed out by Maugham J., in Cambridge University Press v. University Tutorial Press.

[18]*See* Feist v. Rural (1991) 111 S.Ct. 1282.

[19]Goldstein, supra note 178, at Section 2.2.1.

[20]81 F.2d 49 (2nd Cir.).

he observed that "If by some magic a man who had never known it were to compose a new Keats's Ode on a Grecian Urn, he would be an 'author' and, if he copyrighted it, others might not copy the poem, though they might of course copy Keats's."

The United States Supreme Court placed a significant gloss on the originality requirement in the landmark decision of *Feist Publications v. Rural Telephone*[21] involving the copyright-ability of telephone directory white pages sequenced alphabetically. Departing from this conservative and broad definition of originality, the court observed that in addition to independent effort, originality required a 'minimal degree of creativity'.

Moreover before *Feist Publications v. Rural Telephone*[22] courts generally required some expression of creativity only in the case of art reproduction[23] and representational photographs. It might be because, unlike verbal descriptions or paintings that inevitably embody some element of the artist's personality, these works will often appear to be exact mirrors of the image they reflect.[24] *Feist Publications v. Rural Telephone*[25] extended this creativity requirement to factual works such as a telephone directory.

3.1.5 Traditional V. Modern Approach

The issue of creativity, as a component of originality is confined to a small class of works and nowadays ensures that almost all other works easily pass the test of originality. It is in this field that the treatment of originality is likely to affect the copyright-ability of a work because one can merely discover facts and not create them. On the one hand such a work may be copyrightable because it has come into being as a result of independent effort while on the other it may not be given protection because it lacks creativity. There can be arguments both for and against subsistence of copyright in such a work. This work may be very useful and thus liable to duplication. Therefore, it would make sense to give it protection both as incentive to the author and as a deterrent to duplicators.

On the other hand any other person may gather the identical information merely by expenditure of effort. Affording it protection under the copyright regime would allow the author to monopolize information, which actually exists in the public domain and prevents any other person from doing the same. This is where the

---

[21]499 US 340 (1991).

[22]499 US 340 (1991).

[23]This requirement of creativity was expressed by the courts in cases involving art works in various ways. The courts insisted that the creator's contribution must represent more than a 'merely trivial' variation, 'some substantial, not merely trivial originality', a 'modicum of creativity', a 'touch of fresh authorship', or at least a 'distinguishable variation'.

[24]Goldstein, supra note 178, at Section 2.2.1.

[25]499 US 340 (1991).

debate over the sweat of the brow doctrine originates and since it depends entirely on the way originality is interpreted, it may be the case, that its acceptance or rejection is not uniform as approaches to originality. Copyright does not seek to reward an author merely for the effort he has expended in authoring a work, the reward is an incentive to contribute and expand the knowledge or information base in any given field. It should not be the object of the law to protect information that is a part of the public domain and allow an individual to monopolize it merely because he was the first person to gather it.

The Supreme Court of Canada has provided a new dimension to the concept of originality in CCH[26] case. The court acknowledged that the idea of intellectual creation was implicit in the notion of literary and artistic work under Berne Convention. Australian court[27] opined that the main purpose of copyright law is to prohibit copying of other peoples' work. So in case of compilation of facts if the second author does the compilation again by himself, then it is not infringement even if the second work is exactly similar to the first one.[28]

The Canadian court has provided that the concept of originality should be based on the test of skill and labour, i.e., it should not be copied and has added additional requirement that the skill and labour should not be mechanical and negligible. It has deviated from the standard of *Feist Publications v. Rural Telephone*[29] i.e., there should be modicum of creativity and noted that it leads more towards the novelty requirement of patent law. The Canadian position is in between the higher standard of USA and lower standard of UK.[30] The practical problem of Canadian standard will be to decide criteria to satisfy the requirement that skill and labour is neither mechanical nor negligible.

3.1.6 Sweat of the Brow Doctrine

An interesting question that often arises within the realm of copyright law is whether a work that is created merely by investing labour will be afforded protection. In such a situation, the originality requirement would have to be satisfied merely by the expenditure of labour, resulting in an independent creation, though it involves no amount of skill, judgment or creativity. The terminology used in the United States to describe the principle which the courts have applied in holding that copyright may in fact exist in such works is the 'sweat of the brow', signifying that

[26]CCH v. Law Society of Upper Canada [2004] SCC 13. Publishers of legislative text and law reports filed case against Law Society of Ontario as it used to supply photocopies of decisions and legal materials to the lawyers without offering any license fee to collecting society.

[27]Telstra Corp Ltd. v. Desktop Mktg Sys Pvt. Ltd [2001] FCA612.

[28]Gervais D (2005) Copyright in Canada: An Update after CCH. Revue Internationale Du Droit D'author, 203:14.

[29]499 US 340 (1991).

[30]CCH v. Law Society of Upper Canada [2004] SCC 13.

it is protected by law solely because of the expenditure of effort. However, recently this principle has been subject to severe criticism and explicitly overruled in the United States in *Feist Publications v. Rural Telephone.*[31] The research shall endeavour to analyze the rise and fall of the principle and the impact of it on copyright law in general and database in particular will be examined.

3.1.7 Rationale for Sweat Doctrine

Courts have applied sweat of the brow doctrine in cases where it is fit to protect works created merely by the expenditure of labour. Thus the labour of the author is being rewarded in the form of copyright protection. This position is explained by Nimmer who states: "Nonetheless, a discernible tendency formerly existed in some cases, and in some commentary, to find copyright protection for such disparate facts on the theory that plaintiff's labour in researching the copied facts is sufficient to give him a legally protected interest".[32]

The rationale underlying the doctrine revolves around the traditional approach to copyright law. Here copyright is seen to advance the object of rewarding the author's effort, and accordingly originality requires merely independent creation. The early English case of *Walter v. Lane*[33] is an appropriate example of this principle. In this case it was held that copyright subsisted in a newspaper report of a speech reproduced verbatim by a reporter and the newspaper, for whom the reporter worked, the Times, owned that copyright.[34] Thus the reporter's efforts of reproducing the speech were rewarded although it did not involve any creativity or significant amount of skill and judgment.

Moreover, sweat of the brow emerges from the attitude of the courts wanting to prevent other persons from taking undue advantage of the efforts expended by an author in researching and collecting information. This is clearly discernible from the case of *Toksvig v. Bruce Publishing Co*,[35] where the plaintiff had written a biography of Hans Christian Andersen based upon original Danish sources, including letters written by Andersen. The defendant wrote a biography on Andersen deriving his information from English sources including the plaintiff's book. In holding for the plaintiff, the court stated that the question is not whether Hubbard could have obtained the same information by going to the same sources", but rather did she go to the same sources and do her own independent research?" Similarly it has also

---

[31]499 US 340 (1991).

[32]Nimmer M B, Nimmer D (1987) Nimmer On Copyright: A Treatise On The Law Of Literary; Musical And Artistic Property And The Protection Of Ideas. Mathew Bender, New York, Section 2.11 (E).

[33][1900] AC 539.

[34]Bainbridge, supra note 179, at 43.

[35]181 F.2d 664 (7th Cir. 1950).

been held that "If a historian had published a history of the negotiations between the Soviet Union and the United States with respect to nuclear explosions, and copyrighted it, it would be an infringement of the copyright for another historian to publish a history rewritten from the first historian's book without any independent research."[36]

In identifying copyrightable material, courts have often relied on the test that "what is worth copying is *prima facie* worth protecting".[37] This once again highlights the fact that courts were willing to afford protection to works merely because they were useful, despite it lacking any amount of skill, judgement or creativity. According to Nimmer, "These cases generally rested upon the rationale that one should not freely reap the benefit of the industry of another in reporting and researching facts or other public domain material".[38] Sweat of the brow doctrine has resulted from the courts eagerness to reward the labour of the author and to prevent another person from benefiting from the fruits of the author's labour. In doing so, there is danger of protecting uncopyrightable material such as ideas, data and facts.

3.1.8 Origin of Sweat Doctrine

The "sweat of the brow" or "industrious collection" conveyed the underlying notion that copyright was a reward for the hard work that went into compiling facts. The classic formulation of this doctrine appeared in *Jeweler's Circular Publishing Co. v. Keystone Publishing Co.*[39]

The copyright of a book upon which one has spent labour in its preparation does not depend upon whether the materials, which he collected, consist or not of matters, which are *publici juris*, or whether such materials show literary skill or *originality*, either in thought or language. The man who goes through the streets of a town and puts down the names of each of the inhabitants, with their occupations and their street number, acquires material of which he is the author.

Similarly, one district court, acting on the premise that "research can be copyrightable", held that the facts relating to a notorious kidnapping, obtained through a considerable labour and expense, were copyrightable and hence the motion picture which copied such facts from the plaintiff's book constituted an infringement.[40] Though the decision was reversed on appeal, it was no doubt reflective of the sweat of the brow attitude prevalent in some of the courts.

---

[36]Huie v. National Broadcasting Co., 184 F. Supp 198.

[37]University of London Press Ltd. v. University Tutorial Press Ltd., [1916] 2 Chap. 601 at 610.

[38]Nimmer, Nimmer, supra note 205, at Section 3.04 [B][1].

[39]281 F.83 (2d Cir. 1922). In: Feist v. Rural, (1991) 111 S.Ct. 1282.

[40]Miller v. Universal City Studios Inc., 460 F. Supp. The court reasoned: "as it is necessary to reward the effort and ingenuity involved in giving expression to a fact, it is necessary also, if we are to expect individuals to labour on our behalf, to reward the ingenuity involved in obtaining knowledge of the fact".

Public domain material may be freely copied if the copier goes to the original source. Such material may not be copied directly, even if the particular arrangement or original contribution of this work itself is not copied. *Leon v. Pacific Telephone & Telegraph Co*[41] is another particularly apt illustration of this line of cases.[42] In *Leon.*, the plaintiff had compiled a telephone directory with the names and telephone numbers listed in the usual alphabetical order. The defendant copied the names and numbers from the plantiff's directory; but instead of arranging them in alphabetical order, the defendant's directory listed the names in the numerical order of the telephone numbers. Thus, whereas the plantiff's directory was useful for finding a person's telephone number if his name was known, the defendant's directory could be used for identifying the individual who possessed a given telephone number. Despite the fact that the individual names and telephone numbers were not copyrightable *per se*, and the plaintiff's original contribution in the form of his arrangement was not copied the court nevertheless held the defendant to be liable for infringement.

Commenting on the sweat of the brow doctrine Nimmer opined "The desire of the courts in Leon and like cases to protect the industriousness of the researcher is both understandable and in a sense commendable. It is nonetheless incorrect; for those courts fail to apply the standard of originality as it is understood in copyright law".[43]

3.1.9 Implication of Sweat Doctrine

The sweat of the brow doctrine permits any author to claim copyright, and thus protect his work, merely by expending labour in creating it, although it may be devoid of originality in the sense of creativity, or application of skill and judgment. It prevents any other person from taking advantage of this labour expended. Its implications are that it allows the author greater protection than what copyright ought to advance. It especially affects the copyrightability of factual compilations. Since these works comprise of facts, which are available for all in the public domain, and do not originate in the author, ordinarily the author cannot claim copyright in such facts. Ordinarily the author cannot claim copyright in such facts. However if the author expends skill, labour and judgment in the selection, arrangements and the compilation he may claim copyright in these aspects only. The sweat of the brow doctrine, however, goes a step further, by allowing the author, who has expended labour in collecting facts, to prevent others from copying

[41] 91 F.2d 484 (9th Cir. 1937).

[42] Hartfield v. Peterson, 91 F.2d 998 (2d Cir, 1937); Banks v. McDivitt, 2 F. Cas., 759 (1875); Yale University Press v. Row, Peterson & Co., 40 F.2d 290 (S.D.N.Y. 1930); W.H. Anderson v. Baldwin Law Publishing Co., 27 F.2d. 82 (6th Cir. 1928).

[43] Nimmer, Nimmer, supra note 205, at Section 3.04 [B][1].

these facts. It may not mean monopolizing the facts themselves, as sweat of the brow permits use of the same facts so long as they are obtained independently.

This position of law favoured enterprises whose business was to create such factual compilations or databases. Thus creators of telephone directories could protect their labour by claiming copyright infringement even for the copying of facts such as the names, addresses and telephone numbers of individuals. This may appear to make practical sense as it provides an incentive for investment of time, labour and money in collecting facts.

3.1.10 Fall of Sweat Doctrine

To rectify the fallout of sweat of the brow, originality was made an explicit requirement in Copyright Act 1976. With regard to compilations the statute made it clear that though factual compilations were copyrightable the protection would not extend to the facts themselves. Rather, facts contained in existing works may be freely copied because copyright protects only the elements that owe their origin to the compiler—selection, coordination and arrangement of facts.

Despite the Copyright Act, 1976 and decisions of contrary authority,[44] Leon and like cases continued to be followed by some courts, until the Supreme Court laid it to rest in 1991.[45] In *Feist Publications v. RuralTelephone*,[46] the court unanimously rejected the sweat of the brow doctrine by holding "Without a doubt, the sweat of the brow doctrine flouted basic copyright principles."

3.1.11 Is Sweat Doctrine Still Valid?

Original derivative work can be produced by collection, selection and arrangement of pre existing materials if labour, skill and capital have been used in creation of compilation and if resulted work is different in quality from the raw materials.[47] Copyright protection has been given to compilation of information on satisfying these criteria.[48] Database Regulation has defined database as 'collection of

---

[44]Triangle Publications Inc. v. Sports Eye, Inc. 415 F. Supp. 682 (1976); Schroeder v. William Morrow & Co., 566 F.2d 3 (7th Cir. 1977).

[45]The Supreme Court had an opportunity to rule on the sweat of the brow principle as early as 1985 in Harper & Row, Publishers, Inc. v. Nation Enters., 471 US 539 (1985), and though it took note of the unsettled nature of authority in this area it expressly declined to resolve the issue.

[46]499 US 340 (1991).

[47]Macmillan & Co Ltd v. K & J Cooper, (1924) 40 TLR 186.

[48]Time Table Index (Blacklock v. Pearson, [1915] 2 Chap. 376), Trade Catalogue (Purefoy v. Sykes Boxall, [1955] 72 RPC 89), Professional Directory (Waterlow Directories v. Reed Information, [1992] FSR 409, Waterlow Publishers Ltd. v. Rose, [1995] FSR 207), Football

independent works, data or other materials which are arranged in a systematic way and accessible by electronic or other means.[49] The selection or arrangement of the content of database must be original to create a copyrighted work.[50] Chronological list of television programs and alphabetical list of solicitors get copyright protection under UK law, although there is no creativity in the arrangement of the compilation.[51] About application of skill and labour, the court decided that commercial judgement was equally important as the skill.

In *Ladbroke v. William Hills*,[52] the court offered protection to fixture of football pool form though it consisted of a compilation of sixteen known form of bet. The justification for protection was the skill employed in selecting the particular forms of wager which is different from simple labour of compiling.[53] If the effect of compilation is very commonplace like the compilation of day and dates of year, table of weights and measures and postal information in a diary, there cannot be any copyright in the product.[54]

Until the appearance of the 1911 Copyright Act, copyright law in the United Kingdom did not require a work to be 'original' in order to qualify for protection, as *Walter v. Lane*, suggesting that copyright protection would be afforded to works lacking even a modicum of creativity, merely on the basis of the expenditure of labour. Most of the principles relating to copyright-ability, both before and after originality was incorporated as a statutory requirement, have been built by the common law, which relies on non-specification of the meaning of originality. The subconscious application of the sweat of the brow doctrine in the United Kingdom is a result of the cases interpreting the term originality and the acceptance even now of principles applied before 1911.[55]

Over time the courts have used two different and largely inconsistent approaches when determining the meaning of originality, especially in cases involving factual compilations.[56] These approaches are similar to the extent that they focus upon the labour exercised in the creation of the work, but differ in terms of the type of labour that is needed to satisfy the criterion of originality. In one category of cases originality is satisfied through the application of appropriate skill, labour and

(Footnote 48 continued)

Fixtures List (Football League v. Littlewoods, [1959] Chap. 637), Racing Information (Greyhound Services Ltd. v. Wilf Gilbert Ltd, [1994] FSR 723), Television Program Listing (Independent Television Publications v. Time Out, [1984] FSR 64).

[49]Database Regulation 12.

[50]Database Regulation 6.

[51]BBC v. Wireless League Publishing Co, [1926] Chap. 433; Dun & Bradstreet Ltd. v. Typesetting Facilities Ltd, [1992] FSR 320.

[52][1964] 1 WLR 273.

[53]Cornish, Llewelyn, supra note 40, at 389–390.

[54]Cramp v. Smythson, [1944] AC 329.

[55]In Express Newspaper Plc v. News (UK) Ltd, [1990] WLR 1320 it was held that Waler v. Lane was still undeniably good law.

[56]Bentley, Sherman, supranote 189, at 91.

judgement, thus focusing on the quality of labour employed. More controversially, the second category of cases has held that originality can also arise through the application of a sufficient amount of routine labour, thus focusing upon the quantity of labour expended.

The first type of cases conform to the position in the United States, where copyright subsists only in the selection, arrangement and coordination of the work, provided that a substantial amount of skill, labour and judgement has been applied. However, in certain situations courts have accepted that the mere exercise of a substantial amount of routine labour may give rise to an original work. Thus, where a compiler has spent a considerable amount of time and effort in creating a chronological list of television programmes[57] or an alphabetically ordered list of lawyers,[58] the resulting work will be original. That is, even though the author may not have exercised the appropriate quality of work, by the application of skill and judgement, the work may nonetheless be original if the process of compilation involves a sufficient amount of mundane labour.[59] The selection of seven tables at the front of a diary, consisting of days and dates of the year, tables of weights and measures, postal information, was held to be non-original.[60] Similarly, a compilation of a local timetable showing a selection of trains to and from a particular town that was made from official timetables, was held to lack originality.[61]

Instead of asking whether the work is original and can be protected, courts have often focused on the quantity of labour exercised in the creation of the work on the premise that the labour expended by the author must be protected.[62] This is reflected in the maxim: 'what is worth copying is prima facie worth protecting.[63]

Bainbridge is of the opinion that "This approach (the sweat of the brow) is not necessarily at odds with the position in the UK",[64] Bentley and Sherman differ by stating that "The position in the UK where the exercise of non-creative labour can give rise to an original work can be contrasted with the position in other jurisdiction…The UK position is also at odds with the position in the USA where, as the Supreme Court pointed out in the *Feist Publication v. Rural Telephone*[65] decision, a work must have at least a minimal degree of creativity to be protected".[66]

---

[57]BBC v. Wireless League Gazette Publishing Co., [1926] Chap. 433.

[58]Waterlow v. Reed, [1992] FSR 409.

[59]Bentley, Sherman, supranote 189, at 92.

[60]Cramp v. Smythson, [1944] AC 329.

[61]Leslie v. Young, [1894] AC 335.

[62]*See for example* Hogg v. Scott, (1874) L.R. 18 Eq 444. "The principle in all these cases is that the defendant is not at liberty to use or avail himself of the labour which the plaintiff has been invested for the purpose of producing his works; that is merely to take away the result of another man's labour, or in other words another man's property".

[63]Bainbridge, supranote 179, at 40.

[64]University of London Press Ltd. v. University Tutorial Press Ltd., [1916] 2 Chap. 601.

[65]499 US 340 (1991).

[66]Bentley, Sherman, supra note 189, at 93.

US copyright law defines compilation as a work formed by the collection and assembling of pre-existing materials or data that are selected, co-ordinated, arranged in such a way that the resulting work as a whole constitutes an original work of authorship.[67] Copyright in a compilation work does not create any exclusive right in any pre-existing material. A compilation work should be a product of original effort so that it creates more than *de minimis* creativity[68] and it becomes eligible for copyright protection.

Although the standard of originality which is required for the purpose of copyright demands that work must originate from author and it need not be novel but US Supreme court decided that work should have minimum amount of creativity as it denied copyright protection to alphabetical listing of telephone numbers for lack of creativity.[69] Thus copyright protection depends in these cases on the 'distinguishable variation'. It leads to a situation that if the compilation work satisfies the originality and creativity criteria, it will be protected. There is no copyright in facts *per se*[70] but original expression of factual compilation can get copyright protection.

3.1.12 Fallacies of Sweat Doctrine

Rural Telephone Service Company, Inc. carried on its business by providing telephone services in the state of Kansas. As a condition to its monopoly franchise, Rural published a typical telephone directory, consisting of white pages and yellow pages of its subscribers in the State. The white pages listed the names of Rural's subscribers, together with their towns and telephone numbers in alphabetical order. The yellow pages listed Rural's business subscribers alphabetically by category and featured classified advertisements of various sizes.

Feist Publications, Inc., was a publishing company, specializing in area wide telephone directories. Unlike a typical directory, which would cover only a particular calling area, Feist's wide-area directories covered a much larger geographical range, reducing the need to consult multiple directories. Unlike Rural, who

---

[67]17 USC Section 101.

[68]In 1898 US Court of Appeal held in case of a compilation of laws with annotation, index, citation, '... no one can obtain the exclusive right to publish the laws of a state in a book prepared by him ... any person desiring to publish the statutes of a state my use any copy of such statutes to be found in any printed book, whether such book be the property of the state or the property of an individual. ...copyright covers all in his books that may fairly be deemed the result of his labour. Speaking generally this would include marginal references, notes, memoranda, table of contents, indexes, digests of judicial decisions prepared by him from original sources of information.' Howell v. Miller, 91 Fed Rep 129, Court of Appeal, Sixth Circuit, Nov. 1898. In: Hamlin A (1904) Copyright Cases. G.P. Putnam's Sons, New York, p 24.

[69]Feist Publications v. Rural Telephone Services Co., 499 US 340 (1991).

[70]Miller v. Universal City Studio, 650 F. 2d. 1365.

could obtain subscriber information quite easily during the time of application, Feist needed to rely on the telephone companies providing services in various regions. Thus, Feist approached each of the eleven companies operating in Kansas and offered to pay for the right to use its white page listings. Only Rural refused to license its listings. Feist used them without Rural's consent. Rural sued for copyright infringement taking the position that Feist, in compiling its own directory could not use the information contained in Rural's white page listings and they would have to gather this information independently. On the other hand Feist challenged the very subsistence of copyright in the white pages of Rural's directory.

In order to resolve the issue the court studied the objective that copyright law seeks to advance and the concept of originality in copyright. In holding in favour of Feist, the court reasoned that the element of originality that renders a factual compilation worthy of protection must lie in the selection, arrangement and coordination of the facts and not the facts themselves. Moreover referring to the objective of copyright it was held that the primary purpose of the law was to facilitate progress and not merely to reward individual labour.

In the course of its judgment the court reverted to the understandable, yet flawed reasoning of those courts that used copyright as a vehicle for protecting industrious collection. The court noted that an inevitable consequence of the idea/expression dichotomy is that raw facts may be copied at will and each newcomer need not start from scratch. Copyright law intends to make available to all the fruits of the previous research. In doing so the court excluded the application of the sweat of the brow doctrine. Though at first sight the sweat of the brow doctrine may seem commendable, and justified, in as much as it seeks to protect the labour of compilers, it runs contrary to the basic tenets of copyright law. In *Feist Publication v. Rural Telephone*[71] the Supreme Court aptly summed up how the principle runs contrary to the fundamental axioms of copyright law.

Throughout history, copyright law has recognized a greater need to disseminate factual works. But through sweat of the brow Court took a contrary view and offered proprietary interests in facts and declared that authors are absolutely precluded from saving time and effort by relying upon the facts contained in the prior work.

Feist Publication v. Rural Telephones[72] is about copyright infringement in white page telephone directory which was affirmed by the lower court but reversed by Supreme Court. The case draws attention due to its treatment to sweat of the brow doctrine which implies industrious collection. White page telephone directory is nothing but a compilation.[73] The selection, co-ordination or arrangement of the compilation and not the material itself, is protected by copyright. Feist found in its

[71]499 US 340 (1991).

[72]499 US 340 (1991).

[73]Compilation is a work formed by the collection and assembling of pre-existing materials or of data that are selected, co-ordinated or arranged in such a way that the resulting work as a whole constitutes an original work of authorship.

judgement that there is nothing original in the selection, co-ordination or arrangement of the white page of telephone directory and they are of garden variety, without any trace of creativity.

Although for copyright law, originality demands only independent creation and not novelty,[74] in this case Supreme Court added an additional element and that is, the work should have 'modicum of creativity' also. It will be always challenging to find out what lies between 'more that *de minimis* quantum of creativity' which is required for copyright in regular copyright-able work and 'minimal degree of creativity or modicum of creativity' which is required for copyright in databases. Compilations can be protected by copyright law if the selection and arrangement is done independently and it is sufficiently original but the protection is available only for original selection and arrangement of facts and not for the fact itself.

In *Victor Lalli,*[75] court observed that horse racing charts are not copyrightable because they are compilation of information taken from horse racing statistics used for gambling and are of common and similar variety of information. In *Key Publications Inc. v. Chinatown Today Publishing Enterprises Inc.*[76] court held that Chinatown's yellow page directory for New York Chinese American community did not infringe copyright of Key's Chinese American yellow pages. The justification for the decision was that Key had 9000 listing where as Chinatown had only 2000 and out of which 1500 were also common in Key's directory. Moreover Key had 260 categories whereas China town had only 28 categories and out of which 3 categories were common. It appeared that China town had used only one sixth of Key's work. Considering the nature of the directories, overlapping of materials was inevitable and the arrangements of two directories were different. Thus there was no infringement although there was some amount of similarity between two directories. At this point it would not be out of place to mention that this is the object of copyright law.[77]

Feist copied white pages (name, address and telephone number) from Rural's telephone directory. Supreme Court overruled the earlier position that copying of factual compilation constituted infringement and decided that the alleged white page was a garden variety of compilation and had no trace of creativity and thus did not deserve any protection and held that originality must lie in the selection, arrangement and co-ordination of the compilation to get copyright protection. Feist copied only the white pages of Rural, which was not protected, and thus the action was not actionable.

---

[74]*See generally* Nimmer, Nimmer, supra note 205.

[75]Victor Lalli Enters Inc. v. Big Red Apple Inc., 936 F 2d 671 (2nd Cir. 1991).

[76]945 F. 2d 509 (2nd Cir 1991).

[77]To promote the Progress of Science and useful Arts, by securing for limited Times to Authors and Inventors the exclusive Right to their respective Writings and Discoveries. U.S. Constitution Article 1, 8, Cl 8.

In *Mathew Bender & Co. v West Publishing Co*,[78] US Court of Appeal decided that Bender did not infringe copyright of West by inserting star pagination to West's case reporter into its discs. Court followed the standard in *Feist Publication v. Rural Telephone*[79] and decided that originality and intellectual creation criteria of arrangement required more than sweat of the brow approach of selection and arrangement.[80] Copyright in factual compilation is thin.[81] The protection is only for original features of the compilation, that is selection and arrangement and not for the compilations itself. But if there are only limited ways of presenting facts then following merger doctrine, there will be no protection.

3.1.13 Application of the Sweat Doctrine in India

Before analysing the application of sweat of the brow in India, it must be understood that there is negligible literature on the point. Even case laws are few. The base upon which copyright law and principles have developed in India has been the English law. Therefore the law in India prior to *Feist Publication v. Rural Telephone*[82] is in conformity with the position in the U.K. wherein the primary goal of copyright law is to protect an author's labour. According to this view, any unauthorized use of an author's labour would constitute an infringement.

One of the earlier Indian cases that reflect this notion was *Macmillan v. Suresh Chander Deb*[83] where plaintiff was the proprietor of copyright of selection of songs and poems prepared by Palgrave. The defendant published a book containing the same selection of poems and songs as contained in Palgrave's book. The arrangement of the defendant's book differed from that of Palgrave. The plaintiff contended that they were entitled to the copyright in the selection made by Palgrave.

Justice Wilson observed,' In case of works not original in the proper sense of the term but composed of or compiled or prepared from materials which are open to all, the fact that one man has produced such a work does not take away from anyone else the right to produce another work of the same kind and in doing so to use all

[78]158 F. 3d 693, 2nd Circuit, 1998. West Publishing Co. publishes printed compilation of judicial decisions. Mathew Bender manufactures discs containing compilation of judicial decisions. In this compilation Bender indicated the page location of particular text of West's printed version (star pagination). The case involved the issue whether star pagination was infringement of West's copyright in the compilation of judicial decisions. Before Feist, in West Publishing Co. v. Mead Data Central Inc., 799, F2d 1219, 8th Circuit, 1986, circuit court held that LEXIS by using star pagination of West had appropriated the compilation and thus infringement.

[79]499 US 340 (1991).

[80]Halpern S W (2002) Copyright Law. Carolina Academic Press, p 76.

[81]Feist Publications v. Rural Telephone Services Co., 499 US 340 (1991).

[82]499 US 340 (1991).

[83]1890 ILR 17 Cal 951.

the materials open to him…the defendant is not at liberty to use or avail himself of the labour the plaintiff has been at for the purpose of producing his work…such a selection, as Mr. Palgrave has made, obviously requires extensive reading, careful study and comparison and the exercise of taste and judgment in selection. It is open to any-one who pleases to go through a like course of reading and by the exercise of his own taste and judgment to make a selection for himself but if he spares himself this trouble and adopts Mr. Palgrave's selection, he offends against the principle… in the instance…a work consisting of a selection from various authors, two men perhaps make the same selection, but that must be resorting to the original authors, not by taking advantage of the selection already made by another'.

In *Hogg v. Scott*,[84] *the* court held that "The true principle in all these cases is that the defendant is not at the liberty to use or avail himself of the labour which the plaintiff has been at for the purpose of producing his work, that is, in fact, merely to take away another man's labour, or, in other words, his property". Later cases decided by the Indian courts such as *S.K. Dutt v. Law Book Co.*,[85] *Govindan v. Gopalakrishnan*[86] and *N.T. Raghunathan v. All India Reporter*,[87] all have viewed copyright as a tool to prevent the misappropriation of labour, rather than 'to promote the progress of science and useful arts'.

3.2 Impact on Copyright Law

The step from printed book to online media brought many changes in the methodology of education and research and also with the growth of information technology; the Internet became the lifeblood of global information system.[88] Reading the pulse of the situation, publishers put together information and started selling a new product called databases. Periodicals are always important sources of research. How expensive are these journals? The U.S. periodical prices show that the journal prices have increased over the years.[89]

Although publishing is a costly affair and books are quite expensive, researchers need information contained in books or else the research would be affected. Few factors which influenced the situation are financial constrains of public authorities,

[84]1874 (31) LT 163.

[85]AIR 1954 All 570.

[86]AIR 1955 Mad 391.

[87]AIR 1971 Bom 78.

[88]U.K. Commission on Intellectual Property Rights, Integrating Intellectual Property Rights and Development Policy. http://www.iprcommission.org/graphic/documents/final_report.htm. Accessed 13 April 2009, p 107.

[89]Dingley B (2005) US Periodical Prices. http://www.ala.org/ala/alctscontent/alctspubsbucket/alctsresources/general/periodicalsindex/05USPPI.pdf. Accessed 15 April 2009.

technological devises preventing access and prospect of making easy money.[90] If the whole journal is not affordable, then there should be a system of purchasing information which will be cheaper, affordable and adequate for the researcher. The price development of US periodicals indicates that periodical price index is much superior to higher education price index and consumer price index.[91]

Copyright has always been linked with commercial value. The offer of limited monopoly right to authors is made to promote and advance both creativity and profit. Modern copyright law protects works with authorial presence. The protection depends on manifestation of authorial personality and not on taste or talent manifested. A work of high commercial value but low authorial personality has posed a challenge to the modern copyright law.

The unitary and personality based concept of copyright law is a product of nineteenth century and it excludes competing model of copyright law. According to this model, works of original authorship are those which manifest substantial authorial presence and it does not include work of little personal authorship, yet consumes considerable expenditure of labour and capital.[92] Conventional understanding stressed on authorial subjectivity as pre-requisite for original work of authorship as it reflects author's personality and embodies subjective choices of the creator, even in selection and arrangement.[93]

Max Planck Society organized an international conference on 'Open Access to Knowledge in the Sciences and Humanities' in 2003 and it culminated into 'Berlin Declaration on Open Access to Knowledge in the Sciences and Humanities'.[94] The Declaration observed 'The Internet has fundamentally changed the practical and economic realities of distributing scientific knowledge and cultural heritage. For the first time ever, the Internet now offers the chance to constitute a global and interactive representation of human knowledge, including cultural heritage and the guarantee of worldwide accesses.

Believing on these objectives, it was felt that publicly financed research result should not be privatized in line with their publication and free access would not presuppose to get it free of charge. The Declaration offered 'On the one hand, authors and right holders grant to all users a free, irrevocable, worldwide right to access to and a license to copy, use, distribute derivative works, in any digital medium for any responsible purpose, subject to proper attribution of authorship, as well as right to make small numbers of printed copies for their personal use'.

---

[90]Hilty R M (2006) Five Lessons About Copyright in the Information Society: Reaction of the Scientific Community to Over-Protection and What Policy Makers Should Learn. J Copy Soc USA 53:122.

[91]Dingley, supra note 263.

[92]Patterson, Joyce (1969) Monopolizing the Law: The Scope of Copyright Protection for Law Reports and Statutory Compilations. UCLA L Rev 36:719.

[93]Saunders E M (1987) Copyright Protection for Compilations of Facts: Does the Originality Standard Allow Protection on the Basis of Industrious Collection? Norte Dame L Rev 62(4):763.

[94]Berlin Declaration on Open Access. http://www.zim.mpg.de/openaccess-berlin/ber-lin_declaration.pdf. Accessed 15 April 2009.

This open access is aimed at promotion of new open access paradigm to gain maximum benefit from science and society. Keeping these objectives and principles, a balanced system of copyright has to be placed where competition law will offer support from outside. In this alternative approach, intangible good that is produced out of research by public funding may be considered as public good as suggested by Kenneth J. Arrow.[95]

Copyright law in America is based on the theory of providing economic incentive for creative activities, which is reflected through 'work made for hire' but in many cases authors or creators try to assert their interest in contractual dealings with those who would exploit their work.[96] The conflict of interest appears between copyright industry who wants to optimize profit by all means and consumer wants to pay as little as possible to have access to and use copyrighted works.

3.3 Impact of the Feist Judgment on Copyright Law

Feist Publication v. Rural Telephone Service Co. established the conceptual framework under which all factual compilations must be analyzed. It clarified the standard governing the copyright-ability of factual compilations or databases; only those compilations possessing a minimal degree of creativity in the selection, coordination, or arrangements of the factual data qualify for protection.

The specific holding that an alphabetical listing of all the subscribers in a particular telephone service area fails the originality test, implies that not all databases are assured of copyright protection. This holding may also imply that other mechanical arrangements, such as chronology, are also ineligible for protection.

Feist makes it apparent that the database owners will not be able to claim that the effort expended in collecting the factual information constituting the work would justify advancing copyright protection to the facts themselves. The court reaffirmed the axiom that facts are not copyrightable.

3.4 Impact on Databases

The European Directive on Copyright in Information Society observes 'A rigorous, effective system of protection of copyright and related rights is one of the main ways of ensuring that European cultural creativity and production receive the

[95]Arrow K J (1962) Economic Welfare and the Allocation of Resources for Invention, The Rate And Direction Of Inventive Activity: Economic And Social Factors. A Report Of The National Bureau Of Economic Research, p 609. In: Hilty, supra note 264, at 130.

[96]Nimmer D, Menell P, Mc Gimsey D (2003) Pre-existing Confusion in Copyright's Work for Hire Doctrine. J Copy Soc 50:399; Cohen J E (2002) Copyright in a Global Information Economy, p 399. In: Hilty, supra note 264, at 122.

necessary resources and safeguarding the independence and dignity of artistic creators and performers.'[97] The same is true for the other parts of the world as well. The economic principles believe that people respond to incentives and thus copyright industry quite reasonably demands for adequate legal protection for their investment, though defining what is adequate protection is a tricky job. But it is true that unreasonable expansion of copyright protection will affect the balance negatively and disturb dissemination of information.

A disproportionate legal protection may not improve the author's situation but it can jeopardize market of copyright industry. As the industry survives on protection of investment, so a competition based legal regime should be in place.[98] The draft declaration of World Summit on the Information Society, 2003 observes, 'Intellectual Property protection is important to encourage innovation and creativity in the Information Society, similarly, the wide dissemination, diffusion and sharing of knowledge is important to encourage innovation and creativity. Facilitating meaningful participation by all in intellectual property issues and knowledge sharing through full awareness and capacity building is a fundamental part of an inclusive Information Society.'[99]

The copyright industry should be directed towards economic based and competition based approach which can sustain need of information society. Authors are never threatened by users as users are willing to pay reasonable remuneration for using protected works but authors often appear to be weak contractual parties in front of publishing houses and often succumb to unjustified conditions, as authors often work as employees and thus the state should intervene and offer reasonable protection to authors as well as ensure that copyright industry can get back their return of investment.[100]

U.K. Commission on Intellectual Property Rights, Integrating Intellectual Property Rights and Development Policy observed 'The arrival of the digital era provides great opportunities for developing countries in accessing information and knowledge. The development of digital libraries and achieves, Internet based distance learning programs, and the ability of scientist and researchers to access to sophisticated online computer database of technical information in real time, are just some examples. But the arrival of the digital era also poses some new and serious threats for access and dissemination of knowledge. In particular, there is a real risk that the potential of the Internet in the developing world will be lost as rights owners use technology to prevent public access through pay to view system'.[101]

---

[97] Recital 11, Information Society Directive. In: Hilty, supra note 264, at 132.

[98] Hilty, supra note 264, at 134.

[99] Hilty, supra note 264, at 135.

[100] Ginsburg, supra note 132, at 1613; Casamiquela R J (2002) Contractual Assent and Enforceability in Cyberspace. Berk Tech LJ 17:475. In: supra note 264, at 137.

[101] http://www.iprcommission.org/graphic/documents/final_report.htm. Accessed 17 May 2009.

Copyright tries to offer protection on the basis of creativity and if protection is given on the basis of investment the objective will be lost. To protect investment, laws on unfair competition, law on undue enrichment or even law on computer crime can be applied to address the issue of loss caused be the competitors who reproduce without authorization. Misuse of database by authorized users by extending access to unauthorized persons can be handled though licensing terms or contract clauses. For that matter even database manufacturers can use technical solutions encryption or access codes but they must remember that they need to balance between potential loss by unauthorized use and flexibility in the database to ensure consumer-friendliness of the database, especially when lot of alternative suppliers are available in the market.

In most jurisdictions, copyright protects compilation or databases as literary work and protection is given for its selection and arrangement.[102] U.S.C. does not expressly state whether exertion of time, money or effort in compiling database would suffice to trigger copyright protection or would require creativity. It is left to the court in US. In EU due to the Directive, there is direct statutory reference of creativity.[103] The Supreme Court in US rejected the sweat of the brow doctrine for creation of databases. As it observed 'Rural's selection of listing could not be more obvious, it publishes the most basic information—name, town and telephone number—about each person who applies to it for telephone service. This is 'selection' of a sort but it lacks the modicum of creativity necessary to transform mere selection into copyrightable expression. Rural expended sufficient effort to make the white page directory useful but insufficient creativity to make it original'.[104]

The problem of the Feist judgment is that it does not give any guideline as to what type of databases will attract protection. More over in case of computerized databases, it is the comprehensiveness of the content that matters and the value of the database depends on that and not on the selection. This brings the peculiar situation that is the more comprehensive database means more useful and more valuable but less selective and less copyrightable. Arguably a more selective database will be less valuable but more copyrightable.

Jeffrey Wolken observed 'Imposing a definite, physical arrangement on the information contained in a database would severely decrease the database's utility. Even if database producers wanted to gain copyright protection by providing a definite physical arrangement when saving their information, it is not practical for them to do so. In addition to the limitations imposed by the physical process of randomly saving computerized information, any formal arrangement of information would detract from the usefulness of a database.

[102] 17 USC Section 101—A work formed by the collection and assembling of pre-existing materials or of data that are selected, coordinated or arranged, in such a way that the resulting work as a whole constitutes an original work of authorship.

[103] CDPA Section 3A(2).

[104] Feist Publication v. Rural Telephone Service Co., 499 US 340 at 362.

It is the ability of users to search an unrestricted database for the information they want that makes the database valuable. After a search, a user can create for himself the best presentation of the information by imposing this own arrangement on the search results. Generally, the utility of a database is inversely related to the degree of arrangement originally found in the database. More structure equals less utility. Therefore using arrangement as a protectable element of a computerized database is both unfeasible and impractical'.[105]

'Copyright protection is the traditional means of protecting databases. Copyright establishes a surrogate form of ownership by erecting a system of portable fences. These fences, valid against the world and backed by the state, accompany creative effort in their journey from mind to mind'.[106] Databases are protected as compilation under copyright law[107] but as it is a work of low authorial presence, in comparison to a novel which is a work of high authorial presence, often copyright law feels uncomfortable in protecting databases. This uncomfortable-ness is due to failure of recognizing dual role of copyright—creativity and commercial value. In copyright law, facts and ideas are never protected as they are in public domain.[108] This essential feature has been preserved in case of database by following sweat of the brow doctrine,[109] i.e. investment of labour for creation of database and by offering protection to creative element of arrangement.

In the United Kingdom, copyright protection of factual data is based on 'sweat of the brow' or industrious collection where the threshold of originality is very low and the law requires that the work should originate from the author. The amount of skill and labour required for protection depends on fact and circumstances.[110] A substantial similarity between former and later work may lead to assumption of infringement unless created independently. In Waterlow v. Reed[111] the plaintiff sought injunction against the defendant for restraining from infringement of copyright in Solicitor's and Barrister's Directory as the defendant published Butterworth's Law Directory by using plaintiff's directory to get information. Justice Aldous held that there had been copyright infringement as the defendant's work reproduced substantial portion of plaintiff's work.[112]

---

[105]Wolken J C (1998) Just the Facts, Ma'am: A Case for Uniform Federal Regulation of Database in the New Information Age. Syrac L Rev 48:1263.

[106]Reichman J H (1992) Electronic Information Tools—The Outer Edge of World Intellectual Property Law. Univ Dayton L Rev 17:797.

[107]Section 101 US Copyright Act; Callaghan v. Myers, 128 US 617 (1888)—volume of law report was capable of copyright but author had no exclusive right in judicial opinion published.

[108]Feist Publication Inc. v. Rural Telephone Service, 499 US 340—the first person to find and report a particular fact has not created that fact but merely discovered its existence.

[109]Jeweler's Circular Pub Co. v. Keystone Pub. Co., 281 F.83 (2nd Cir. 1922).

[110]In Cramp v. Smythson, (1944) AC 329, table of information in a pocket diary were held not to attract copyright as there was no element of originality or skill for arranging those information.

[111](1990) 20 IPR 69.

[112]In Tele Direct (Publications) Inc. v. American Business Information Inc., (1996) 35 IPR 121, Tele Direct published a yellow pages directory. American Business Systems Inc. produced various

In the United States, before Feist, there were two ways of protection for factual compilations—one is under sweat of the brow and the other is creative element of compilation. If the facts or ideas are considered as building blocks of understanding or hard ideas to which doctrine of merger should apply whereas, soft ideas which are mostly author's opinion, for them merger doctrine may be used as they are not fundamental for understanding.[113] Sweat of the brow is criticized of giving too much of protection, almost in the form of de facto monopoly in factual compilation. It forces the subsequent compiler to collect raw data afresh and thus it encourages inefficiency instead of offering incentive. Feist on the other hand offers minimal protection to database as it has been observed 'Feist left database naked in the market place vulnerable to parasitic competitors, users and information Samaritans'.[114]

The problem of originality is that 'true originality is an illusion and every act of authorship is a process of adaptation, transformation and recombination of existing materials'.[115] The other problem of Feist is that the scope of creativity is so less, that those only few compilations will be eligible for copyright as arrangement for most of the database is mundane. This problem aggravates in case of electronic database as they do not have unique compilation. Rather they concentrate more on exhaustive material, efficient retrieval system and robust search facilities. Proving infringement is also a difficult matter in case of databases. In case of informational product, the subsequent author has so limited option for different expressions, unless there is verbatim reproduction or very close paraphrasing, it is difficult to have a case for infringement. Thus the protection turns out to be thin. The difference of 'hard fact' and 'soft fact 'is not beyond debate and the reversal of sweat of the brow by judicial decision cannot be ruled out. The question still remains 'why should only subjective selections be protected while useful but objective material not be protected? Even the distinction is debatable, there is much subjectivity in even apparently objective presentations of facts and subjective information is easily objectified'.[116]

(Footnote 112 continued)

business information publications. Justice Mc Gill referred to Waterlow to take the point on 'an important consideration in determining the question of substantial similarity in relation to directories is whether is whether the two works are in competition with each other' and held that as there is no competition between the parties and as plaintiff had merely acquired data not protected by copyright and sorted it according to common criteria in the industry, so there was no infringement.

[113]If expressions available to subsequent authors to express are very limited then ideas are felt to be merged with expression and in that case the copyright infringement issue will not stand. In Kargos v. Associated Press, 937 F.2d. 700 (2nd Circuit 1991).

[114]Hunsucker G M (1997) The European Database Directive: Regional Stepping Stone to an International Model? Fordham Intell Prop Media & Ent L J 7:697.

[115]Litman, supra note 147, at 965.

[116]Ginsburg J (1997) Copyright, Common Law and *Sui Generis* Protection of Databases in the United States and Abroad. Univ Cin L Rev 66:151.

The copyright protection of database can be supplemented by contract or technology but both have their own demerits. Contractual protection often turns out to be weak protection as information does not physically reside with only the receiver and contractual terms are binding on the parties to the contract only. The technological protection can prove to be effective depending on the standard of technology but technology cannot succeed sharing of contents among consented parties. Thus both technology and contract must be combined to achieve desirable protection. The monopolistic nature of database industry will further aggravate with the help of this techno-contractual protection.[117] Online databases coupled with technology to track will enable the database producers to their own collecting society. Pay per use system will affect the research communities. Overall the non-copyrightable information will happen to enjoy over-protection.

Sherman and Bently observed that pre-modern (before 1850) intellectual property law was not divided into categories like copyright, patent, trade mark and design but rather it was subject specific.[118] Its focus was on mental or creative labour embodied in the protected work.[119] But the focus of modern intellectual property law is not the labour embodied in the work but its own right.[120] In pre-modern era, authorial presence in informational works of law like compilations were often issues of dispute. They were granted copyright if the work was original,[121] in the sense that something new was brought to existence[122] and the work was product of mental labour. In Gray v. Russell, the plaintiff alleged that the

[117]Reichman and Samuelson observed that private database industry is largely characterized by niche marketers who dominate specific market segment. The monopolistic nature of database industry may be attributed to a number of factors like start up cost, not realizing prospect of market share, data not available from public sector etc. Reichman, Samuelson P (1997) Intellectual Property Rights in Data? V and L Rev 50:51

C-203/02.

[118]Sherman, Bently (1999) The Making Of Modern Intellectual Property Law: The British Experience (1760–1911), p 147.

[119]The Statute of Anne 1710—An Act for the encouragement of learning, by vesting the copies of printed books in the authors or purchasers of such copies during the time therein mentioned.

[120]Baron, supra note 74, at 912.

[121]Although the individual works could be copied, the originality requirement was that the work as a whole should exist for the first time, that is not be copied from an existing work. Longman v. Winchester, 16 Ves. 269, Eng Rep. 987 (1809); No man writes exclusively form his own thoughts, unaided and uninstructed by the thought of others. The thought so every man are more or less a combination of what other men have thought and expressed, although they may be modified, exalted, or improved by his own genius or reflection. Emerson v. Davies., 8 F. Cas 615 (C. C. D. 1845) (No. 4436).

[122]'The idea when once reduced to writing is susceptible of identity and becomes the subject of property.' Wheaton v. Peters, 33 US 591;' To compile is to copy from various authors into one work. in this the judgment may be said to be exercised to some extent in selecting and combining the extracts. Such a work entitles the compiler… to a right of property. The right may be compared to that of a patentee, who by a combination of known mechanical structures has produced a new result'. Story v. Halcombe, 23 F. Cas. 171 (C.C.D. Ohio 1847) (No. 13, 497). In: Baron, supra note 74, at 913.

defendant infringed copyright in his Latin Grammar. The defendant claimed that there was nothing new in the notes of the Plaintiff and all could be found in antecedent works.

Justice Story observed 'The true question is whether these notes are to be found collected and embodied in any former single work. It is admitted that they are not so found. The most, that is contended for is that (the plaintiff) has selected his notes from various authors, who have written at different periods and that any other person might, by a diligent examination of the same works, have made a similar selection...Now certainly the preparation and collection of these notes from these various sources, must have been the work of no small labour and intellectual exertion. The plan, the arrangement and the combination of these notes in the form, in which they are collectively exhibited in Gould's Grammar, belong exclusively to this gentleman'.[123] One of the reasons for keeping so low threshold for granting copyright was the assumption that no work of authorship is original and no work in literature, arts and science would qualify for protection if true originality is looked for. It was also true that the author had no right to appropriate to himself something which was common to all people before the work was made.

Learning can be best encouraged by ensuring that the learner had free access to advances in literature and science to be found in useful books. It is true that ideas and facts are to be protected as common property but denial of protection to information products can have its own repercussions. In Lewis v. Fullarton,[124] injunction was sought for copyright infringement in The Topographical Dictionary of England and while granting injunction, the Court observed 'it is plain no protection whatsoever could be given to any work in the nature of a gazetteer, dictionary, road book, calendar, map, or any other work the subject matter of which is open to common observation and enquiry and that every man who had bestowed any amount of labour and expense in collecting and arranging the information requisite for the production of such a work, might immediately on its publication, be deprived of the fruit of his industry and ability'.

Court struck a deal between the creator and the state by not depriving the creator the fruit of his labour and at the same time without conferring unlimited monopoly. 'That every man is entitled to the fruit of his own labour must be admitted but he can enjoy them only except the statutory provision, under the rules of property which regulates the society and which defines the right of thing in general'.[125] Court tried to balance between two equally important extremes 'that men of ability who have employed their time for the service of the community may not be deprived of their just merit and the reward for their ingenuity and labour and the world may not be deprived of improvements and nor the progress of the arts be retarded'[126] as it was observed that Statute of Anne ought to receive a liberal

[123] 10 F Cas. 1035 (C.C.D.Mass. 1839) (No. 5728). In: Baron, supra note 74, at 913.

[124] 48 Eng. Rep. 1080 (1839). In: Baron, supra note 74, at 915.

[125] Wheaton v. Peters, 33 US 591. In: Baron, supra note 74, at 916.

[126] Gyles v. Wilcox, 26 Eng. Rep. 489 (1740). In: Baron, supra note 74, at 916.

construction, for it is very far from being a monopoly as it is intended to secure the property of books in the authors themselves or the purchaser of the copy as some recompense for their pains and labour in such work as may be of use to the learned world'.

The Principle of Roman natural law based on occupancy as primary form of acquisition influenced Locke's view 'a person who mixed her labour with an un-owned object became morally entitled to property in that object'.[127] This labour can comprehend both creativity and sweat of the brow. A compiler cannot have right over the information derived from common stock of knowledge. The independent work can cover both gathering of information and also creative presentation of existing information. During the late 19th and early 20th century, more emphasis was given on individualism and author's presence in the final work became deciding factor for copyright-ability. 'In what respect does the right of an author differ from that of an individual who has invented a most useful and valuable machine? In the production of this, his mind has been as intensely engaged as long and perhaps as usually to the public as any distinguished author in the composition of his book. The result of their labour may be equally beneficial to the society and in their respective spheres they may be alike distinguished for mental vigour'.[128]

During pre-modern stage, granting of copyright was liberal but copyright infringement was limited as there were extensive list of authorized uses. 'The author's exclusive property in the creation of his mind cannot be vested in the author as abstraction but only in the concrete form which he has given them and the language in which he has clothed them. When he had sold his book, the only property which he reserves to himself or which the law gives to him, is the exclusive right to multiply the copies of that particular combination of characters which exhibits to the eyes of another the ideas intended to be conveyed. That is what is the law terms copy or copyright. The inquiry is not whether the defendant has used the thoughts, conceptions, information or discoveries promulgated by the original but whether his composition may be considered a new work requiring invention, learning and judgment or only a mere transcript of the whole or parts of the original with merely colourable variations'.[129]

For the purpose of determining infringement in case of wholesale appropriation, is relatively an easier job. Even incorporating large portion of whole work into a larger work may constitute infringement depending on time value of the portion taken and its effect on the sale of the original work. 'It is certainly not necessary to constitute an invasion of copyright that the whole of a work should be copied or even a large portion of it in form or substance. If so much is taken, the value of the original is sensibly diminished, or the labours of the original author are substantially to an injurious extent appropriated by another, that is sufficient in point of law, to constitute a piracy pro tanto. The entirety of the copyright is the property of the

[127]Yen, supra note 116, at 523.

[128]Wheaton v. Peters, 33 US 591. In: Baron, supra note 74, at 917.

[129]Stowe v. Thomas, 23 F. Cas. 201 (C.C.E.D. Penn. 1853) (No. 13, 514).

author and it is no defense that another person has appropriated a part and not the whole of any property. Neither does it necessarily depends upon the quantity taken, whether it is an infringement of the copyright or not. It is often affected by other considerations, the value of the materials taken and the importance of it to the sale of the original work'.[130]

During the pre-modern era, infringement used to be assessed against the legitimate use of the work. 'The only fair use you can make of the work of another of this kind is where you take a number of such works, catalogues, dictionaries, digests and look over them all and then compile an original work of your own, founded on the information you have extracted from each and all of them but it is of vital importance that such new work should not have no mere copying, no merely colourable alternations, no blind repetition of obvious errors'.[131] It is always open to come out with a work similar to the previous one independently by the second comer but there is no public interest served by reproducing the first work even if the purpose is to offer it at a much cheaper price.

'If great errors have not previously existed or unusual ignorance to be corrected no great novelty is practicable or useful, unless it tries to add new discoveries or inventions, new names or words, decisions—so as to post up the subject to more recent periods—or unless it be to abridge and omit details and condense a more voluminous work into a smaller and cheaper form, so as to bring its purchase and use within the reach of new and less wealthy classes in society. Some similarities and some use of prior works, even to copying of small parts are in such cases tolerated, if the main design and execution are in reality novel or improved and not a mere cover for important piracies from others'.[132]

In determining infringement court often looks at *animus furandi*—intention to steal. 'That part of the work of one author is found in another is not of itself piracy or sufficient to support an action, a man may fairly adopt part of the work from another, he may so make use of another's labour for the promotion of science and benefit of the public but having done so, the question will be: was the matter so taken used fairly with the view and without what may term the *animus furandi*?'.[133] Lack of guilty intent can exonerate a defendant but a defendant can be held liable even if there is no *animus furandi*. In Scott v. Stanford,[134] Scott was a clerk and registrar of Coal Market of London. He published certain statistical data relating to importation of coal. He alleged that Stanford infringed his copyright as one third of Stanford's book, 'Mineral Statistic for the use of Great Britain and Ireland' reproduced verbatim from Scott's book. It was held 'if the bulk of a plaintiff's publication had been appropriated and published in a form that would materially injure his copyright, mere honest intention or the part of appropriator would not

[130]Falsom v. Mars, 9 F. Cas. at 345. In: Baron, supra note 74, at 921.

[131]Hotten v. Arthur, 1 H & M 603. In: Baron, supra note 74, at 921.

[132]Webb v. Powers, 29 F. Cas at 517. In: Baron, supra note 74, at 923.

[133]Cary v. Kearsley, 170 Eng. Rep. 679 (1802). In: Baron, supra note 74, at 923.

[134]3 LR-Eq 718 (1867). In: Baron, supra note 74, at 924.

suffice to avoid a finding of infringement'. To decide whether the original work will be materially injured, following factors are to be considered—nature of selection of portion copied, quantity and value of the material used.

A second comer can legitimately use a pre-existing work so long it is not essentially a reduplication of the earlier work. Pre-existing work can be used to create something completely new. The original work can be used to create a new work which does not compete with the original work in the market. For example digest, abridgement and reviews do not substitute the original work. 'The question is whether the defendant's publication would serve as a substitute for it? A review will not in general serve as a substitute for the book reviewed and even there if so much is extracted that it communicates the same knowledge with the original work, it is an actionable violation of literary property. The intention to pirate is not necessary in an action of this sort, it is enough that the publication complained of is in substance a copy whereby a work vested in another is prejudiced'.[135]

If the subsequent author decides to create an identical work, he has two options —to compensate the original author for the market loss or to repeat the original research process. This second option which is known as verification can be criticized as it involves expenditure of time labour in duplicating the original author's work. 'The defendant had not made a map from actual surveys, employing persons to improve or correct but took a copy with merely colourable alterations. It might be asked how is it possible to have a copyright in a map of the Island of St. Domingo? Must not mountains have the same position, the rivers the same course? Must not the points of land, the coast connecting them, the names given by the inhabitants, everything constituting a map be the same? All those objections were urged. The answer was that the subject of the plaintiff's claim was a map, made at great expense, from actual surveys, distinguished from former maps by improvements, that were manifest, the defendant's map was a servile imitation, requiring no expense, no ingenuity, possessing nothing that could confer copyright. Must not the latitude and longitude of the several points upon the adjoining shores and the soundings, be the same as they were placed by nature? They must be the same or the chart must destroy the mariner. What room can there be for originality upon such a subject? That may be the reason for not making new charts or map but it is no reason for a servile imitation'.[136]

To summarize, pre-modern copyright law granted copyright on the basis of mental labour which could encompass both creativity and sweat of the brow. There was no proprietary right over facts. Appropriation of original work through illegitimate use could cause infringement. Illegitimate use meant where second work could replace the original work or could prejudice it in the market. There was no penalty for relying on the original work to create a new one. Legitimate use for research and non-competitive use were permitted. A subsequent author could make

---

[135]Roworth v. Wilkes, 170 Eng. Rep. 889 (1807). In: Baron, supra note 74, at 926.

[136]Mathewson v. Stockdale, 33 Eng. Rep. 103 (1806). In: Baron, supra note 74, at 927.

an identical competing work but he had to compensate the original author and had to do the research afresh by himself.[137]

3.5 Importance of Copyright in Protecting Databases

To incorporate the pre-modern copyright law in case of database protection, this will give more protection than Feist as it does not require any creativity to be proved. The ambit of protection offered by pre-modern copyright law is narrower than sweat of the brow as it does not allow derivative or adaptation right. Fair use will remain to be crucial for determining infringement. Pre-modern copyright law would offer more access to database than *sui generis* structure as it allows competitors to access the original database to create new database. There will not be perpetual protection but at the same time the duration of protection shall not be like copyright, but rather 5–10 years and if existing database is amended significantly, it will be protected as a new work and the old work will go to public domain. There has to be some measures to be taken to address the problem that many databases are inaccessible to public which needs to be brought into the public domain.

As the objective of copyright law is to promote learning and progress and not to create monopoly over information, it increases the healthy stock of common knowledge and offers a limited monopoly in exchange of public access to copyrighted work. In case of *sui generis* protection, the privilege is given without any assurance of public access. Moreover the term of protection being perpetual, the database may never enter into public domain. A *sui generis* model coupled with pre-modern copyright law principles will offer protection against illegitimate use while encouraging legitimate use for creation of new databases and thus it will make a balance between protection to database maker and public access.

After deciding the subject matter for copyright protection, the next difficult job is to decide infringement. Facts and ideas are excluded from protection and thus from a copyrighted material also facts and ideas can be copied. The idea-expression dichotomy allows borrowing the idea and facts from earlier work and presenting them in different form. If ideas and facts can be extracted and exploited by others so easily then in formational work how will the author enjoy his limited monopoly? If the work is not an original one, it can be copied verbatim but if the work is original then only the form of expression can not be copied. Thus ultimately it boils down to the question as to whether the work is an original one or not and in case of informational work the job becomes more difficult to determine the originality of the work.[138] The original authorship approach does not pay attention to sweat of the

[137]Baron, supra note 74, at 928.

[138]Francione (1986) Facing The Nation: The Standard for Copyright Infringement and Fair Use of Factual Works. Univ PAL Rev 134:519.

brow type argument for low authorial informational work.[139] In case of works like map, directories, arrangement has little connection with the value of the work as source of information. As informational work creates its value because of its information, so the author's personality manifesting characteristics do not hold good in these cases. De facto protection of commercial value of compiled facts is the most troublesome aspect of copyright protection.[140]

There are two kinds of copyright—1. copyright in high authorship works such as novels where copyright protects the authorial presence in the work, 2. copyright in low authorship works such as telephone directory and compilation where copyright protects labour and resources invested in the work. Thus copyright is concerned with both creativity and commercial value. If it is observed that personality based approach has completely replaced the investment model then the balance inside the copyright law will be affected but co-existence of these two approaches will absorb conflicting views regarding aim and objective of copyright law.[141] If low authorship works are considered as unoriginal and thus are not given any protection, it will harm the system in the same way as if the information gatherer becomes the proprietor of all possible recombination within a dataset and can exclude the second comers to create any variant information work.[142] The appropriate balance will offer incentive to the first compiler to undertake collection of information and will also allow the second comer to create further informational work relying on earlier collection which will increase over all access to broad variety of works of information.

'In reading the cases in the (English) Reports for the last 100 years, you cannot overlook the literary insignificance of the contending volumes. The big authors and the big books stand majestically on one side—the combatants are all small fry. The question of literary larceny chiefly illustrated by disputes between book makers and rival proprietors of works of references …'[143] Work on the deposit records of all works registered for federal copyright protection during the first 10 years of the first copyright statute also shows a great preponderance of informational and

[139]Denicola, supra note 112, at 516.

[140]Haungs M J (1990) Copyright of Factual Compilations: Public Policy and the First Amendment. Colum J L & Soc Prob 23:347.

[141]There has been some amount of dis-uniformity with respect of US Copyright law—Section 111 (c) compulsory license for cable retransmission, Section 113 permitting certain unlicensed reproduction of pictorial, graphic or sculptural works in the context of advertising, Section 114 scope of protection of sound recording extend neither to imitation of recorded sound nor to public performance, Section 115 compulsory license for mechanical recording, Section 116 compulsory license for juke box performance of non dramatic musical composition Section 117 owner of copies of computer program entitled to make archival copies and to copy and adapt programs in conjunction with their use in computer, Section 118 compulsory license for certain public broadcasting performances, Section 119 compulsory license for receipt of broadcast signals by home satellite dishes. Ginsburg, supra note 132, at 1886.

[142]Ginsburg, supra note 132, at 1866.

[143]Birrell A (1971) Seven Lectures On The Law And History Of Copyright In Books. Kelley, New York, p 195.

instructional works.[144] It is possible that due to this overwhelming presence of informational work, English and American statutes have described copyright as instrument for promotion and advancement of knowledge.[145]

Although there is constitutional text for incentive model of copyright objectives, the role of copyright for inducement to creation received very less attention in the early stage of its development in the United States but in the present age copyright is mainly perceived as incentive for creation.[146] Till the middle of the nineteenth century, if the work was produced by the author with his own effort, the work would be eligible for copyright. Towards the end of the nineteenth century, copyright was seen from a different perspective where authorship was considered as reflection of author's personality, as the work incorporated unique individuality of the author. With this conception, criteria for originality transferred from author's labour to distinctiveness of the execution of the work.

The criteria became subjective to judgment from objective issues like investment of time and labour. This distinctiveness or subjectivity did not imply a higher level of criteria as it was argued that every author is a distinct individual and it was this individuality which made the difference between the works. 'In ordinary life no two descriptions of same fact will be in the same words…The order of each man's words is as singular as his countenance…'[147] So what is required is that the author should contribute something more than mere trivial variation. Originality here implies author's addition, however poor artistically it may be. If original skill and labour is expended then the work will qualify for copyright protection.[148] During nineteenth and twentieth century, concept of originality embraced both original authorship and original creative act.[149]

In the United States, in Emerson v. Davies,[150] it was held 'A man has a right to the copy-right of a map of a state or country, which he has surveyed or caused to be compiled from existing materials, at his own expense, or skill or labour or money. Another man may publish another map of the same state or country, by using the

[144]Federal Copyright Records 1790–1800. Ginsburg A (1990) A Tale of Two Copyrights: Literary Property in Revolutionary France and America. Tul L Rev 64:991.

[145]An Act for Encouragement of Learning/Congress shall have power….To promote the Progress of Science and Useful Arts.

[146]Ginsburg, supra note 132, at 1873.

[147]Jeffery v. Boosey, 10 Eng. Rep. 703. 'No photograph however simple, can be unaffected by the personal influence of the author and no tow will be absolutely alike', Jeweler Circular Publishing Co. v. Keystone Publishing Co., 274 F. 932.

[148]Copyright on plastic bank copied from cast iron version held invalid because this trivial variation did not satisfy originality requirement. L. Batlin & Sons v. Snyder, 536 F.2d 99 (2nf Cir.). But highly detailed art reproduction entitled to copyright protection on grounds of originality in copying, a copy of the requisite exactitude and faithfulness to the source cannot be made without great skill and effort, Kuddle Toy Inc. v. Pussycat Toy Co., 183 U.S.P.Q. 642.

[149]Ginsburg, supra note 132, at 1875.

[150]8 F. Cas 615 (C.C.D. Mass. 1845) (No. 4436). In: Ginsburg, supra note 132, at 1873.

like means or materials and the same skill, labour and expense. But then he has no right to publish a map taken substantially and designedly from the map of other person, without any such exercise of skill or labour or expense.' Thus the author must need something produced by him. It may be original and unpublished thought, principle or new combination of old thoughts and ideas, new application of common materials or new collection which is the result of his industry and skill. To claim exclusive privilege, the author must show something which law can prove as product of his labour and not another's labour.[151]

It has been claimed that the true test of originality is whether the production is the result of independent labour or of copying.[152] The concept of copyright-ability based on labour investment can justify all kinds of informational products. A map or navigational chart of a new territory may not be very relevant for showing subjective authorship but they are important because of their value and importance of the information they offer.[153] This justification for copyrightability of informational works however cannot indicate a pointer for infringement. Initially the scope of copyright was modest and thus the first creator of work could not prohibit the second comer to create a competing work.

'If a person collects an account of natural curiosities or of works of art or of mere matters of statistical or geographical information and employs the labour of his mind in giving a description of them, his own description may be the subject of copyright. It is equally competent to any other person to compile and publish a similar work. But it must be made substantially new and original like the first work, by resort to the original sources and must not copy or adopt from other, upon the notion that the subject is common'.[154] If second comer's appropriation from the first author can be characterized by enough new, developed, indicating new toil and talent then new property right will be vested in the last author. So new toil gives rise to new intellectual property. In such situation if all the subsequent authors are prevented by copyright to come out with improved version of the basic text, there is no guarantee that the first author will undertake more toil to produce new and improved versions, resulting the basic text will remain in the society as the only

---

[151]Curtis G T (2005) Treatise On The Law Of Copyright In Books; Dramatic And Musical Compositions; Letter And Other Manuscripts, Engravings And Sculptures; As Enacted And Administered In England And America. Little Brown & Co., Boston, p 169.

[152]Drone E S (1879) A Treatise On The Law Of Property In Intellectual Productions In Great Britain And The United States. Little Brown & Co, Boston, p 44.

[153]Take the instance of a map, describing a particular county and a map of the same county, afterwards published by another person. If the description is accurate in both, they must be pretty much the same but it is clear that latter publisher cannot on that account justify in sparing himself the labour and expenses of actual survey and copying the map, previously published by another…. A work consisting of a selection from various authors, two men might perhaps make the same selection but that must be resorting to the original authors, not by taking advantage of the selection, already made be another. Longman v. Winchester, 33 Eng. Rep. 987 (1809). In: Ginsburg, supra note 132, at 1873.

[154]Curtis, supra note 325, at 169.

source of information. Thus there will not be any more improvement and the society will be affected.

It is often said that early copyright jurisprudence recognized the reproduction right but not the adaptation right as earlier copyright did not prohibit the unauthorized re manipulation of data but in certain cases it recognized infringement by reference—to use the first author's data to save independent research effort and expenses for engaging into the same research once again. Till the twentieth century, copyright law recognized the labour of the author and prohibited free riding.[155] 'The right and duties of compiler of books which are not original in their character but are compilations of facts from common and universal sources of information, of which books, directories, maps, guide books, road books, statistical tables and digests are the most familiar examples, are well settled. No compiler of such a book has a monopoly of the subject of which the book treats. Any other person is permitted to enter that department of literature and make a similar book. But the subsequent investigator must investigate for himself, from the original source which are open to all. He cannot use the labour of a previous compiler, *animo furandi* and save his own time by copying the result of the previous compilers study, although the same result could have been attained by independent labour. The compiler of a digest, road book, directory or map can search or survey for him in the fields which all labourers are permitted to occupy but cannot adopt as his owns the product of another's toil'.[156]

Information product is duly protected when a rival engages in creating similar product without effort of his own. It is protected either as copyright infringement or misappropriation tort under unfair competition.[157] In Edward Thompson Co. v. American Law Book Co.,[158] it was held that it was not infringement to use the plaintiff's legal encyclopaedia as source for citation of cases when the defendant used his own commentaries. Otherwise if it were held that an author could not consult authorities collected by his predecessor, it would deviate from the objective of copyright law, instead of progress of arts and science, and it would retard progress.

[155]Ginsburg, supra note 132, at 1878.

[156]Banks v. Mc Divitt, 2 F.Cas. 759 (1875). In: Ginsburg, supra note 132, at 1879.

[157]In International News Services v. Associated Press, 248 US 215 (1918), the Supreme Court held quasi property right in dissemination of information. Here news published by Associated Press was copied by INS and supplied it to Mid West or West Coast rival papers ahead of AP's local counterparts. Information was not copyrighted. The judgment was for information relating to current events and was enforceable against competitors and not against public at large. As the Court observed 'Defendant admits that it is taking material that has been acquired by complainant as the result of organization and the expenditure of labour, skill and money and which is salable by complainant for money and that defendant in appropriating it and selling it as it own is endeavouring to reap where it has not sown and by disposing of it to newspapers that are competitors of complainant's members is appropriating to itself the harvest of those who have sown'.

[158]122 F. 922 (2nd Cir).

During early nineteenth century, there was a trend to think of every authorship as an expression of individual personality.[159] In Jefferys v. Boosey,[160] it was observed 'The order of each man's word is as singular as his countenance and although if two authors composed originally with the same order of words, each would have a property therein, still the probability of such an occurrence is less than that there should be two countenances that could not be discriminated'. The Nature has given so much scope of variety that manners of several excellent authors are as different as their faces.

3.6 Position of Database v. Protection

In digital era, collection of data in electronic form has new significance and value. The technology makes this collection of information vulnerable to copying. Collection, arrangement and presentation of information is a must for business and financial services, government, scientific and educational institutions and consumers. It is an industry by itself. A data is 'known facts or things used as a basis for inference or reckoning, quantities, or characters operated by computer'.[161]

Database is structured data which is independently accessible. Database is a reference point where information is stored. Ancient Indian literature called Rig Veda is collection of Sanskrit hymns which can also be described as database and was created as early as during 1500–900 B.C.[162] Shakespeare's First Folio is also a type of database as it is a compilation of all the plays of Shakespeare.[163] Databases like any other intellectual property are indivisible, inexhaustible and ubiquitous.[164] They are not only important for economy[165] but also contribute in cultural,

[159]'By a spirit of imitation we counteract nature and thwart her design. She brings us into the world all originals. No two faces, no two minds are just alike but all bear nature's evident mark of separation on them.' Yong E (1759) Conjectures On Original Composition. In: Ginsburg, supra note 132, at 1881.

[160]10 Eng. Rep. 681.

[161]The Concise Oxford Dictionary of Current English (1997) (8th edition), p 294.

[162]Suthersanen U (2000–2001) A Comparative Review of Database Protection in the European Union and United States. The ATRIP Papers 2000–2001.

[163]Id.

[164]Reichman J H (1995) Charting the Collapse of the Patent—Copyright Dichotomy: Premises for a Restructured International Property System. Cardozo Arts & Ent LJ 13:475.

[165]Between 1991 and 1997 the number of databases in the US increased from 7637 to 10,338. There has also been a marked commercialization of database industry. In 1977, 78 % of databases were produced by the public sector but by 1997 this figure had dropped to 22 % while the private sector share increased to 78 %. Williams M E (1999) The State Of Databases Today. In: Baron, supra note 74, at 880.

scientific and technical progress. For these social utilities, generally investment in databases is encouraged.[166]

'Developing, compiling, distributing and maintaining commercially significant collection requires substantial investment of time, personnel, effort and money. But several recent legal and technological developments threaten to derail this progress by the incentives for continued investment needed to maintain and build upon the US lead in the world market for electronic information resources'.[167] Right in a compilation can be traced to Article 8 of Prussian Law 1837 which offered 30 year right for educational and research institute over work including work which in one or several volumes constitute a single edition.[168]

More recent reference to legal protection of database is found in Berne Convention. 'Collection of literary and artistic work such as encyclopaedias and anthologies which by reason of the selection and arrangement of their contents, constitute intellectual creations'.[169] Database is defined as collection of independent works, data or other materials arranged in a systematic or methodical way and individually accessible by electronic or other means.[170] Prior to widespread use of computer technology, most of the compilations used to be on paper with the help of labour intensive process of filing and indexing.

Computer technology has offered faster retrieval, more storage, and more accuracy.[171] Even an electronic database comprising several hundred collective

---

[166]Databases are essential tools for improving productivity, advancing education and training. These are also the linchpins of a world leading dynamic commercial information industry in the United States. H.R. Rep. No. 106–349 (1999).

[167]H.R. Rep. No. 106–349 (1999). Under the present scope, copyright provides more protection for creativity and labour when invested in an entertaining work, at the expense of having too little of everything else. Lunney G S (1996) Reexamining Copyright's Incentive-Access Paradigm. V and L Rev 49:483.

[168]Suthersanen, supra note 336.

[169]Article 2(5), Berne Convention for the Protection of Literary and Artistic Works (Paris Version 1971).

[170]Article 1, Database Dierctive. Article 2(1), WIPO Draft Treaty—database is a collection of independent works, data or other materials arranged in a systematic manner or methodical way and capable of being accessed by electronic or other means. Section 101(1) (A), The Consumer and Investor Access to Information Bill—database is a collection of a large number of discrete items of information that have been collected and organized in a single place, or in such a way as to be accessible through a single source, through the investment of substantial monetary or other resources, for the purpose of providing access to those discrete items of information by users of the database. Such term does not include works that are combined and ordered in a logical progression or other meaningful way in order to tell a story, communicate a message, represent an idea or achieve a result. Section 1401(1) The Collection of Information Anti Piracy Bill—collection of information means information that has been collected and has been organized for the purpose of bringing discrete items of information together in one place or through one source so that persons may access them.

[171]Technology has also helped sometime to ruin the market of a database as copying, re-manipulation and dissemination have been widely influenced by the technology. Again threat to an online database is different from a database in a CD. Monnotti A (1992) Copyright Protection of Computerized Databases. Austl Intell Prop J 3:135.

agreements on a CD-ROM was considered as original thematic presentation of data and thus deserved copyright protection. With the rise in computing power and better digital storage technology, demand and supply of databases have increased to a great extent. Database can cover different type of products like e-book, directories, online information services and even the whole Internet is conceptually a database. The concept of database is broad enough to include telephone directory, collection of university courses, collection of genetic information or satellite information, collection of metrological records, horse racing records, TV program guides, collection of legal or commercial information, compilation of observations in the field of physics, chemistry or biology.

Database can cover wide area like consumer data (spending habits—for super markets' target marketing, health insurance, and financial status), educational and scientific information (Lexis, West Law, and Genomics Online Database), travel companies (flight schedules and hotel accommodation information) and online shopping companies (Amazon's clientele).[172] Hunsucker felt that commercial competition could be observed in three database market—1. one stop shopping market, where general information content offered to a broad customer base, 2. problem focused market, where specific information content focused on particular problem offered to industry groups and 3. industry focused market, where both general and specific information offered to specific industry market.[173]

Under-protection and over-protection of databases are equally damaging. The argument in favour of strong protection for non-original databases is based on guaranteeing appropriate return from the investment needed to create, maintain and update the database, especially when due to information technology copying and distribution has become so easy.[174] This argument is based on the concept of industrious collection or sweat of the brow and it believes that without the adequate protection, production of databases would be less than what is socially desirable. The argument against the protection to non-original database is that it goes against conventional notion of intellectual property regime and it does not support the idea of promotion of creativity and new ideas. Along with that there is no specific indication that database industry has been damaged due to lack of this protection.[175]

[172]Lipton J (2003) Balancing Private Right and Public Policies: Reconceptualising Property in Databases. Berk Tech L J 18:773.

[173]Hunsucker, supra note 288, at 697.

[174]The vulnerability of products that bear their know-how on their face enables second comer to undercut the originator in the market. This is because the second comer does not need to cover the cost incurred by the originator. The originator therefore lacks a natural lead time in which to recoup his or her investment and make profit. Baron, supra note 74, at 880.

[175]'Nevertheless, the interviews and research conducted for this paper did not find a single instance in which a commercial publisher decided not to start a project because it lacked statutory protection. Maurer, supra note 70.' Movements in the share-prices of companies in the sector show no sign that the profitability of the business is falling in the USA, in spite of the apparent lack of protection', Maurer S M, Hugenholtz P B, Onsrud H J (2001) Europe's Database Experiment. Sci 294:789. There is no empirical evidence to determine the real size and rate of growth of database market, measured in terms of money. Supra note 7, at 11.

It has been argued that if there is a need for greater protection for databases that could be achieved through changes to the unfair competition legislation which would protect database owners against piracy by competitors without affecting user's access to information.[176] The culture of science involves combining new data with existing databases to create more powerful research tools. Allowing scientists to reuse facts, rather than requiring them to reinvent the wheel ensures that research moves forward. Research and development is an important foundation for all commercial activity.[177]

Apart from technological threat and database piracy, there is one more element which negatively influences the database market and they are known as 'information samaritan', who collect data from databases without authorization and disseminate it among public for free and thereby erodes the market for databases.[178] The effect of it is the same like regular database piracy. These actions deter investment and call for better legal protection in database which will not only encourage more investment but also influences international trade as legal regime like in EU makes it obligatory to create an equivalent legal regime to claim equal protection in Europe like European databases.

The balance between incentive and access is a delicate one.[179] Legal protection needs to be designed tactfully to avoid cycle of overprotection and under-protection. Under-protection will undermine the incentive to collate information as there will be free riding to the work and over-protection will remove necessary information out of public domain. So a careful balance has to be maintained so that database industry will develop and society will not be affected. The fear of inhibiting information flow raises debate over database protection. The debate is about whether the new right created for database protection will serve both the purposes—encouraging investment as well as ensuring access to information. The debate also address whether the purpose to be achieved by a database law with exceptions or by competition law with clauses on unfair restriction and unjust enrichment. Digital technology has greatly influenced the search facility in a database and any exclusive right must ensure the balance between interest of producers and consumers.

---

[176]Maurer, Hugenholtz, Onsrud, id., p 789.

[177]Preamble, WIPO DOC. CRNR/DC/6, 1996. In: Baron, supra note 74, at 885.

[178]In United States v. LaMacchia, 871 F. Supp 535 (1994)—in this case La Macchia devised a scheme to allow free dissemination of popular software and games through an electronic board. This destroys incentive to produce. Hunsucker, supra note 288, at 697.

[179]The information infrastructure has the potential to demolish a careful balancing of public good and private interest that has emerged from the evolution of US intellectual property law over past 200 years. The report claims that the challenge is to provide sufficient control to authors to motivate them, but not so much control as to threaten important policy goals. The balance is not however straightforward. Polivy notes that the argument for public access to fact works such as databases can be turned on its head so as to argue that societal need for fact works justifies greater incentives for authors. Polivy D R (1998) Feist Applied: Imagination Protects but Perspiration Persists—The Bases of Copyright Protection for Factual Compilations. Fordham Intell Prop Media & Ent L J 8:773.

Database or collection of information used to be protected initially as compilation under copyright law.[180] Under copyright system original works are protected and the level of originality is generally low, although the term original has not been defined. In case of compilation, emphasis was on selection and arrangement. UK court felt that skill, labour and judgment in selection and arrangement should be the deciding factors and not the creativity.[181] It offered extended protection but it was only limited to expression as per regular notion of copyright.

European States set a higher standard for originality as it was asked for the author's own creation to get the author's right.[182] US Supreme Court held that white page of telephone directory was not protected by copyright.[183] According to Ginsburg, the decision of Feist supported the free access to information. In *Australia Telestra Corporation Ltd. v. Desktop Marketing Systems Pvt Ltd.*, the court held that copyright subsisted in white page and yellow page of directory.

The Database Directive proposed for two-tier structure for protection of database—copyright protection for original databases and *sui generis* protection for non-original databases. The apprehension for *sui generis* right is that it may even protect the underlying information contained in a database. This apprehension is more in case of sole source databases. The BHB decision has to some extent curtailed the extent of protection given by Database Directive.[184] The Directive also while adopting dropped the provision related to compulsory licensing. It is possible that time has come to consider reintroducing of this provision back into the Directive.[185] The WIPO and US initiatives did not see the light of the day.[186] According to Catherine Colston, UK has three tier protections—database copyright through the Directive, copyright in compilation and *sui generis* right. A new format of protection may consider following options to handle the threat of creating monopoly over information—stronger regime on unfair competition, expanding existing exceptions, reintroducing compulsory licensing.

Books that record fact or existing data have been considered as original for the purpose of copyright. Thus dictionary[187] and encyclopaedia[188] are copyrightable works. Where the author has added nothing of his own to the existing data that have

---

[180]Article 2(5) Berne Convention.

[181]Ladbroke (Football) Ltd v. William Hill (Football) Ltd., 1964 HL 175.

[182]Dutch Supreme Court required selection of words for a dictionary to include author's own view. Van dale v. Romme (1991) Ned. Jur. 608. In: Cornish (1999) Intellectual Property: Patents, Copyright, Trade Marks And Allied Rights. Sweet & Maxwell, p 385. In: Colston, supra note 72.

[183]Feist Publication v. Rural Telephone, 499 US 340 (1991). Court rejected the argument of sweat of the brow.

[184]British Horseracing Board Ltd. v. William Hill Organization Ltd., C-203/02 (2004) ECJ.

[185]Colston, supra note 72.

[186]http://www.wipo.int/pressroom/en/updates/1999/upd99_58.htm. Accessed 20 Dec 2009. The Database Investment and Intellectual property Piracy Act. HR 3531, Collection of Information Antipiracy Act, HR 354, Consumer and Investor Access to Information Act HR 1858.

[187]Barfield v. Nicholson, (1824) 57 ER 245.

[188]Mawman v.Tegg, (1826) 38 ER 868.

been recorded, originality can be found in the arrangement and selection and thus can get copyright. Compilation as a piece of work is a different character from work of art or literature. It is more correct in case of compilation of facts which are available in public domain. To create this type of compilation, facts are to be selected, collected, arranged in a particular fashion which can some time generate the level of originality required to get protection.

The level of originality required in case of compilation is different from other works. It is suggested that as the level of originality in case of compilation is different, a person who brought out a directory in consequence of an expensive, complicated and well-organized venture, it can get copyright even if there is no creativity in selection and arrangement. In Hotten v. Arthur,[189] the plaintiff a bookseller claimed copyright in a catalogue of stock. The catalogue consisted not only the name, author and price of the book but also a short account of the book and a summary of the contents. Wood VC found that there was copyright as he observed 'This is not mere a dry list of names like a personal directory, court guide or anything of that sort which must be substantially the same by whatever number of person issued and however independently compiled'. What happens if there is no creativity in selecting and arranging factual data?

There exists one line of argument according to which to establish originality in compilation of facts, it is not necessary to show any intellectual effort in the creation of work. It is enough if it is shown that there has been sufficient work involved and expense incurred in gathering facts and according to this argument copyright is given as a reward for the author's investment of time and money, even if there is no creativity in the work. In Matthewson v. Stockdale,[190] the plaintiff brought an action to prevent the defendant from publishing an East India calendar which the plaintiff alleged infringed his copyright. Lord Erskine observed 'If a man from his situation having access to the repositories in the India House has be considerable expense and labour procured with correctness all the names and appointments of the Indian establishment, he has a copyright in that particular work, which has cost him considerable expenses and labour and employed him at a loss in other respects, though there can be no copyright in an Indian Calendar generally'.

In Kelly v. Morris[191] the plaintiff claimed copyright in a street dictionary, which was alleged being copied by the defendant. Wood VC observed 'the defendant has been most completely mistaken in what he assumes to be his right to deal with labour and property of others. In the case of a dictionary, map, guide book, directory, when there are certain common objects of information which must if described correctly, be described in the same words, a subsequent compiler is bound to set about doing for himself that which the first compiler has done. In case of a road book, he must count the milestones for himself…generally, he is not entitled to take one word of the information published previously without

[189]71 ER 264.

[190]33 ER 103.

[191]33 ER 103.

independently working out the matter for himself, so as to arrive at the same result from the same common source of information and the only use he can legitimately make of a previous publication is to verify his own calculation and results when obtained. So in the present case the defendant could not take a single line of the plaintiff's directory for the purpose of saving himself labour and trouble in getting his information'.[192]

Halsbury LC observed 'A man goes along a street, collects the name, address, occupation of each dwellers therein. What is the original composition of which according to Court of Appeal he is the author? The name of the street? The number of the street? The name of the dwellers in several houses? What is the distinction which the Court of Appeal makes in giving copyright to the result of this labour and reducing it into writing? What is it that makes it an original writing? But further where do the words original composition come from? …If the producer of such a book can be an author within the meaning of the Act, I am unable to understand why the labour of reproducing spoken words into writing or print and first publishing as book does not make the person who has so acted as much as an author as the person who writes down the name and addresses of the persons who live in a street. Though the copyright law was designed to encourage literary merit and accordingly it was intellectual labour that constituted authorship. But it appears to me that although it may be true that a preamble may be a guide to the general objects of the statute, it undoubtedly is unquestioned law that it can neither restrict nor limit express enactment. And though I think in these compositions there is literary merit and intellectual labour, yet the statute does not seem to me to require either, or originality either in thought or in language'.[193]

In the same case Lord Davey observed 'Copyright has nothing to do with the originality or literary merit of the author or composer. It may exist in the information given by a street directory or by a list of deeds of agreements or in a list of advertisements.' Copyright unlike patent does not create monopoly as another person can do the same work independently and its term of protection is also lesser than patent. More over the term originality is also interpreted in a much wider way than it is meant through novelty in patent law. So the monopoly right[194] created by copyright has to be understood in a different way.

---

[192]A similar line of argument can be found in Walter v. Lane, (1900) AC 539 where the issue was whether reporters of The Times were entitled to get copyright in a report of number of public speeches delivered by Lord Rosebery. The speeches were taken down in short hand and then written, corrected, revised and published. The defendant argued that for a copyright there must be something more than mere writing down author's word. Reporters argued that although there was so literary skill and originality but the industrious collection would suffice. The plaintiff succeeded.

[193]Walter v. Lane, (1900) AC 539.

[194]The monopoly privileges that Congress may authorize are neither unlimited nor primarily designed to provide a special private benefit. Rather, the limited grant is a means by which an important public purpose may be achieved. It is intended to motivate the creative activity of authors and inventors by the provision of a special reward and to allow the public access to the products of their genius after the limited period of exclusive control has expired. Sony Corp of America v. Universal City Studio Inc., 464 US 417.

In H Blacklock & Co Ltd v. C Arthur Pearson Ltd,[195] publisher of Bradshaw, a compilation of current timetables of every railway in England and Ireland, brought an action against the defendant for reproducing the index of Bradshaw for use in a competition. The defendant argued that there could be no copyright in a bundle of timetables. Judge Joyce held that there was copyright in the index and observed 'the compilation of this index, in particular the making up of the list of names of stations from the time table, though it be not entirely new every month, would obviously be a work of labour and therefore of expense.'

In Leslie v. J Young & Sons,[196] proprietor of a monthly railway timetable sought an injunction against the respondent, publisher of a competing time table to restrain the sale of time table for infringement of copyright. The House of Lords decided that proprietor was not entitled for injunction with respect to railway timetables.[197] In the United States, in Jeweler's Circular Publishing Co. v. Keystone Publishing Co,[198] it was observed 'The right to copyright a book upon which one has expended labour in its preparation does not depend upon whether the materials he has collected consist or not of matters which are publici juris, or whether such materials show literary skill or originality, either in thought or in language, or anything more than industrious collection. The man who goes through the streets of a town and puts down the names of each of the inhabitants, with their occupations and their street number, acquires material of which he is the author. He produces by his labour a meritorious composition, in which he may obtain a copyright, and thus obtain the exclusive right of multiplying copies of his work.'

Justice Yates observed in his dissenting note, 'that every man is entitled to the fruit of his labour I really admit. But he can only be entitled to this, according to the fixed constitution of things and subject of the general rights of mankind and the general rules of property. He must not expect that these fruits shall be eternal that he is to monopolize them to infinity that every vegetation and increase shall be confined to himself alone and never revert to the common mass'.[199] Although copyright creates exclusive right but due to the very nature of it, the degree of monopoly is relatively diluted. The anti-competitiveness is further adjusted due to the fact that ideas are not protected and thus competitors are free to make different works from

---

[195](1915) 2 Chap. 376.

[196](1894) AC 335.

[197]The information in these time-tables was of course derived by the pursuer from sources which were as open to the defenders as to himself, and he does not and cannot claim any right to the information as such; he can only claim copyright in them, if they are the result in some respect or other of independent work on his part, and if advantage has been substantially taken by the defenders of that independent labour. The mere publication in any particular order of the timetables which are to be found in railway guides and the publications of the different railway companies could not be claimed as a subject-matter of copyright. Proceedings could not be taken against a person who merely published that information which it was open to all the world to publish and to obtain from the same source.

[198]281 F 83 (2nd Circuit 1922).

[199]Millar v. Taylor, (1769) 4 Burr. 157.

same materials. The list of fair uses also helps to dilute the effect of monopoly. It is also felt that incentive to create new works would not be affected by copyright, as the primary objective of copyright has remained to be recognition of work rather than securing economic advantage.[200]

In Feist Publications Inc. v. Rural Telephone Service Co,[201] Judge O'Connor held 'original as the term used in copyright means only that the work is independently created by the author as opposed to copied from other work and that it possesses at least minimal degree of creativity. The test of originality would be justified by vast majority of compilations but there remains a narrow category of works in which the creative spark is utterly lacking or so trivial as to be virtually non-existent. The selection and arrangement of facts cannot be so mechanical or routine as to require no creativity whatsoever.'

In Key Publications Inc. v. Chinatown Today Publishing Enterprises Inc[202] plaintiff collected business cared from businesses believed to be of particular interest to Chinese American community and sorted those information and placed each business under appropriate category and listed name, address and telephone number. Court observed that business categories were original and the arrangement was in no sense mechanical and it involved creativity. In Canada copyright of yellow page was discussed in Tele-Direct (Publications) Inc v. American Business Information Inc.[203] and was held that copyright did not subsist in the directory as it had only minimal degree of skill or judgment which was not enough to claim originality.[204]

---

[200]'Many of our best and noblest authors have published their work from more generous views than pecuniary profit. Some have written for fame and the benefit of mankind.' Wheaton v. Peters, 33 US 591 (1834). Kreiss observed that the argument that some authors are not motivated by economic considerations to be irrelevant as most authors put in hard work because of potential to earn income from the commercialization of new works. Kreiss, supra note 115, at 1.

[201]499 US 340 (1991).

[202]945 F2d 509 (2nd Cir.).

[203](1997) 154 DLR 4th 328.

[204]In Data Access Corporation v. Powerflex Services Pvt. Ltd., (1999) 73 ALJR 1435, the appellant had developed a computer program, being a set of instructions to cause a computer to perform a particular function. The instructions took the form of a computer language. The language comprised a set of reserved words used in accordance with the rules governing the use of each word. The words were found in a users guide. Many of the words were ordinary English words suggesting a particular function, for example, check, clear, insert, and loop. Some were unique to the plaintiff's program, but most were in common use. The High Court was required to determine whether there was copyright in the users guide. In a joint judgment the Court said 'The appellant did not submit that any of the Reserved Words themselves were traditional literary works protected by copyright, no doubt because they would face significant hurdles in the form of originality and substantiality. Given that the reserved words are arranged in alphabetical order in the Dataflex User's Guide, very little skill or labour was involved in compiling the reserved words in the form in which they appear in the User's Guide over and above the sum of the skill and labour involved in devising each individual reserved word'. As the Full Court said: 'this is not a case where disconnected words are used in a particular order so that the order becomes the linchpin for copyright. Furthermore, as we have already said, each of the Reserved Words is suggestive of

The more correct approach was given in Ladbroke (Football) Ltd v. William Hill (Football) Ltd,[205] according to which first it has to be determined whether the plaintiff's work as whole is original and protected by copyright. There are three landmarks in debate on database—1. the decision of US Supreme Court in Feist case which held that non-original databases were not protected by copyright law, 2.the adoption of EU Directive which established *sui generis* protection for non-original databases, 3. the collapse of 1996 treaty on databases by WIPO.[206] The interest of database owners can be protected through electronic mechanism such as copy indicator, encoding, authenticator, encryption, password etc.[207] The possible impact of *sui generis* protection to non-original databases is that journals will increasingly digitize their contents and university libraries will shift more to electronic journals and as a result, scope of fair use exemption will be reduced remarkably. At the same time, database suppliers sometimes offer differential prices to some customers such as universities, students etc. If adequate protection is not given to the database owners, then this concession to universities or students will be discontinued. The other possibility is to offer subsidy. For sole source databases, anti-monopoly legislation can be applied.

The computer database is an information compendium but stored in a computer and thus automated. As it is computerized, information can be accessed, manipulated and used in many ways. Westlaw or Lexis is examples of computer databases. The problem of protecting database is that many a times, information compiled will be in public knowledge. A person can always call all attorneys in the city and ask whether they specialize in computer law. If he can put the name and address of all those attorneys who replied yes, a computer database will be created. Any one after him can also follow the same method and create an identical database. The arrangement can also be very general like alphabetical. As names and addresses cannot be owned so both databases will exist side by side. The first person who came with the idea of making a database of computer law attorneys will not be able to stop the second person from doing it.[208]

Computer databases can be protected by contract, trade secret and copyright. Sometimes even unfair competition can come for help. To prepare such database requires significant expenditure of time, effort and money but a database maker just discovers them and does not create them and thus many people can make a database of attorneys who practise computer law. The sweat of the brow doctrine of

(Footnote 204 continued)

the function it performs. In many cases, it is an ordinary English word, or a concatenation of two or more ordinary English words. Even if the skill and labour involved in devising each individual Reserved Word is combined and consideration given to the total skill and labour, there may still be a real question as to whether there is sufficient originality for copyright to subsist in the combination'.

[205](1964) 1 WLR 273.

[206]Supra note 7, at 2.

[207]Baron, supra note 74, at 880.

[208]Mazer v. Stein, 347 US 201.

copyright law can make or bring large area of source materials within protection and can threaten access to information. This doctrine even can protect data itself and thus can overturn the basic principle of copyright law.[209]

In cases where the author makes and creates data and database, data can get some protection. For example, if the author makes a bibliographic database and gives his own input regarding each entry, then he gets protection for both the compilation and the content. Sweat of the brow should be removed as in case of computers, functionality of a computer program is not allowed be protected.[210] If a computer database is protected under trade secret, court will try to find out whether there has been reasonable attempt to keep it secret. Customer list in a computer can also be protected as trade secret and it can be created as computer database. Parties can prevent the content of a computer database from being disclosed through non disclosure agreement, even though the content of database is not a trade secret but in that case the agreement must specifically mention that the other party will not disclose the content of the database and the licensee is contractually bound to maintain that. Some time deliberate errors and omissions are kept in the database to detect copying. Programmer of database may put signature also into the computer database which can help to detect if there is any copy at a future date. Apart from these, regular non-copying measures can be used to make computer database more secure.[211]

A database has two principal components and both can constitute as digital property—raw data which is source of knowledge and the program which is required to store, communicate and manipulate. Some databases are heavily dependent on the raw data and their value is for the richness of data and some database are heavily dependent on the program and their utility is more because of the program. A combination of these two can make the database a really valuable property and an example of this is Lexis-Nexis or Westlaw. Mining of data and expanding search facility of program can make this knowledge product very effective.

Raw data which is otherwise less valuable can generate extremely useful property such as raw data of grocery stores which are otherwise less valuable and can be processed by a program to create data on individual's purchasing habit and which can be valuable property for business organizations as they can use it to make their future business plan. Apart from this, copying and editing capacity can create new derivative properties with new compilations. This makes otherwise a human labour intensive work a very technical one by reducing the sweat and perspiration and increasing the effectively and innovation.

[209]Losey R C. Practical and Legal Protection of Computer Databases. www.floridalawfirm.com/article.html. Accessed 1 Sept 2006.

[210]Lotus Development Corporation v. Paperback Software International, 740 F. Supp. 221.

[211]Losey, supra note 383.

The database industry has opted for technological solutions precisely because law has proved to be out-dated, slow and inconsistent. Technological protection for digital property can be achieved through server and file control, encryption, keys and digital signatures and together with these unauthorized access can be restricted and exclusivity can be enhanced. Access control can be of three types—1. completely uncontrolled where full content of the server are available without restriction, 2. partially controlled where only certain data on the server can be accessed without restriction, 3. completely controlled where no uncontrolled access is given. At the server level, control is maintained through user identification and authentication. Control through hardware key system requires user to verify by inserting a hardware device like credit card into the computer system and without hardware key, server cannot be accessed.

Coupled with this, rendering software can exercise control by fixing up the level of 'who to what extent' and also by establishing rights like to read, write, delete and copy. Encryption can also promote exclusivity by restricting access. In encryption, mathematical algorithm is used to scramble or unscramble data. Earlier encryption used the technology called single key system but stealing or changing of this key compromised security and access. Today public key system is in place where encryption is done with a public key but decryption is done with private key. The only danger in this case is that if the file can be decrypted and three is no other security arrangement, then any one can reproduce and distribute. Digital signature can also offer substantial security benefit as it authenticates the source of the document and verifies the original content of the document. In case of digital signature, algorithm called hash function which produces a shorter, scrambled digest of the message is used by both the sender and the receiver and compares with the message digests as well as verifies the source. All these technological advancements regarding the restriction and access do not dilute the demand of necessity of the legal protection.

Database comprises of data, effort in locating, originality involved in selection, tool for search etc. The owner of database generally likes to permit authorized person to use, to prevent unauthorized persons from using it, to prevent competition. Database can cover wide range of products like from telephone book to complex aggregation of data dispersed through Internet. The legal status of data remains unaffected by the process of compilation as rights are passed through from compiler to end user but data as raw material remains in the public domain.[212] Compilation can be of information which are in public domain as well as of copyrighted works where the compiler has to take permission from the owner of copyright. If the raw material of a compilation is trade secret, then users should be placed under contractual obligation of confidentiality.

[212]Conley J M, Bemelmans K (1997) Intellectual Property Implications of Multimedia Products: A Case Study. Info Comm Tech L 6:3.

3.7 Role of Competition Law in Maintaining Balance

In IMS Health GmbH & Co. OHG v. NDC Health GmbH & Co KG[213] three questions on the interpretation of Article 82[214] of E C Treaty were referred. The litigation cam up due to use by NDC Health a brick structure developed by IMS for the provision of German regional sales data on pharmaceutical products. IMS and NDC were engaged in tracking sales of pharmaceutical and health care products. IMS provided data on regional sales of pharmaceutical products in Germany to pharmaceutical laboratories formatted according to the brick structure which were created by taking into account various criteria like boundaries of municipalities, postcodes, population density, transport connections and geographical distribution of pharmacies and doctors.

The national court found that IMS not only marketed brick structure but also distributed them free of charge to pharmacies and that practice helped those structure to become normal industry standard. IMS brought this litigation to prohibit NDC from using any brick structure. The brick structure used by IMS was a database. NDC argued that refusal to grant license to use brick structure by IMS amounted to infringement of Article 82 EC Treaty. In 2001 the Commission took an interim measure[215] by asking IMS to grant license to use brick structure to all the undertakings and the Commission held that the refusal of access to that structure without any objective justification would be likely to eliminate all competition on the market as without it, it was impossible to compete on the relevant market. INS brought an action in the court of first instance requesting suspension of operation of the order of the Commission and court ordered suspension of the order and appeal against this order was also dismissed. Consequently the Commission withdrew its earlier decision (Decision 2002/165).

As INS pursued its objective of prohibiting NDC from using brick structure and Landgericht Frankfurt felt that INS cannot exercise its right to get interim injunction prohibiting all from using, the case was referred to ECJ. One of the questions referred was—1. whether Article 82 to be interpreted in such a way that there is abusive conduct by an undertaking with a dominant position on the market where it refuses to grant license agreement for the use of databank to an undertaking which seeks access to the same geographical and product market. A balance has to be

[213]C-418/01.

[214]Any abuse by one or more undertakings of a dominant position within the common market or in a substantial part of it shall be prohibited as incompatible with the common market insofar as it may affect trade between Member States. Such abuse may, in particular, consist in: (a) directly or indirectly imposing unfair purchase or selling prices or other unfair trading conditions; (b) limiting production, markets or technical development to the prejudice of consumers; (c) applying dissimilar conditions to equivalent transactions with other trading parties, thereby placing them at a competitive disadvantage; (d) making the conclusion of contracts subject to acceptance by the other parties of supplementary obligations which, by their nature or according to commercial usage, have no connection with the subject of such contracts.

[215]OJ 2002 L 59, p 18.

maintained between the interest in protection of intellectual property rights and economic freedom of its owner against the interest in protection of free competition. The interest in protection of free market will prevail if refusal to grant license prevents development of secondary market to the detriment of consumers. Here we need to be careful that sometimes upstream product becomes indispensable for supply of downstream products.

In Bronner[216] judgment a press undertaking with a very large share of the daily newspaper market which operates only nationwide newspaper home delivery scheme refuses access to that scheme to the publisher of a rival news paper which by reason of its small circulation is unable either alone or in cooperation with other publisher to set up and operates its own home delivery scheme under economically reasonable condition constitutes abuse of a dominant position. Whether the undertaking which requested license does not limit essentially to duplicate goods or services already offered on the secondary market by the owner of intellectual property rights or intends to produce new goods and services not offered by the owner of intellectual property rights and for which there is potential consumer demand is very important criteria in ascertaining abuse of dominant position.

It is observed that in order for a refusal of license to be considered abusive, it is not necessary that there has to be two distinct markets, it is sufficient if the undertaking in a dominant position in a market has monopoly over an infrastructure which is indispensable in order to compete with it in the market.[217] The opinion of the Court was that for the purpose of examining whether the refusal by an undertaking in a dominant position to grant a license for a brick structure protected by intellectual property right which it owns is abusive, the degree of participation by users in the development of structure and the outlay, particularly in term of cost, on the part of potential users in order to purchase studies on regional sales of pharmaceuticals products presented on the basis of an alternate structure are factors which must be taken into consideration in order to determine whether the protected structure is indispensable to the marketing of studies of that kind.

The refusal by an undertaking which holds dominant position and owns an intellectual property right in a brick structure indispensable to the presentation of regional sales data on pharmaceutical product to grant a license to use the structure to another undertaking which also wishes to provide such data constitutes abuse of dominant position if 1. the undertaking which requested for license intends to offer new product or service not offered by the owner of intellectual property rights and for which there is potential consumer demand, 2. refusal is not justified by objective consideration, 3. refusal is such as to reserve to the owner of the intellectual property right the market for supply of data on sales of pharmaceutical products by eliminating all competition in the said market.

The US aggressively uses trade sanctions to create pressure on other countries to increase intellectual property protection and open market from American goods.

---

[216]C 7/97, (1998) ECR I-7791.

[217]Magill (RTE and ITP v. Commission), (1995) ECR I-743.

Rural Telephone Service Co. Inc. is a certified public which provides telephone service to several communities in northwest Kansas. Rural publishes telephone directory containing white and yellow pages to distribute to its subscribers annually. The white page contains names of Rural's subscribers in alphabetical order together with town and telephone number. The yellow page contains names of Rural's business subscribers alphabetically by category together with telephone number. This directory is distributed free of cost to Rural's subscribers but Rural earns revenue from Yellow page advertisement. Rural collects information from its subscribers at the time of offering telephone connection.

Feist Publications Inc. is a publishing company, which publishes area wide telephone directory. It covers 11 telephone service areas in 15 counties and contains 46878 white page listing.[218] Feist approached all these 11 telephone companies and offered them to pay for using their white page listing. Only Rural refused to license its listing which created a problem for Feist as its directory would become incomplete and less attractive publication without these data.

Feist eventually used Rural's white page listing without its permission. 1309 entries out of 46878 listing in Feist's directory were identical to listing of Rural. Four of them were fictitious listing that Rural entered into its directory to detect copying.[219]

Rural sued Feist for copyright infringement in the District Court of Kansas. Rural argued that Feist could not use information contained in its white pages while compiling its own directory. Rural felt that Feist must travel door to door of the county and conduct survey to collect the same information for them. Feist countered that information was beyond copyright protection. District Court granted judgment to Rural. Judge Richard Dean Rogers held that telephone directories are copyrightable.[220] Court of Appeal for Tenth Circuit also affirmed the judgment of the District Court.[221] Justice O'Connor of the Supreme Court held that names, towns and telephone numbers of subscribers were un-copyrightable facts and they were not arranged in an original way in the white pages to deserve copyright protection and thus reversed the judgment of the Court of Appeal.

In the Supreme Court, Justice Blackmun concurred with Justice O'Connor. This case deals with two important positions of copyright law. One of them is that facts are not copyrightable and the other one is that compilation of facts is generally copyrightable. No author can copyright his ideas or facts he narrates as facts and discoveries are not subject to copyright protection.[222] As many compilations consist of raw data and has no original expression, so there is no ground to give them copyright protection. Sine qua non of copyright is originality. Original means that

[218]499 US 340 (1991).

[219]499 US 340 (1991).

[220]663 F.Supp. 214.

[221]916 F.2d. 718.

[222]Harper & Row Publishers Inc. v. Nation Enterprises, 471 US 539 (1985).

the works is independently created by the author and it is not copied.[223] Most of the works manage to satisfy the requirement of originality as they possess some element of creativity, however crude or obvious they may be. Originality does not mean novelty. A work may be original even though it can closely resemble with another, so long there is no copying.[224]

The originality is a constitutional mandate for all works.[225] No one can claim originality as to facts as facts do not owe their origin to any act of authorship. Census reports are not the original works as the author do not create the data; rather they copy from the world around him. The same is with historical and scientific facts. They are part of public domain and are available to every person. Selection and arrangement of a factual compilation may be protected if they are done independently and possess minimum degree of creativity. A work is copyrighted does not mean that every element of that work is protected but rather copyright extends to those elements who can satisfy the originality requirement.

The format of selection or arrangement may be original but facts will never be original. The primary object of copyright law is not to reward the labour of author but to promote Progress of Science and useful Arts.[226] The same fact may be reshuffled or restated by second author although the fact was first discovered by the first author. This is known as idea—expression dichotomy. Raw facts may be copied at will but the presentations or expressions should be original. That is how copyright leads to progress of arts and science. 'The very object of publishing a book on science or useful arts is to communicate to the world the useful knowledge which it contains. But this object would be frustrated if the knowledge could not be used without incurring the guilt of piracy of the book.[227] 'The statute does not define originality but since the author is referred as creator or originator, so work of author is required to be original work'.[228]

In Jeweler's Circular Publishing Co v. Keystone Publishing Co.,[229] it was observed that copyright was a reward for the hard work that went into compiling facts and the principle was referred as sweat of the brow or industrious collection. 'The man who goes through the streets of a town and puts down names of each of the inhabitants, with their occupations and their street number, acquires material of which he is the author'. The defect of this sweat of the brow doctrine is that it tends to protect the facts as it prevents subsequent compiler from taking information published earlier; rather the subsequent compiler has to work out the matter for

---

[223]Nimmer, Nimmer, supra note 205, Section 2.01.

[224]Sheldon v. Metro-Goldwyn Pictures Corp., 81 F. 2d 49.

[225]Patterson, Joyce, supra note 266, at 719.

[226]Twentieth Century Music Corp v. Aiken, 422 US 151 (1975).

[227]Baker v. Seldon, 101 US 99 (1880).

[228]Nimmer, Nimmer, supra note 205, Section 2.01.

[229]281 F 83 (2nd Cir 1922).

himself so that he may arrive at the same result from same common source. But no one can copyright fact or idea.[230]

Information is not the creation of the writer but it is report of matters which are ordinarily in publici juris. Sweat of the brow doctrine undoubtedly flouted basic principles of copyright.[231] Remedies for issues relating to result of research may be some time available under unfair competition theory but protecting them through copyright distorts copyright principle and creates monopoly over public domain material.[232] In Copyright Act 1976, the phrase 'all the writings of an author' was replaced by 'original work of authorship'. The word original was purposefully left undefined so that the established standard of originality set by the Court would be maintained.[233]

Section 102(b) of 1976 Act prohibited copyright of facts.[234] This section neither expanded nor contracted the scope of protection; it merely clarified the law without changing ambit.[235] Compilation is defined as a work formed by the collection and assembling of pre-existing materials or of data that are selected, coordinated or arranged in such a way that the resulting work as a whole constitutes an original work of authorship.[236] Thus collection of facts is not copyrightable *per se*. It requires three elements—1. collection and assembly of pre-existing materials, fact or data, 2. selection, coordination or arrangement of those materials, 3. creation by virtue of particular selection, arrangement, of original work of authorship.[237] So every collection of facts does not enjoy copyright protection. Only those collections that are considered as original work of authorship will receive copyright protection.

As novelty is required for compilations, so compiler can take clue from other existing arrangements. Originality demands that the author should do the compilation independently without copying from other source. As a result of this requirement most of the compilation will pass the test but not that all compilation will be able to satisfy the requirement. Facts contained in an existing work may be copied as copyright protects only the selection, arrangement of facts. Mere use of information contained in a directory, without substantially copying the format does not constitute infringement. The sweat of the brow doctrine used in Jeweler's Circular Publishing Co v. Keystone Publishing Co[238] has been repudiated.

---

[230]Miller v. Universal City Studio, 650 F. 2d 1372.

[231]499 US 340 (1991).

[232]Nimmer, Nimmer, supra note 205, Section 3.04.

[233]Report of the Registrar of Copyright on the General Revision of the U.S Copyright Law, 87th Congress, 1st Session, p 9. In: 499 US 330 (1991).

[234]In no case copyright protection for an original work of authorship extend to any idea, procedure, process system, method of operation, concept, principle or discovery, regardless, of the form in which it is described, explained, illustrated or embodied, in such work.

[235]Nimmer, Nimmer, supra note 205, Section 2.03 (E).

[236]Section 101, Copyright Act, 1976.

[237]499 US 340 (1991).

[238]281 F 83 (2nd Cir 1922).

Rural was first to record the names, towns, telephone numbers but this data did not owe to Rural. These are un-copyrightable facts and they existed even before Rural recorded them. Rural cannot be called author of these names, towns and telephone numbers. Regarding the selection, Rural's selection was alphabetical. For the purpose of copyright protection, selection and arrangement need not be innovative but it cannot be so mechanical and routine that it has no creativity. The standard of originality is low but it definitely exists.[239] The garden variety of white page directory of Rural was devoid of slightest trace of creativity. Thus Rural's database lacked de minimis quantum of creativity and disqualified to become an original work of authorship and consequently loses copyright protection. Feist's use of listing of Rural was not an infringement and decision of Court of Appeal was reversed.

In Telstra Corp.v. Desktop Marketing Systems,[240] Judge Finkelstein felt that Justice O'Connor in Feist was wrong in observing that limiting copyright in compilations to those where there had been an exercise of judgment would not affect many publication. It was also observed that many obvious method of grouping like alphabetical, chronological, sequential would be denied originality according to Feist, though these type of grouping would make the database valuable. Judge Finkelstein observed 'There are policy reasons both for and against the result in Feist.

On the one hand, the ability to prevent others from appropriating information in a compilation of facts will severely limit the ability of later authors to build upon earlier works. This may impair progress in both the sciences and the arts. On the other hand, there are those who argue that the abandonment of the 'sweat of the brow' theory has threatened the progress of information. The argument is that the collection of factual material is essential to the economy. Databases provide a wealth of information to business people, professionals, scientists and consumers. If copyright protection is not given, the investment of time and money that is required to produce these compilations will not be forthcoming'.[241]

Jeweler's Circular Publishing Co. v. Keystone Publishing Co[242] deals with an infringement issue related to a compilation of trademarks of various firms engaged in jewellery and allied trades. The Jeweler's Circular Publishing Co was the owner of copyright (No. 391,804) in a compilation called 'Trade Marks of the Jewelry and Kindred Trades'.

The Jeweler's Circular Publishing Co alleged that the Keystone Publishing Co while preparing its book 'The Jeweler's Index' unfairly used and pirated the result of Jeweler's Circular Publishing's labour and expenditure, instead of resort to original sources. Evidences indicated the Keystone Publishing Co's compilation of trademark of firms and individuals involved in jewellery business followed

---

[239]Patterson, Joyce, supra note 266, at 719.

[240](2001) F.C.A.612.

[241](2001) F.C.A. 612.

[242]281 F. 83.

the same classification of Jeweler's Circular Publishing Co's compilation and reproduced errors, observed similarity in arrangement and language. The Keystone Publishing Co denied the allegation. The lower Court held that the copyright of Jeweler's Circular Publishing Co was valid and the Keystone Publishing Co did infringe the copyright and granted injunction.

Justice Holmes in Bleistein v. Donaldson Lithographic Co[243] observed that speaks of directories was being capable of copyright. Contrary to the prevailing notion, Congress by enacting Section 5[244] of Copyright Act 1909 removed all doubts about copyright-ability of directories. Keystone Publishing Co argued that as Jeweler's Circular Publishing Co's directory contained trade mark, it would not be copyrightable as per the Copyright Act[245] of 1874 (18 Stat. 78, c.301) which was not repealed by the Act of 1909. Keystone's argument was that trade mark being sole property of the manufacturer; mere copy of a mark did not have sufficient originality to deserve copyright protection. Keystone took help of Royal Sales Co. v. Gaynor[246] which decided that copyright of a book did not cover a monogram of a campaign described therein but it was not a relevant precedent as monogram was not a 'cut, print or engraving'.

Keystone also took help of J. L. Mott Iron Works v. Clow[247] where Court of Appeal of Seventh Circuit decided that a publication containing trade catalogue and photographic illustrations of bathroom appliances not copyright-able as they were advertisement and had no aesthetic value. This view was subsequently reversed[248] as picture none the less a copyrightable work even though used as advertisement and if a picture could command attention of public, then it must have commercial value and the taste of public could not be treated with contempt by describing them as devoid of aesthetic value.

A person's name, occupation, place of business, residence is not subject of copyright but a compilation of this information is copyrightable, though the separate parts of which it is composed are not copyrightable. Thus individual trade mark may not be copyrightable but compilation of trademarks should be copyrightable. 'The right to copyright a book upon which one has expended labour in its preparation does not depend upon whether the materials which he has collected consists or not of matters which are publici juris or whether such materials show literary skill or originality, either in thought or in language or anything more than industrious collection.

[243]188 US 239.

[244]Books including composite and cyclopaedic works, directories, gazetteers and other compilations.

[245]The words 'engraving', 'cut', 'print', shall be only applied to pictorial illustrations or works connected to the fine arts and no prints or labels designed to be used for any other articles of manufacture shall be entered by the Copyright Law but may be registered in the Patent Office.

[246]164 Fed 207.

[247]82 Fed 316.

[248]Bleistein v. Donaldson Lithographic Co., 188 US 239S.

The man who goes through the streets of a town and puts downs the names of each inhabitants, with their occupation and street number, acquires material of which he is the author. He produces by his labour a meritorious composition, in which he may obtain a copyright and thus obtain the exclusive right of multiplying copies of his work'.[249] A similar view was taken in Walter v. Lane,[250] where a reporter who took down in shorthand speeches delivered by Lord Roseberry on public occasion and published them was entitled to copyright. In case of a directory, map or guide book, directory, there is certain information which has to be described in a particular way and in these cases subsequent compiler is bound to follow the way the first compiler has done. But he must go through the whole process once again. He is not allowed to take information published earlier without doing it independently so as to reach same result using the same common source of information. The only thing which he can legitimately do is that after preparing the compilation he can use the earlier material to verify the content of his own creation.

'No one has right to take the result of the labour and expenses incurred by another for the purpose of rival publication and thereby save himself the expenses and labour of working out and arriving at these results by some independent road. If this was not so, there would be practically no copyright in such work as directory'.[251] So it is not lawful for the defendant to cut slips from the plaintiff's directory and insert into their own directory.

In Pike v. Nicholas,[252] two rival works were published with reference to the same subject—matter but the defendant had been guided by the plaintiff's book so far as the authorities were concerned which the plaintiff used in his book. It was legitimate action on the part of the defendant to refer to the plaintiff's book and use it as guide because the defendant went to the original authorities and complied from there without making any unfair use of the plaintiff's book. In Moffat v. Gill,[253] this had been summed up as rule 'you cannot where another man has compiled a directory, simply take his sheet of paper and reprint them in your name, you are entitled, taking the sheet with you, to go and see whether the existing facts concur with the description in the sheet and if you do that, you may publish the result as your own'.

In Edward Thompson Co. v. American Law Book Co[254] the question came up whether the above mentioned logic can be applied in case of quotation. Then it lead to that being directed by a reference to a particular quotation, to go and look to the author and see whether the quotation corresponds with the text and if so, text being common property, he was at liberty to annex the quotation. Using the same

[249] 281 F. 83.

[250] L.R. (1900) A.C. 539.

[251] Kelly v. Morris, L.R. 1 Eq. 696. In: Jeweler's Circular Publishing Co. v. Keystone Publishing Co, 281 F 83 (2nd Cir 1922).

[252] L.R. 5 Chap. 251.

[253] 86 Law Times 465.

[254] 122 Fed. 922.

argument in case of directories would lead to that if in the publication of directory, giving the name of all the inhabitants of a place, with the street numbers and another person simply took the sheet and verified for himself whether facts concurs with statement in the sheet, could publish without copying from the sheet. This would be doing something recognized by law and as of right to do without taking one word from information published previously without working independently to reach the same result from same common source of information.

In Edward Thompson Co. v. American Law Book Co[255] the question came up 'is a copyrighted law book infringed by a subsequent work on the same subject matter where the only accusation against the second author is that he collected all available citations including those found in the copyrighted book and after examining them in the text book and reports, used those which he considered applicable to support his own original text?'. The Court replied in negative and observed that writer of law text book might use a copyrighted digest of decisions and might copy the list of cases to assist him in running down the cases and such use is a fair one but pointed out that copying or paraphrasing of syllabi from copyrighted reports of law cases by subsequent publisher of a similar report or digest of cases constituted infringement.

In List Publishing Co. v. Keller[256] it was observed that the compiler of a general directory was not at liberty to copy any part of the previous directory, however small, to save himself the trouble of collecting the material form original sources, otherwise practically there would be no copyright in such book as the content of the rival publication of this kind be identical. 'When the selection is made, each compiler must of necessity reproduce the same name and addresses, so far as the selection coincide and must arrange them in alphabetical order. The law of Copyright only requires the subsequent compiler to do for himself that which the first compiler has done. The same source of original information is open to each. Either of the present parties could lawfully use the general city directory to obtain the correct addresses, of the selected persons, nor is it doubted that the defendant had right to use complainant's book for the purpose of verifying, the correctness of name and addresses of the persons selected. But if the defendant has used the list of the plaintiff to save himself the trouble of making an independent selection or classification of persons selected, though he may have done it to a very limited extent, he has infringed copyright'.[257]

In Jeweler's Circular Publishing Co. v. Keystone Publishing Co,[258] number of instances was recorded to illustrate the copying of trademarks—1. in large number of instances where defendant reproduced trade mark of manufacturers which appeared in plaintiff's book, no one representing defendant ever called manufacturer for trade mark information, 2. in number of instances where the address given

[255]122 Fed. 922.

[256]30 Fed. 772.

[257]30 Fed. 772.

[258]281 F 83 (2nd Cir 1922).

in plaintiff's book were wrong when defendant started its work but they had not been rectified, 3. in number of instances the sequences of plaintiff's arrangement had been followed by the defendant, 4. in number of instances where names of manufactures feature in plaintiff's book had been copied but they went out of business by the time defendant started its work, 5. in number of instances errors and misspellings of plaintiff had been continued with by the defendant. Presumption arising out of identity of inaccuracies had been given more importance as it was held that when a considerable number of passages were proved to have been copied by the copying of the blunders in them, other passages must be presumed prima facie to be similarly copied though no blunders occurred in them.[259]

Judge Hough in his dissenting judgment pointed out 'copyright protects only arrangement, selection of printed matters and infringement of such copyright consists only in copying material part of such selection'.[260] He objected in granting proprietary interest to an advertising list maker over whatever trade mark he decided to list. Consequently the trade mark owner if wished to copy his own trade mark from the advertising trade list would be infringing the interest of the list maker.

As Article 11 of the Database Directive provides that E.U will extend the right to other countries only on the basis of reciprocity, so if US wants to protect its database producers then US needs to adopt a domestic legislation comparable with the Directive. It has been argued that abandonment of 'sweat of the brow' would threaten the progress of information. The argument is that the collection of factual material is essential to the economy and databases provide a wealth of information to business people, professionals, scientists, consumers. The investment of time and money that is required to produce these compilations would not be forth coming.[261] It is possible that the risk of losing out information product led to the proposal of alternative legislations. 'In the United States of America, various bills have been put forward on the subject (legal protection of non-original database), although none has been approved by the national legislative authorities, largely due to opposition both from the scientific and academic communities—citing restrictions on the free circulation of data which characterizes research activity and from various companies in the telecommunications and IT sectors'.[262]

Before the Feist,[263] American court granted copyright protection for efforts involved in finding and assembling data on the basis of sweat of the brow doctrine or industrious collection doctrine whether or not materials collected were in public domain or whether or not there was originality or literary skill in thought or

[259]Mawman v. Tegg, 2 Russ 394. In: Jeweler's Circular Publishing Co. v. Keystone Publishing Co., 30 Fed. 772.

[260]Jeweler's Circular Publishing Co. v. Keystone Publishing Co., 30 Fed. 772.

[261]Boyarski J R (1999) The Highest of Feist: Protections for Collections of Information and the Possible Federalization of Hot News. Cardozo L Rev 21:871.

[262]Supra note 7, at 2.

[263]Feist Publications Inc. v. Rural Telephone Services Co. Inc., 499 US 340 (1991).

language. In those cases defendant had to go to the original sources for collection of raw materials in order to avoid infringement suit. Copyright protection was dependent on quantity and not on quality. The Feist[264] explicitly rejected the sweat of the brow doctrine and held that copyright protection would depend on quality and originality and not on quantity.

In International News Services v. Associated Press[265] held that factual items that comprise news are not literary work eligible for copyright protection but can get support from common law of unfair competition which does not allow a competitor to reap where it has not sown. This claim on misappropriation needs some extra element than copyright like time sensitive value of facts, free riding by defendants, and threat to plaintiff's product. Apart from copyright, product of industrious collection can also be protected through contract where users have to enter into contract to get access, although it is sometime difficult to establish police and enforce contractual relations. In cases of contract through Internet, click on license can be adopted for download and access which will ensure some return of proprietor's effort but the material will go out of the control of proprietor after download. Contractual enforceability is an important question for high end limited access databases.

In ProCD Inc. v. Zeidenberg,[266] enforceability of shrink-wrap contract has been affirmed just like regular contract. But the advantage for copyright law is that copyright is a right against the world but contractual rights are only bound between parties to the contract. Facts are not protected under copyright and any attempt to protect fact through other mechanism would not be appreciated from legal perspective.

Compilation is defined as a work formed by the collection and assembling of pre existing materials or of data that are selected, coordinated or arranged in such a way that the resulting work as a whole constitutes an original work of authorship. The Fiest[267] is considered to be authority for originality and the standard for originality is 'original as the term is used in copyright means only that the work was created by the author and that it possesses some minimal degree of creativity. The requisite level of creativity is extremely low, even a slight amount will suffice'.[268]

A white page directory is expected to be the least creative compilation and thus every other compilation will involve stronger position than the Feist.[269] So in this regard the Feist[270] can be considered as weakest possible case for standard of originality and possibly every other compilation will have more creativity than the

[264] 499 US 340 (1991).
[265] 248 US 215 (1918).
[266] 86 F.3d. 1447 (7th Cir 1996).
[267] 499 US 340 (1991).
[268] 17 U.S.C. Section 101 (1994).
[269] 499 US 340 (1991).
[270] 499 US 340 (1991).

Feist,[271] although the Supreme Court did not give any guideline for the lower court regarding how much more creativity than white page is required to qualify for copyright.

In Key Publications Inc. v. Chinatown Today Publishing Enterprises Inc.[272] plaintiff Key Publication collected business cards from business and professional people and copied some restaurant listing from another directory and created yellow page. The US Court of Appeal held that impugned directory was eligible for copyright protection as it was sufficiently creative to satisfy the Feist test and rejected the claim of copyright infringement on the basis of substantial similarity. In Oasis Publishing Co. v. West Publishing Co.[273] Oasis planned to convert the decisions in West's Florida Cases to CD-ROM format without copying head notes and synopses. It also planned to display parallel first page citations to Florida Cases and also to star paginate its cases. West claimed that citations and page numbers were part of copyrighted case arrangements and using star pagination would infringe their copyright although using parallel first page citation would be fair use.

It is to be remembered that in West Publishing Co. v. Mead Data Central Inc.[274] West's internal pagination was considered as expression of copyrighted case arrangement and thus could not be copied by competitors. In Mead Data[275] the court observed that act of creativity involved in West's arranging of cases as West first divided cases by state and then by court level and arranged the decisions according to their nature such as memoranda, opinion and then organized it on the basis of date and alphabets. Oasis contended that if usage of citation of first page of a case could be considered as fair use, then use of subsequent page number could not command copyright protection but the court rejected the argument on the basis of Mead Data.[276]

In Mathew Bender & Co. Inc. v. West Publishing Co[277] US Court of Appeal for the Second Circuit denied copyright protection to many selection and arrangement of West‘s case reporter. Hyperlaw, a CD-ROM compilation of Federal judgments, copied text of the opinion and some enhancement features which West added like information about parties, court, counsel, date of decision, subsequent procedural development from West but did not copy West's syllabi, head notes, key numbers. West asserted that enhancement features were creative choices of West but the court held that they were factual in nature the compilation and arrangement did not reflect minimum creativity prescribed by Feist. West argued 'indirect infringement theory'—Bender's star pagination would infringe by allowing users to perceive West's arrangement of cases exactly as published by West. Court observed that Bender's

---

[271] 499 US 340 (1991).

[272] 945 F. 2d. 509 (2nd Cir 1991).

[273] 924 F.Supp 918 (D. Minn 1996).

[274] 799 F2d. 1219 (8th Cir 1986).

[275] 799 F2d. 1219 (8th Cir 1986).

[276] 799 F2d. 1219 (8th Cir 1986).

[277] 158 F.3d 674 (2nd Cir 1998).

work was not substantially similar to West's. Nor could Bender be charged with contributory infringement as West failed to identify any primary infringer.

In Warren Publishing Inc. v. Microdos Data Corporation[278] Warren owned a Television and Cable Factbook. Microdos copied elements from the Factbook. Court of Appeal found that Warren's Factbook would fail the originality test as Warren selected and included every cable system listed by FCC and thus there was no selection at all. In Kregos v. Associated Press[279] Kregos has a compilation of statistics about the starting pitches in upcoming baseball games. The District Court relied on blank form and held that Kregos' form was not copyrightable as it did not have sufficient originality. The Court of Appeal remanded for reconsideration and on remand District Court found sufficient originality butheld that there was not substantial similarity between Kregos' form and defendant's service. The Second Circuit reiterated that pitching form was sufficiently original to deserve copyright protection and held that the merger doctrine did not apply, as there were varieties of selections Kregos could have chosen from.

Feist has contributed by raising the level of originality. Although the standard is minimal but none the less there is a standard. Feist was dealing with conventional paper based compilation but there are so many electronic and Internet based databases for which Feist doctrine may not be as effective as in case of paper based databases. Moreover only very little thing is known to us so far as electronic databases are concerned. The more comprehensive the databases are, the less possibility of getting copyright in it. As Warren directory included all cable operators, so there was no selection and thus there was no copyright but the fact remains that the database by itself was a comprehensive one. The selection and arrangement of the compilation should be original to the database creator and should not be dictated by function, practice or market like alphabetical listing, pitching form, basic information etc. The search and organization tools for database get protection like any other program through copyright law and patent law.

[278]115 F.3d 1509 (11th Cir. 1997).

[279]3 F.3d. 656 (2nd Cir. 1993).

Chapter 4
Database Protection: European Experience

After discussing conventional method of protecting databases through copyright law or similar laws in the earlier chapter, current chapter will focus on new method of protecting databases through a relatively new type of legal regime in Europe.

The European Union has adopted a Directive known as Directive 96/9/EC on Legal Protection of Databases to protect non-original databases. The Directive is a secondary community law which harmonizes the law of the members of the EU but requires implementation through domestic law by each country. Database protection law as required by the Directive has been enacted by Austria, Belgium, Denmark, Finland, France, Germany, Great Britain, Spain, and Sweden. The original version of the Directive was based on Nordic Catalogue Rule, which offered short-term protection for compilation which was not eligible for copyright protection and prevented slavish reproduction of the compilation for 10 years.

4.1 Role of Database Directive in Protecting Database

The Directive has offered a high level of protection for databases. Similar initiative at the international level did not materialize.[1] To differentiate with copyright, the protection under the Directive is perpetual as it can renew term of protection if there is substantial change. The scope of protection offered by the Directive is also wider than that of copyright as the Directive confers exclusive right of extraction and reutilization. The fair uses allowed by the Directive are circumscribed than that

[1]In December 1996, representatives from over 180 countries met to recognize three new international copyright protection treaties that addressed advantages of technology. One of the proposals originally scheduled for negotiation was the Basic Proposal for the Substantive Provisions of the Treaty on Intellectual Property in Respect of Databases, WIPO CRNR/DC/6, August 30, 1996. Negotiations on this proposal were delayed until later in 1997. At its Governing Bodies meeting in March 20 and 21 1997, WIPO convened a Committee of Experts which met September 10–12, 1997 to consider a draft of a 'Treaty on Intellectual Property in Respect of Databases'.

A. Mazumder, *Database Law*, DOI 10.1007/978-981-10-2200-5_4

offered by copyright law as the exceptions under the Directive should not be used in such a way as to prejudice the legitimate interest of the maker of database.

The Directive attempts to protect skill, labour and financial resources invested in the database. The Directive was developed based on the following principles—1. Databases were not sufficiently protected by existing legislation, 2. Difference in legal protection of databases offered by different legislation might negatively affect functioning of databases, 3. Copyright protection over database might have different forms, 4. Emphasis on prevention of unauthorized extraction or reutilization of the content of database, 5. Making of database involves investment of considerable human, technical and financial resources, 6. Unauthorized extraction or reutilization of contents of database might have serious economic and technical consequences, 7. Databases being vital tool for information market, 8. Worldwide exponential growth in the amount of information generated and processed annually in all sectors of commerce and industry requires investment, 9. Investment in modern information storage and processing system would not take place unless a stable and uniform legal protection regime is in place, 10. Protection requires for compilation of works stored, accessed by electronic, electromagnetic or electro-optical process, 11. Protection should also cover non-electronic databases, 12. Author's intellectual creation would be the eligibility criterion for copyright protection in databases, 13. Database should include literary, artistic, musical works and material can be text, sound, image and facts, 14. Database should not include compilation of musical performances on a CD, 15. Copyright of works which constitute database would not be affected, 16. There would not be any moral right for the database, 16. Exceptions to the restricted use should be listed, 17. Maker of a database should be a person who takes initiative and risk of investing for generating database, 18. Right to prevent unauthorized extraction or reutilization should not extend to copyright protection to mere facts or data, 19. Extraction of database should be allowed for the purpose of teaching and scientific research, substantial new investment leading to substantial modification should be basis for new term of protection, 20. There should be appropriate remedies for unauthorized extraction or reutilization.

The Database Directive influences harmonization of member state's copyright laws.[2] From the adoption of the Directive, European Commission promoted database right as model for database protection outside the European Union by making it part of trade agreement.[3]

---

[2]In Netherland, comprehensive and non-selective compilation is protected for limited term as non-original writing. Article 10(1)(I) Dutch Author's Right Law 1912. Jehoram C. (1999) International Copyright Law. In: Suthersanen, supra note 336. Scandinavian countries provided limited term of protection to producers of non original compilations under catalogue rule. Garrigues C (1997) Database: A Subject matter for Copyright or for a Neighbouring Right Regime. EIPR3.

[3]At present over 50 states have adopted or are soon to adopt database right legislation, including most states of Eastern Europe, the former Soviet Union and even Mexico. Hugenholtz, supra note 114.

4.1.1 *Definition of Database*

The Directive defines database as a collection of independent works,[4] data or other materials arranged in a systematic or methodical way and individually accessible by electronic or other means.[5] Let us take Recital 6[6] and Recital 40[7] of the Directive and read them together. This will raise the issue whether unfair competition remedy is a better option for databases? Cornish is of the view that the *sui generis* right has its place in the Database Directive because there is no harmonized law of unfair competition between EC States by which undue misappropriation of information could be addressed.[8] A joint reading of Recital 45[9] and 46[10] of the Directive indicates that the purpose of the Directive is not to create any new right in the underlying data and to preserve the traditional copyright balance between protection and access. The Directive protects not only electronic databases but also databases in paper form, such as telephone directories. Databases which by reason of the selection or arrangement of their contents, constitute author's intellectual creation, shall be protected by copyright.[11] As per Recital 12, a collection of unorganized data fixed on a hard disk would qualify as database if combined with database management software, enabling retrieval of data but the software would not be protected in this case. A database is more than a mere collection of simple data. A collection of works of authorship such as anthology, encyclopaedia, or multimedia, non-original photograph shall qualify as database as 'information' should be interpreted in widest sense of the term. But a collection of moving images together constituting a film does not become a database and in the same way a music file consisting of collection of digital data does not become eligible to get protection as database. Database protection can be given to telephonic directories,

[4]The question comes whether collection of items, for example a museum can fall within the definition of database? Supra note 7, at 5.

[5]Article 1.

[6]Whereas, nevertheless, in the absence of a harmonized system of unfair competition legislation or of case-law, other measures are required in addition to prevent the unauthorized extraction and/or reutilization of the contents of a database.

[7]Whereas the object of this *sui generis* right is to ensure protection of any investment in obtaining, verifying, or presenting, the contents of a database of the limited duration of the right; whereas such investment may consist in the deployment of financial resources and/or expending of time, effort and energy.

[8]Cornish, Llewelyn, supra note 40, at 786.

[9]Whereas the right to prevent unauthorized extraction and/or re-utilization does not in any way constitute an extension of copyright protection to mere facts or data.

[10]Whereas the existence of a right to prevent the unauthorized extraction and/or re-utilization of the whole or a substantial part of works, data or materials from a database should not give rise to the creation of a new right in the works, data or materials themselves.

[11]Article 3.

collection of legal materials, radio or television guides, real estate information websites, bibliographies, encyclopaedia, address lists, company registries, catalogues, collection of hyperlinks etc.

4.1.2 Substantial Investment

The maker of database has been given a *sui generis* right to prevent extraction or reutilization of whole or substantial part of the content of database, evaluated qualitatively or quantitatively if there has been substantial investment, evaluated quantitatively or qualitatively, in obtaining, verification and presentation of the contents.[12] Qualitative investment means employing expertise of a professional, for example, lexicographer selecting keywords for a dictionary. Quantitative investment means deployment of financial resources, time, labour etc.

As the word 'substantial' has not been defined, so in case of a small database even one data can constitute substantial part and thereby facts would get de facto intellectual property right protection. 'Obtaining' refers to collection of data, works or other materials comprising the database. 'Verification' means checking, correcting and updating data already existing in the database. 'Presentation' refers to retrieval and communication of compiled data. It must be understood that expression 'investment in obtaining, verification or presentation' means investment in the creation of the database as such as the purpose of the protection is to promote the establishment of storage and processing systems for existing information and not the creation of materials capable of being used subsequently in a database. This substantial investment test is important as it prevents database right being abused to create a legal monopoly in derivative information market.[13]

Obtaining content of fixtures, monitoring its accuracy and presenting it, do not require any particular effort from the maker of the database. Thus investment refers to the resources used to seek out existing independent materials and collect them into databases and not the resource used for creation of independent materials as such. In the context of drawing up a fixture list for the purpose of organizing football league fixture does not cover resources used to establish date, time and team pairing of various matches in the league.

It was observed that the expression 'investment in obtaining, verification and presentation of the contents' generally refers to the investment in creation of that database as such. The purpose of the *sui generis* protection is to promote establishment of storage and processing systems for existing information and not creation of materials capable of being collected subsequently in a database. The objective of the Directive as reflected in 39th Recital excludes creation of material contained in a database from the definition of 'obtaining'. Investment in creation of

[12]Article 7.

[13]Hugenholtz, supra note 114.

database may consist in deployment of human, financial or technical resources but it must be substantial in qualitative or quantitative terms. The qualitative assessment refers to efforts which cannot be quantified like intellectual effort or energy and quantitative assessment refers to quantifiable resources.

Presentation of football fixture is also closely linked to creation of data. So there is no substantial investment in obtaining, verification and presentation of content to justify *sui generis* protection. Thus investment refers to the resources used to seek out existing independent materials and collect them into databases and not the resource used for creation of independent materials as such. In the context of drawing up a fixture list for the purpose of organizing football league fixture does not cover resources used to establish date, time and team pairing of various matches in the league.

Creation of database may be sometime linked to the creation of materials used in creating database, thus what is to be proved is that obtaining, verification and presentation of materials required investment which is independent of resources required in creating those materials. The search for data or verification of data do not require special resources as either the database maker has created those data or they are available to him but their collection, systematic arrangement and verification of their accuracy during their operation requires substantial investment which require protection. Thus for organizing horserace, some amount of data is created relating to horses who join in the race and which are predominantly the contents of the database of BHB. So the investment for creating this database cannot be termed as investment for obtaining the content of the database, rather it is for creation of materials which constitute contents of the database.

At the time of making an entry of a horse into a horse-racing list, certain things are to be checked, like characteristics of the horse, classification of the horse, its owner, its jockey. The investment required for checking these are investment for creating the list and thus for creating the data and not for obtaining or verification of the contents of the database. The investment in obtaining the content of the database refers to resources used to identify existing independent materials and collect them in a database and it does not cover resources used for the creation of material which make up the contents of database.

The investment for verification of the contents of the database refers to the resources used with a view to ensure the reliability of the information contained in the database and to monitor the accuracy of the materials contained in the database. The resources used to verify the content during the stage of creation of material does not come within the ambit of the protection. The resources used to draw up a list of horses in a race and to carry out checks in that regards do not constitute investment in obtaining and verification of the contents of the database. It is not very clear whether *sui generis* right covers use of data which although derived originally from protected database but user obtained form a source other than the database.

4.1.3 Creation, Extraction and Reutilization

This bring the debate on the meaning of 'creation'—whether it means generation or gathering. This interpretation will play vital role in case of de facto monopolization. Creation and use of databases are considered as life blood of research activity and if the Directive contemplates that the researcher will take prior permission that would definitely block research activities. When more people are involved in making of a database and trying to assert right over the database, considering it to be their intellectual property, the database may start disappearing from public domain. Human genome research is an example of such situation. The non-availability of human genome sequences as public scientific resources will have a serious blow to the scientific activities.[14] If creation of database is linked to the exercise of a principal activity in which the person creating database is also the creator of the materials contained in the database, although search for data and verification of their accuracy do not require the maker of the database to use particular resource because data are those he created and are available with him but their collection, arrangement and verification will require substantial investment to get protection. In the present case, resource deployed for the purpose of making the football fixtures, considering date, time, venue of every match, home and away match etc. are essentially investment in the creation of fixture list and such investment relates to organization like football league to create data and thus it cannot get protection under the Directive.

Extraction means transfer of the content of database to another medium and reutilization means making available to public by distribution of copies, renting, and online transfer. This right includes downloading, copying, printing or other reproduction in whatever form. Public lending is not considered as extraction. Article 7(2) of the Directive provides that *sui generis* right covers act of extraction and reutilization of data and it does not cover act of consultation and thus act of consultation of database is not covered by database maker's exclusive right.[15] The *sui generis* right created by the Directive is not very clear in its scope as the terms used by the Directive are not defined and do not have an established interpretation in the copyright law.

First sale of a copy of database will exhaust the right to control resale of that copy. 'Reutilization' means making available the content of database by distribution, transmission, renting etc.

---

[14] European Bureau of Library, Information and Document Association (2006) Response to the European Commission on the Evaluation of EU Rules on Database. www.eblida.org/position/Database_Response_March06.htm. Accessed 15 March 2006.

[15] ECJ case, C-203/02. First Evaluation of Directive 96/9/EC on Legal Protection of Databases, Commission of The European Communities, Brussels, 12 Dec 2005, p 22.

In Fixtures Marketing Ltd. v. Svenska Spel AB[16] the issue was concerning interpretation of the provisions of the Directive 96/9/EC. The litigation came up as Fixtures Marketing Ltd. filed case against Svenska Spel AB for using information taken from fixtures list for English and Scottish football league for the purpose of organizing betting games. In England professional football is organized by the Football Association Premier League Ltd. and the Football League Ltd. and in Scotland by the Scottish Football League. Fixture lists are drawn up for the matches to be played during the session. The data are stored electronically and published in printed booklets. The organizer retained Football Fixtures Ltd. to handle exploitation of the fixture list through licensing. Sevenska Spel operates pool games in which bets can be placed on the result of football matches and for the purpose of those games it reproduces data concerning those matches. Fixtures filed a case against Sevenska claiming compensation for using the data as the use of data by Sevenska constituted breach of intellectual property rights. It was decided that the fixtures list were covered by catalogue protection as it involved substantial investment but Sevenska's use of data did not make any infringement. On appeal the judgment of first instance was upheld. Fixtures appealed further but the Court raised doubt whether purpose of the database should be given importance in deciding the ambit of *sui generis* protection, what sort of human or financial investment required for making an investment substantial and also what interpretation should be given for 'extraction', 're-utilization' and 'normal exploitation'. The issues which were referred to ECJ were—1. Whether investment for a product independent of database should be considered for assessing substantial investment, 2. Whether database enjoys protection in respect of activities covered by the objectives of the database, 3. What should be proper interpretation of terms like 'substantial investment evaluated qualitatively or quantitatively', 'extraction', 're-utilization' and 'normal exploitation'.

The Directive offers the power to the maker of database that he can prevent extraction and reutilization of full or substantial part of the database and in some cases even insubstantial part of the database so long it is going to prejudice the interest of the maker of the database.[17] 'Extraction' is defined as permanent or temporary transfer of all or substantial part of the content of a database to another medium by any means and in any form.[18] The expression 'by any means and in any form' suggests that the clause requires wide interpretation. Any act of appropriating and making available to public without consent of the maker of the database which affect the investment and deprive the maker from revenue can be sufficient ground to invoke the *sui generis* right.

[16]C-338/02.

[17]Article 7.

[18]Article 7(2)(a).

'Reutilization' is defined as any form of making available to the public all or substantial part of the contents of a database by distribution of copies, by renting, by online or other forms of transmission.[19] The term extraction and reutilization have been created to protect the maker of the database from acts of user which go beyond the legitimate right of the user and thereby harm the investment made by the maker of the database. The Directive, among its many objectives, has tried to guarantee the return of the investment made in creation and maintenance of the database. For the purpose of assessing the scope of the *sui generis* right, it is not relevant to find out whether the extraction and reutilization is for creating another database or for other use as the Directive suggests that the *sui generis* right is not only to prevent manufacturing a parasitical competing product but also to prevent act which causes detriment to the investment.[20]

The first sale of a copy of the database within the community by the maker or with his consent shall exhaust the right to control resale of that copy within the community.[21] This exhaustion principle does not cover the right to control extraction and reutilization of the content from that copy of the database. Since act of unauthorized extraction and reutilization by user from a source other than the database would affect the maker so far as the investment is concerned, in the same way as the unauthorized extraction and reutilization from the database, so extraction and reutilization include both direct and indirect access to the database.

It has to be remembered also that *sui generis* right is applicable only for extraction and reutilization and it does not apply in case of consulting the database. The maker of a database can always limit the accessibility to few limited people but if the database is made available to public, then he cannot prevent consulting the database. If maker of a database authorizes its reutilization, it makes an alternative way to gain access to the contents of the database. Any authorization to reutilize by the maker of the database does not prevent the maker to recover the cost of investment and thus he can always collect fee for reutilization or subsequent consultation of the database.

If the maker of the database has given authorization to a user to consult the database, the maker can always prevent that user from extraction and reutilization of the database. So the authorization for consultation of database does not exhaust the *sui generis* right. In case of online transmission, right to prohibit reutilization is not exhausted as regards the database or copy of the database made by the addressee with the consent of the right-holder.[22] The act of extraction—transferring the content of the database to another medium and act of reutilization—making it available to public, require the authorization of the maker even if the database is made accessible to public.

---

[19]Article 7(2)(b).

[20]Recital 42.

[21]Article 7(2)(b).

[22]Recital 43.

Extraction and reutilization refers to any act of appropriation and distribution to public, either whole or part of the database and it is not limited to only direct access to database. The fact that the database has been made accessible to the public, does not mean the right to prevent extraction and reutilization have been relinquished. It will not be out of place to mention that the maker of the database is the person who takes initiative in obtaining, verifying and presenting contents of database and takes the risk of investing for the same and the maker of the database is regarded as first owner of the database.[23]

4.1.4 Exceptions

Exception can be made for extraction and reutilization for private purpose in case of non-electronic database, in case of teaching and scientific research so long as source is indicated and used for non commercial purpose and in case of public security, administrative and judicial procedure.[24] Although Recital 50[25] does not differentiate between electronic and non-electronic database so far as its objective is concerned, but no general right to private use is given for electronic databases in Article 9. According to Chalton and Rees, a careful drafting of license may restrict the user to limited parts of database and for limited uses.[26]

4.1.5 Term of Protection

The term of protection for databases is 15 years from the date of completion of database. Any substantial change, evaluated qualitatively or quantitatively, to the contents of database so as to consider that there is substantial new investment, will offer database a fresh term of protection.[27] A regularly updated database can get perpetual protection.[28] The Directive requires a report to be submitted periodically to examine the application of the *sui generis* right and to verify whether it has lead

[23]Reg. 14(1), Copyright and Rights in Databases Regulation 1997.

[24]Article 9.

[25]Whereas the Member States should be given the option of providing for exceptions to the right to prevent the unauthorized extraction and/or reutilization of a substantial part of the contents of the database in case of extraction for private purposes....

[26]*See* Rees, Chalton, supra note 1. In: Colston, supra note 72.

[27]Article 10.

[28]Article 3—Any substantial change evaluated qualitatively or quantitatively, to the contents of the database, including any substantial change resulting from the accumulation of successive additions, deletions, alteration which would result in the database being considered to be a substantial new investment, evaluated quantitatively or qualitatively, shall qualify the database resulting from that investment for its own term of protection.

to abuse of dominant position or interference with free competition.[29] The Directive is capable of offering an exclusive right of everlasting duration with limited exception.

The ownership of a database made by an employee in the course of employment will be with the employer. However it is dependent on the employment contract. The database right exists for 15 years from the end of the completion of the calendar year in which database was completed. A substantial change to the database due to substantial investment will give a fresh term of 15 years of protection. To get a renewed term the database must be considered as new and separate database.[30]

4.2 Role of Database Directive in Limiting Monopoly

In *Magill,*[31] European Commission observed that three public television broadcasters had abused their dominant position in market by refusing to license Magill to publish in its magazine, a comprehensive television guide including television program timetable as without television program timetable, a television magazine could not compete in the market. The European Court of Justice agreed that unjustified refusal to license information which was indispensable for carrying on business and thus prevented the introduction into the market of a new product for which a potential consumer demand existed and this amounted to abuse of dominant position. This Magill doctrine has later on been used in IMS litigation[32] and has become a useful instrument to counter balance the monopoly power of the Directive.

Prof. Hugenholtz observed that it was unfortunate that the Directive did not incorporate the rule of Magill[33] although it came after 1 year of Magill[34] and thus today one needs to depend on court or competition authority instead of statutory rule. The District Court of The Hague observed that collecting and maintaining up to date information about several thousands of real estate properties amounted to substantial investment.[35] To the contrary newspaper headlines were regarded as

[29]Article 16.

[30]British Horseracing Board Ltd. and others v. William Hill Organization Ltd., C-203/02.

[31]Radio Telefis Eireann (RTE) and Independent Television Publication (ITP) Ltd. v. Commission of Europe Communities, C-214/91 P, April 6, 1995. First Evaluation of Directive 96/9/EC on Legal Protection of Databases, Commission of The European Communities, Brussels, 12 Dec 2005, p 8.

[32]Health GmbH & Co. v. NDC Health GmbH & Co., (C-418/01).

[33]Radio Telefis Eireann (RTE) and Independent Television Publication (ITP) Ltd. v. Commission of Europe Communities, C-214/91 P.

[34]Hugenholtz, supra note 114.

[35]NVM v. De Telegraaf, 12th Sept. 2000. First Evaluation of Directive 96/9/EC on Legal Protection of Databases, Commission of The European Communities, Brussels, 12 Dec 2005, p 11.

spin off of newspaper publication (spin off databases do not enjoy *sui generis* right protection) and thus did not constitute substantial investment as held by the District Court of Rotterdam.[36] Again collecting and verifying data for weekly top 10 hit musical titles were considered to constitute substantial investment.[37]

In Fixtures Marketing Ltd. v. Oy Veikkaus Ab,[38] the litigation arose from the use by Veikkaus for the purpose of organizing betting games, of information taken from fixture list for English football league. The litigation was concerning the interpretation of provisions of Directive 96/9/EC. In England professional football is organized by the Football Association Premier League Ltd. and the Football League Ltd. Fixture lists are drawn up for the matches to be played during the session. The preparation of fixture list requires number of factors to be taken into account such as need to ensure the alteration of home and away matches, several clubs from the same town are not playing at home on the same day, clashing with international fixtures, other public events, availability of police etc. Veikkaus has the exclusive right to organize gambling activities in Finland.

In that connection Veikkaus uses data concerning matches in English league football. In order to organize such betting, Veikkaus collects data regarding 400 matches per week from the Internet, newspaper, directly from the football clubs. In 1996, it was held that fixture list was a list which contained large quantity of data and under Article 49 of Copyright law it enjoyed copyright in it and thus Veikkaus infringed the copyright. On appeal this judgment was set aside and the Supreme Court refused leave to appeal. After the Directive came into force, Fixtures brought an action against Veikkaus for unlawfully using its database. The Court accepted the argument that it was a database but held that Veikkaus did not infringe the right. The questions which were referred to the ECJ were 1. Does 'obtaining' referred in the Directive connected to the investment and making of databases, considering that in the present case, investment is directed to determining the dates of matches and pairing the teams, 2. Whether protection should be given in such a way that person other than author of fixtures may not without authorization use the data for commercial purposes, 3. Whether using one week's data by Veikkaus in one week constitutes substantial use, evaluated qualitatively and/or quantitatively.

It had been observed that the relation between Fixtures and English Foot ball League was not expressed in clear terms. Considering the objectives specified in the Recital, meaning of the expression investment in obtaining… means resources used to seek out existing independent materials and collect them into databases and not the resource used for creation as such of independent materials as the purpose of the *sui generis* is to promote establishment of storage and processing systems for existing information and not creation of materials capable of being collected

[36]Algemeen Dagblad v. Eureka, 22nd August 2000. First Evaluation of Directive 96/9/EC on Legal Protection of Databases, Commission of The European Communities, Brussels, 12 Dec 2005, p 11.

[37]Hit Bilanz, 21 July 2005. First Evaluation of Directive 96/9/EC on Legal Protection of Databases, Commission of The European Communities, Brussels, 12 Dec 2005, p 12.

[38]C-46/02.

subsequently in a database. Finding and collecting data which make up a football fixture do not require any particular effort from the Professional League as those activities are indivisibly linked to creation of those data. Professional League does not need to put particular effort in monitoring accuracy of data as the League is directly involved in creating those data.

Similarly headings, URL, summary of press articles and hyper linking of headings were considered not to constitute substantial investment and thereby not infringing *sui generis* right.[39] In British Horseracing Board[40] ECJ emphasized that the resources used to draw up a list of horses in a race did not constitute investment in obtaining and verification of contents of database. According to the Court there is a difference between using resources to create material which form the content of database and obtaining the data to assemble the content of database. The former one is not protected under *sui generis* right but the later one is protected. Thus the bodies that create data will not get protection under *sui generis* right but bodies who do not create data, rather obtain data from others, will be protected under *sui generis* right.

European Court held that on-line betting on football matches or horse races by betting companies did not infringe the database right of the producer of the database as they did not prejudice the substantial investment in creation of these database.[41] This position leads to protect publishers of directories, maps, and listings, so long they do not create their own data but obtains these data from others. It is possible that following the judgment of ECJ, only fewer databases will be protected under *sui generis* right.

The judgment of ECJ[42] has narrowed down the scope of the Directive by interpreting the difference between creating and obtaining data. The ambiguity is still not clear whether *sui generis* right comes very close to the protecting of raw data itself which is definitely not the object of copyright law and which have been upheld in the *Feist*[43] case as well. Database is blessed with the strongest intellectual property protection after patents, though there has been no novelty type requirement for it except the fact that collation of information requires investment. Recreating database after collecting information from the available source will be economically ineffective and due to the monopolistic structure in the market, creating secondary product from database may lead to abuse of market power.

[39]First Evaluation of Directive 96/9/EC on Legal Protection of Databases, Commission of The European Communities, Brussels, 12 Dec 2005, p 12.

[40]British Horseracing Board Ltd. and others v. William Hill Organization Ltd., C-203/02.

[41]Organizers of Football matches or horse races, make the calendar by pairing the team, setting up home and away matches, which are part of basic activity of organizing such events and this setting up of the fixtures are by product of the basic activity and does not require substantial investment to seek protection. British Horseracing Board Ltd. and others v. William Hill Organization Ltd., C-203/02, Fixtures Marketing Ltd. v. Svenska Spel, AB C-338/02.

[42]British Horseracing Board Ltd. and others v. William Hill Organization Ltd., C-203/02.

[43]Feist Publications v. Rural Telephone Service Company, 499 US 340 (1991).

The Sui *generis* right has the potential to make use of information through pay per view model and can monopolize the information in sole source databank. Explanatory Memorandum indicated that compulsory licensing provision can be invoked against Stock Exchange with respect to stock market data but not against operator of earth observation satellite as collection of remote sensing data cannot be considered as sole source data producer. The provision relating to competition between rival database manufacturers will play important role in this regard.[44]

In *RTE* and *ITP v. EC,*[45] court held that refusal to license the information to third party constituted abuse of dominant position. The Netherlands Competition Authority regarded broadcaster's refusal to license radio and television program listing was an abuse of dominant position.[46] This interpretation is in line with the first proposal of the Directive. According to this provision had one provision—if the works or materials contained in a database which is made publicly available could not be independently created, collected or obtained from any other source, the right to extract and re-utilize, in whole or substantial part, works or materials from database for commercial purposes shall be licensed on fair and non-discriminatory terms.[47] This provision was removed after the close door meeting of the Council of Ministers in 1995.[48]

In most cases where information is available with one person, information will be considered as confidential and will not be available in public. In these cases, licensing clause would be very effective. Cases where production of competing database is uneconomic, access to information will be hindered in absence of an effective licensing clause.[49] In spite of existence of both legislation and technical means to protect investment in creation and maintenance of databases, problem related to enforcement and circumvention measure of technical protection can lead to losses to database owners. Through the Directive, it is possible to protect any type of compilation, as the criteria of substantiality do not work well in practice for, e.g., if someone extracts insubstantial data but of a high value to the person extracting it, then it can become a legally questionable act.[50]

---

[44]Recital 47, The Database Directive. The protection given by the sui generis right must not be afforded in such a way as to facilitate abuse of dominant position, in particular, as regards the creation and distribution of new products and services which have an intellectual, documentary, technical, economic or commercial added value.

[45]1995 FSR 530.

[46]De Telegraaf v. NOS and HMG, Netherlands Competition Authority, 10 September 1998. In: Hugenholtz, supra note 114. The Dutch Competition Authority raised doubt whether investments were substantial as program listing were spin off of the broadcaster's main activity. http://www.ivir.nl/publications/hugenholtz/fordham2001.html.

[47]Article 8(1), First Proposal Draft of Directive.

[48]Council Common Position No. 95/20, Statement of Council's Reasons, OJC 288/02.

[49]See generally, Lloyd I (2000) Information Technology Law. Butterworths, London.

[50]Hugenholtz (2001) The New Database Right: Early Case Law from Europe, Ninth Annual Conference on International IP Law & Policy, Fordham University, School of Law, 2001.

Most of the cases involve companies that create synthetic data like telephone numbers, TV listing, date of sport event which cannot be protected through the Directive.[51] The critique of the Directive is mainly on issues like possibility of granting protection in perpetuity, restricted fair use exceptions, not having adequate safeguard for ensuring access to information for research and educational communities (exception to be used in a manner which does not unreasonably prejudices the right holder's legitimate interest for exploitation of database and databases can be extracted for scientific purposes but can not be reused[52]), absence of compulsory licensing procedure, ban on making copies even for backup copies.[53]

It was observed that the Directive did not envisage the need to protect free access to information either for competitors who did not have access to protected databases or for third parties wishing to use the same information for a purpose other than creating a new database.[54] The regime contributed by the Directive would create a de facto monopoly on factual content of protected databases with consequent risk to the generation of knowledge and a threat to the conventional difference between protection of expression and protection of ideas.

Online databases upgrade so frequently that copying it does not become cost effective and useful. More over manufactures make sure that information can be accessed one at a time. Producers of single source data like public telephone service operator, broadcasting companies, organizers of sporting events can use database right to monopolize downstream market in telephone subscriber data, television guide, off-track betting etc. This situation can be remedied through two possible ways that is by applying general anti-competition laws and by interpreting substantial investment test as it would be difficult to prove substantial investment criteria in case of spin off databases.

The Directive is not very clear as to how much 'blood, sweat and tear' the producer must shed to qualify for *sui generis* protection. Before *Fixtures Marketing*[55] litigation it was not clear whether investment in case where the database was by-product (spin off) of services offered to the public, would be considered to be substantial. In other words whether for measuring investment for producing databases involving radio, television program listing, railway and airlines schedule, telephone directory, stock exchange out puts, sporting event schedules, the investment for producing these synthetic data should be considered or not.

In Netherlands, questions were raised about the fate of database like list of restaurants, compilations of stars in galaxy, listing of radio programs and the Minister of Justice accepted that the investments were not directed towards creating databases and they were spin off of other activities.[56] Here it will be interesting to

---

[51]Maurer, Hugenholtz, Onsrud, supra note 349, at 789.

[52]Colston, supra note 72.

[53]Reichman, Samuelson, supra note 72. In: Colston, supra note 72.

[54]Supra note 7, at 21.

[55]Fixtures Marketing Ltd. v. Svenska Spel, AB C-338/02.

[56]Hugenholtz, supra note 114.

note the difference between copyright and database right. The idea—expression dichotomy in copyright law does not create downstream monopolization. Moreover it leaves enough material in the public domain so that competitors can freely extract materials from that without incurring liability.

Although the Directive makes it clear that *sui generis* right does not protect data contained in a database but there is no demarcation between data and database as it exists in idea and expression. Prof. Hugenholtz has also pointed out the differences between the First Proposal of the Database Directive and the Directive as the First proposal offered special rule of unfair competition instead of exclusive right. He also pointed out that *sui generis* right is an economic right which is different from unfair competition as it does not sanction behaviour a posteriori.[57] The provision on compulsory licensing which was present in the First Proposal but missing from the Directive is very useful provision against information monopolists. If the Directive is compared with the First Proposal, it can be found that an ex post remedy based on unfair competition has been transformed into a powerful intellectual property right offering ex ante right. The broad but vague protection offered by the Directive coupled with potential perpetual protection can drastically dilute the public domain.

It has been observed that existing form of *sui generis* protection is the most deviant example of *sui generis* protection demanded by the breakdown of traditional copyright/patent dichotomized model of intellectual property.[58]

The *sui generis* law is to induce other countries to offer greater protection to databases. The *sui generis* protection grants perpetual protection and restricts the use of researchers and potential users and it is difficult to defend it in terms of social benefit. The existing *sui generis* protection, being termed neither too strong nor too weak but just right has proved to be elusive. The copyright protection is too little and sweat of the brow is too much protection for database makers and protection through unfair competition has proved to be too uncertain.

4.3 Evaluation of Database Directive

The European Commission conducted an evaluation of the Directive 96/9/EC on legal protection of databases.[59] The purpose of the evaluation was to assess whether the policy behind the Directive had been achieved and to assess whether there was any adverse effect on competition. The evaluation[60] was to find out whether the rate of growth of European database industry increased after the introduction of the

[57]Hugenholtz, supra note 503.

[58]Reichman, Samuelson, supra note 291, at 51.

[59]First Evaluation of Directive 96/9/EC on Legal Protection of Databases, Commission of The European Communities, Brussels, 12 Dec 2005.

[60]The evaluation was conducted through restricted on line survey addressed to European database industry. 500 European companies including publishers, suppliers of data, database manufacturer, distributors were involved in the survey and 101 replied were received.

Directive that is to say whether the beneficiaries of the Directive produced more databases than they would have produced prior to the Directive.

The evaluation reflects that the European database industry would like to continue with the *sui generis* right along with copyright protection. The repealing of *sui generis* right might lead to introduction of the sweat of the brow doctrine and thereby reopening the controversy related to standard of originality. The evaluation concludes that as the ECJ judgments have reduced the scope of the protection and thereby limited the possibility of negatively affecting competition, so the Directive may be left unchanged for the time being.

The Commission observed that the database producers of countries which had clear protection for database were in a more advantageous position than database producer of countries having uncertain protection of databases. The Commission believed that the investment in creation of databases required to be protected against misappropriation of the fruit of financial and professional investment in obtaining and collection of data. The Commission argued that the investment in production of databases could not be encouraged unless the manufacturers of databases in EU[61] were awarded at par with other trading partners.

The Directive has more or less maintained the right balance between the interest of the right holders and users. Though publishers felt that the Directive offered incentive for further development of the market and thus it should not be changed; many users like libraries, academic institutions expressed concern for the over-broad protection offered by *sui generis* right.[62] From user's point of view, they would like to expand the scope of exception to the *sui generis* right by allowing private use in digital database, by introducing regular fair use principle like reporting of current events etc. in case of *sui generis* right and by creating new exception like concession for disabled persons.

In comparison with United States, the on line survey conducted by the European Commission indicated that the *sui generis* right had helped the European database industry to catch up with that of United States but the *sui generis* right did not improve the global competitiveness of the European database industry.

Many of the database producers felt that the *sui generis* right has offered legal certainty and created more business opportunities for databases. It is also suggested that the Directive may be repealed, as it did not offer encouraging growth in the database industry in Europe. But if the whole Directive is repealed, then there will be possibility of going back to sweat of the brow doctrine. Again withdrawal of *sui generis* right may encourage companies dealing with factual compilation to protect their works by contract or by technology. An amendment of the Directive has been

---

[61]The total turnover of the database and directory publishing industries in 2000 amounted to 8.2 billion euro and the software, database and print industry contributed to 1 % of EU GDP. EADP Annual Report. www.eadp.org. Accessed 21 April 2006. First Evaluation of Directive 96/9/EC on Legal Protection of Databases, Commission of The European Communities, Brussels, 12 Dec 2005, p 16.

[62]First Evaluation of Directive 96/9/EC on Legal Protection of Databases, Commission of The European Communities, Brussels, 12 Dec 2005, p 21.

suggested as one of the options by the Commission.[63] The amendment may throw light on the issue of protection in case where creation of data takes place concurrently with collection. The amendment may also indicate the position of single source database for the purpose of protection and cases where producing database is a secondary activity. The amendment may also be helpful for clarifying what constitutes substantial investment. Alternatively the status quo may be maintained so far as the Directive is concerned till more feedback is received regarding the options suggested by the Commission.[64]

The continuing success of US publishing and database production without any *sui generis* protection is a troubling factor for continuance of database right in EU. Before introduction of *sui generis* right for non-original databases legal and factual analysis should have been more carefully done and the need for such measure should have been more carefully evaluated. According to a Max Planck Institute study, database right should have been introduced only after ex-ante consideration and balancing of possible benefits and drawbacks. Once legislation is enacted, discarding it can be done only in exceptional cases and thus subsequent evaluation cannot be an effective idea but rather a thorough homework beforehand is desirable.[65] The general notion about database right is that it has offered extra protection and it will have some impact on competition and freedom of information but as because there is no clear proof of the negative effect of database right, repealing it altogether is not a feasible idea.

It is true that after ECJ's decision,[66] possible negative impact of database right has been substantially reduced. Still there is inhibition about the fact that if the market is blocked by the copyright protection of databases, remedy can be secured under competition law.[67] Amendment of the Directive must address the issue of substantial investment, issue of creation of data currently with collection of it, issue of scope of the Directive—whether to include only the primary producer of databases or also the databases which are spin off of main activity and the issue of single source databases. The amendment should not counteract the judgment of ECJ.[68]

To deal with single source databases, competition rules must be interpreted strictly. But relying on external solutions like competition rules may not be a desirable situation as it is dependent on the interpretation of courts and other bodies, rather there should be provision for non-voluntary licenses within database law. Database protection should not be available when the creator of database is not a private commercial actor but rather a public authority that collects information as a

---

[63]First Evaluation of Directive 96/9/EC on Legal Protection of Databases, Commission of The European Communities, Brussels, 12 Dec 2005, p 26.

[64]Id., p 27.

[65]Position paper by the Max Planck Institute for Intellectual Property, Competition and Tax Law on First Evaluation of Directive 96/9/EC on the Legal Protection of Databases, p 1.

[66]British Horseracing Board v. William Hill, C-203/02.

[67]IMS Health GmbH & Co. OHG v. NDC Health GmbH & Co. KG, ECJ C-418/01.

[68]Supra note 520, at 5.

part of official assignment.[69] Any amendment of the Directive must categorically contain the difference between primary database and database which is a spinoff of main activity as suggested in the judgment of ECJ.[70] This judgment may not be helpful in cases where investment in data creation and investment in data collection cannot be distinguished.[71] A distinction may be made between inventing data and measuring pre existing data and it may be helpful in identifying cases worth protecting as the former will not get protection but the later one will get protection and it will not affect the competitors.[72]

Competition law can apply in all cases whether or not it gets protection. The exemptions and limitations of *sui generis* right need to be properly drafted. The exemptions and limitations of copyright may also be applicable to database right. The amendment should address the relation between database right and unfair competition. Rules relating to unfair competition are not prejudiced by database protection. The Directive aims at offering minimum level of protection and keeping access of compilation of data free so long the requirement for protection has not been fulfilled.

The European Bureau of Library, Information and Document Association (EBLIDA) expressed the view that the Database Directive is a confusing law and complying with it will be difficult for ordinary persons though use of database is a regular activity.[73] According to it the Directive is ambiguous and not clear where copyright and *sui generis* right begins and ends. It has been observed that cases where databases resulting from original creation, copyright protection and *sui generis* right subsists concurrently.[74] It has been apprehended that complying with the Directive would be difficult because both copyright and *sui generis* right have different terms and different exceptions but qualitative investment giving way to *sui generis* right cannot be distinguished from intellectual creation, giving rise to copyright protection.

---

[69]Supra note 520, at 6.

[70]British Horseracing Board v. William Hill, C-203/02.

[71]Leistner, Comment to BHB v. Hill, 36 IIC 592 (2005), p 593.

[72]Proposed amendment to Article 7.1—Member States shall provide for a right for the maker of a database which shows that there has been qualitatively and/or quantitatively a substantial investment in either the obtaining, verification or presentation of the contents to prevent extraction and/or re-utilization of the whole or of a substantial part, evaluated qualitatively or quantitatively, of the content of that database. Where the substantial investment concerns the creation of data which forms the contents of the database, the right shall not be available in so far as the data have been made up or invented by the database maker, rather than resulting from the measurement and/or collection of pre-existing phenomena. 1a. Paragraph 1 1st sentence does not apply to databases created monitored by public authorities or entities in performance of their official functions and tasks. Supra note 520, at 8.

[73]Response to the European Commission on the Evaluation of EU Rules on Database, European Bureau of Library, Information and Document Association. www.eblida.org/position/Database_Response_March06.htm. Accessed 15 May 2006.

[74]Id.

Considering the fact that the Directive did not achieve the purpose—to offer European commercial database producers an edge over their competitors from other continent and acknowledging that creation and use of database are immensely beneficial for education and research, EBLIDA offered some suggestions,[75] so that the Directive does not create obstruction and creates workable intellectual property principle which can be respected—1. sui generis right should subsist only in electronic database, 2. sui generis right should arise only when a database is reutilized for commercial purpose so that maker of new database need to take prior permission from the maker of existing database before exploiting it commercially, 3. exceptions to sui generis right should be same as exception to copyright, 4. term of sui generis right should be limited to 15 years.

The Database Directive has been described as the most deviant examples of the trend toward *sui generis* protection for intellectual property falling between the cracks of mature paradigm of patent and copyright.[76] It has also been described as one of the least balanced and most potentially anti-competitive intellectual property regime ever created.[77] It has been apprehended that the Directive will stifle access to information, retard competition in database industry and impede basic scientific research.[78] The database industry has three different types of markets—1. 'one stop-shopping' market, a market which offers general information to a broad customer base, 2. 'Problem-focused' market, a market which offers specific information focused on particular problem, 3. 'Industry focused' market which offers specific information to specific industry or professionals like medical legal or news etc. This can be well understood if copy right protection is compared with Nordic Catalogue Rule which used to protect catalogue, tables and similar compilations in which a large number of particulars have been summarized including database for 10 years after first publication. The Directive concentrates on extraction and reutilization but does not refer about use and reuse. The Directive also refers about a positive act—transmission for the purpose of extraction. The liability of downstream innocent users who may unknowingly reuse database contents made available by an initial infringer is not clear.

The *sui generis* right is available without prejudice to other rights and obligations in the content of database and it exists independently from copyright protection to the contents of database. It requires users or potential competitors either to collect information independently or to pay the database maker for collected information.

The beneficiaries of the protection are an identified to be designated by a geographical location (like country, European Union, contracting parties) related through categories like national, habitual residence, registered office, place of

[75]Id.

[76]Reichman, supra note 338, at 475.

[77]Reichman, Samuelson, supra note 291, at 51.

[78]Simon CV (1995) Feist or Famine: American Database Copyright as an Economic Model for the European Union. Brook J Int'l L20:729.

operating business. To offer supplementary protection, importation, manufacture, distribution, of devices whose primary purpose is to defeat or circumvent self-protection measure taken by database maker to prevent unauthorized extraction should be prohibited. There exists protection for incorporating database management information in the database.[79]

The Database Directive tries to harmonize European copyright law and simultaneously creates a renewable but potentially perpetual 15 year toll fence which prohibits unauthorized extraction and reutilization of whole or substantial part of electronic or non electronic database. The toll fence tries to protect commercial interest and it can be extended by proving substantial investment in obtaining, verifying and presenting data. The Directive tries to protect public interest by allowing 1. Insubstantial extraction, 2. Member states to frame fair use exception, 3. Extinguishing database maker's right to control resale after first sale.

Moreover if information producers abuse their dominant position, competition law will come in force to safeguard public interest. The major concerns about the Directive are that it can negatively affect the free flow of information, it is anti competitive and it will retard the long-term growth of database industry. The Directive created a legal barrier to misappropriation of database maker's investment in data collection. No doubt the Directive creates two quasi property rights—right to prevent extraction of content of database and right to prevent reutilization of content of database but none extends copyright protection to underlying data or facts.

ProCD v. Zeidenberg[80] underscores the need for a *sui generis* regime to protect compilers from the mal-competitive behaviour of free riders or information Samaritans. Zeidenberg's investment in creating the database and justification to claim ownership over the content is beyond any doubt.[81] Now if free rider purchases the listing on compact disc for less than $200 and extracts, recompiles the listing and makes it available over Internet, it definitely commercially destroys Zeidenberg. In this litigation, the District Court accepted the argument that free rider's action was unfair but did not accept that it amounted to copyright infringement or breach of contract or unfair competition which indirectly allowed free rider and information Samaritans to extract information from database at a fraction of cost of the maker of database and then make it available for free.

To apply the Database Directive in similar situation, free rider's act of electronic extraction of 20 million telephone listing out of 90 million listing would amount to violation of *sui generis* right as it violates right to prevent extraction of the database maker. In the same way making these listing available in the Internet would amount to violation of *sui generis* right too as it violates the right to prevent reutilization of substantial part of database. Even the act of the free rider to extract listings from

[79]Section 11 HR 3531.

[80]908 F.Supp. 640 (7th Cir. 1996).

[81]Zeidenberg spent approximately $10 million in compiling more than 95 million residential and commercial listing from approximately 3000 telephone directories. 908 F.Supp. 640 (7th Cir. 1996).

compact disk and make it available in the Internet would not be protected by the exception clause, considering that the amount was not substantial enough to attract the *sui generis* right violation as it could be argued that the utilization amounted to repeated act of insubstantial utilization which could unreasonably prejudice the maker's right.[82]

As many users will like to get the advantage of the free access than to pay for the compact disk, making the content of database available in the Internet will unreasonably prejudice the database maker's right and the maker of database should ideally be compensated. The Directive can offer protection to the maker of database both from the competitors who want to gain a competitive advantage by free riding and also from information Samaritans. If the compiler's aim is to contribute in promotion of knowledge through investment in data collection rather than on selection and arrangement, court should focus on protecting commercial interest of the database maker from the parasitic competitors and misappropriations.

The Directive does not completely insulate the maker of database from all possible competition. It only prohibits extraction and utilization. It does not extend copyright protection to facts or data. It does not remove data or fact from public domain. In Copyright law, independent creation is a good defense and thus if the second work is similar to that of the first and if the second author had the access to the first work, to deny the claim of copying can be blocked by the defense of independent creation. In case of database of non-proprietary facts, cost of gathering public domain material can be used to make out a case for independent creation. So any one is free to create identical database so long it is not done by appropriating content of a protected database. Thus under the Directive, if someone collects the same data but independently, compiles and markets, nothing in *sui generis* right is infringed. The Directive not only offers sword to protect public interest but also shield to protect the interest of those who have invested to create databases.

The *sui generis* rights are limited by national or community rules and thus if there is anti-competitive behaviour of database maker, then complaint can be filed both before the European Commission and the national forum. Article 86 of EEC Treaty which prohibits abuse of dominant position within the common market or in a substantial part of the common market that affects trade between Member States can be used to gather compulsory license.

As in RTE v. Commission[83] (Magill), ECJ upheld compulsory licensing order forcing television broadcaster to supply their weekly program listing to someone who sought to produce a value added product, television guide which was not otherwise available in the market. If this was the approach of ECJ, then what would be its approach towards scientific and technical progress? As there is increasing willingness of European firms to abandon anticompetitive behaviour when challenged by the Commission it shows that it should be sufficient to protect interest by

---

[82]ProCD's website permitted extraction of 1000 listing per search and the website was accessed for 20,000 times per day approximately before the litigation. 908 F.Supp. 640 (7th Cir. 1996).

[83]241/91 and 242/91 (1995) E.C.R. 743, 837.

forcing to supply data on reasonable terms. Moreover the Directive calls for review of the *sui generis* right after every 3 year to assess the state of free competition and to protect public interest and even the need for incorporating compulsory licenses. The public lending of database should not be considered as act of extraction and reutilization but even this exception should work within the limits of the Directive or else competitors will circumvent protection offered by *sui generis* right by accessing databases from libraries.

The Directive has substantially reduced the scope of fair use clause by incorporating the requirement of not conflicting with normal exploitation of the database. Thus the interest of users has been covered under the commercial focus of the Directive to protect the interest of database makers and as such users will have to work carefully so that they do not prejudice the commercial interests. It will be interesting to find out whether a scientist recompiling insubstantial portions of old data for non-commercial purpose will be considered as prejudicing the commercial interest of database maker. If this database is famous because of timeliness of its data, than extracting old data may be considered as not prejudicing database maker's legitimate and commercial interest. So for determining the nature of extraction, one should examine the nature of commercial interest affected. Court, while deciding substantiality may look at the activity of users through a commercial lens. Extracting one week old data can be considered as less harmful than extracting data of current week.

Although the Directive allows Member States to adopt the fair use clause as optional requirement, the distinction between electronic and non-electronic database were illogical as high speed scanner and optical character recognition software can convert non electronic database into electronic database quite easily. The fair use clause on teaching or scientific research requires source to be indicated and use should be non-commercial. Along with this legitimate interest of the database maker it also limits the user's ability to use the content of the database. Here it has to be remembered that even an individual academician or scientific or technical institution can become database maker and in that case they can potentially become gatekeeper of scientific or technical data. In this respect the requirement of the Directive to review the impact of *sui generis* right on anti-competition behaviour and information flow in every 3 years is very much required.

In Europe, the Directive along with national or supra national competition law regime can offer ameliorative mechanism to offset downstream adjustment to compensate problem associated with a regime which allows de facto if not de jure ownership right in sole source data. In international level, *sui generis* will also look for support of similar mechanism to ensure value added information products are kept out of the market by someone who refuses to license sole source data. A mechanism which can support such situation is compulsory licensing system almost modelled on the similar line as it is done in copyright law. This will enhance competition in a commercialized information market.

A database is a complex work. A computer program may be used in developing a database but protection given to the computer program is different from the protection of the database, developed by that computer program. Unprotected works, data will not come under copyright even if they form part of a database. Copyright in a database is given to the selection and arrangement. Some sort of intellectual input of the author goes into the selection and the method of arrangement of database. This will have some impact on the protection of databases.

As per the practice in Germany, Belgium and Portugal, investment means resources used to identify existing independent materials and collect them in databases and not resources used for creation of such independent materials. The purpose of the Directive is also to promote the establishment of storage and processing systems for existing information and not the creation of materials capable of being collected subsequently in a database. Among these questions, reference was mainly to get interpretation of extraction, re-utilization, substantial, insubstantial part and substantial change. Substantial investment criterion is not satisfied by putting different things together. 'Obtaining' means identifying independent materials and collecting them in the database. Resources used for creation of materials which form content of database is not covered under 'obtaining'.

The fact that compilations of several recordings of musical performances on a CD does not qualify for substantial investment required for *sui generis* right, shows that resources used for creation of works included in database cannot be deemed to be equivalent to investment in obtaining the contents of database. The investment in verification of content means resources used with a view to ensure the reliability of the information contained in the database and to monitor accuracy of the materials collected when database was created. The resources used to verify materials during the stage of creation of data are considered resources used in creating database and thus cannot be considered for *sui generis* right.

The database right will be infringed if there is unauthorized extraction or reutilization of substantial part of the content of the database.[84] In qualitative terms whether the part is substantial is like the assessment in quantitative terms, referring to the investment in creation of the database, so that it is not detriment to the investment. The expression 'substantial part evaluated quantitatively' refers to volume of data extracted from the database and it must be assessed in comparison with the whole of the database. If the user extracts or reutilizes quantitatively significant part of the database whose creation required substantial resources, investment in extracted part is proportionately substantial. The expression 'substantial part evaluated qualitatively' refers to scale of investment in obtaining, verification and presentation of the content of the database, regardless of whether it represents a quantitatively substantial part of the general content of the protected database. A quantitatively negligible part of the content of a database may contain significant human, technical and financial investment in terms of obtaining, verification and presentation. The intrinsic value of the material affected by act of extraction does not make it substantial. Any part which does not fall within the definition of substantial part evaluated both quantitatively and qualitatively falls within the definition of insubstantial part.

---

[84]Reg. 16(1) Copyright and Rights in Databases Regulation 1997.

The database right is not infringed if the data is extracted by lawful user or extracted for the purpose of teaching and research after indicating the source.[85] It has to be remembered that the maker of a database cannot prevent user from extracting and reutilizing insubstantial part of database. This lack of protection for insubstantial part of database does not encourage it to be repeatedly and systematically extracted. This has been done because if insubstantial part of database is extracted repeatedly and systematically, it will prejudice the investment and it may lead to reconstitution of the whole database or substantial part of it without authorization of the maker of the database.

Incidentally in Germany it was held to be an infringement of database right to scan telephone directories by a competitor.[86] Using information in public domain has a potential risk of tracing it to be derived from protected databases. The Court of Appeal, Hague did not allow database right to broadcasting listing as there was no evidence of substantial investment in compiling the listing which might also be regarded as spin off from broadcasting activity.[87] It would be appropriate to offer a narrow protection to compilation, not extending to underlying information and covering only reprinting or copying the information in same or similar compilation.

> Probably the strongest argument against introducing a *sui generis* regime for non-original databases similar to that has been introduced in the EU in 1996 is that such a regime would be designed to protect not the databases themselves as new and/or creative products but rather the information embodied in them with the attendant risk of limits being set on the latter's circulation, including that of information that hitherto has remained in the public domain. In other words, the creation of new IPRs for databases could upset the balance between protection and dissemination, tipping it dangerously towards the former. The threats in the latter eventuality are to be seen not only in the highly-sensitive areas of science and education, but also in the commercial field itself against the background of the development of Internet, for instance.... This regime would not be directed towards generating new ideas or goods or even creative effort but rather basically towards investment in the collection and organization of information of various kinds. That in principle would run counter to both the tradition and objectives of copyright.[88]

Reichman and Samuelson[89] expressed their concern about the Directive in the following manner—1. The final version of the Directive moves away from notion of unfair or unauthorized uses of database contents, instead of favouring the exclusive right of database makers to prevent extraction and re-use of a substantial part of database's contents, 2. The Directive's 15 year term for property right in a database can be indefinitely extended, 3. The Directive does not require creativity

[85]Reg. 20, Copyright and Rights in Databases Regulation 1997.

[86]Tele-Info-CD, Federal Supreme Court, Germany, May 6, 1999, Case No. IZR 199/96, Telephone directories generally do not enjoy copyright protection pursuant to Copyright Act. A telephone directory is a database. The marketing of electronic telephone subscriber list on CD-ROM constitutes unfair misappropriation if data stored therein is taken directly from the official telephone directory.

[87]Colston, supra note 72.

[88]Supra note 7, at 2.

[89]Reichman, Samuelson, supra note 291, at 51.

or novel contribution to attract database protection but requires only substantial investment in obtaining, verifying or presenting database contents, 4. The Directive offers no guidelines to determine the level of investment required to justify the property right in the database or extend the duration of existing right, 5. The Directive's database right potentially erodes the idea—expression dichotomy from copyright law, 6. The Directive's potentially unlimited term of protection coupled with the strong proprietary nature of protection and the lack of significant fair use exception to the property right dramatically erodes the public domain and potentially converts information products into a commodity, 7. The Directive's deletion of compulsory licensing provision for sole source provider of information creates nearly insurmountable barrier to entry for potential second-comers into information market and secondary market.

In the United Kingdom the Copyright and Rights in Databases Regulations 1997 defines database to include both paper based and electronic databases. It confers database right if there has been substantial investment in obtaining, verifying or presenting the content of database[90] and thus it does not require any creativity or innovation. According to this regulation, infringement occurs if any one extracts or reutilizes all or substantial part of content of database without authorization.[91] Repeated and systematic extraction of insubstantial part of database also can lead to infringement. The term of protection is 15 years but extendable if there is substantial changes to the contents of database.[92]

The UK Regulation defines lawful user as a person who has the right to use the database under a license and allowed to do acts which are otherwise prohibited. A lawful user is allowed to extract or reutilize insubstantial part of database for any purpose and substantial part for teaching and research if there is no commercial purpose and if the source is indicated.[93] It may be difficult to interpret the commercial purpose as institutions can get involved in commercial activities so far as teaching material and research products are concerned in competition with other institutions. The database law of the United Kingdom has created broad database right with narrow and vague exceptions.[94]

[90]Rule 13(1).

[91]Rule 12(1).

[92]Rule 17(1).

[93]Rule 20(1).

[94]Lipton, supra note 346.

4.4 BHB Factor

In British Horseracing Board Ltd. and Others v. William Hill Organization Ltd.,[95] the litigation cropped up as William Hill Organization[96] used information from BHB database[97] for the purpose of organizing betting on horseracing. The first instance judgment of BHB litigation has contributed following views[98]—1. Protection lies for underlying information contained in a database, 2. Protection is potentially eternal where the database is dynamic, regularly updated and it renews protection to earlier versions, 3. Copyright principles are not to be applied to new right by analogy, 4. Use of information derived from a protected database amounts to extraction. The case was referred to European Court of Justice.[99]

---

[95]C-203/02.

[96]William Hill is a subscriber to both Declaration Feed (forwarded by Racing Pages Ltd.) and Raw Data Feed (supplied by Satellite Information Services Ltd.) and is one of the leading providers of off-course bookmaking services in the United Kingdom. William Hill launched on-line betting services on two Internet sites. Interested persons can use information offered by William Hill. Information offered by William Hill is obtained from newspapers and from Raw Data Feed. Information displayed in William Hill's website represents a very small portion of total amount of data of BHB database. The information of William Hill's site mainly contains name of horses, date and time of race, name of racecourse.

[97]The BHB and others managed the horse racing industry in the United Kingdom and in various capacities compile and maintain BHB database which contains a large amount of information supplied by the horse owners, trainers, horse race organizers and others involved in the racing industry. The database contains information on the pedigrees of some 1 million horses, pre race information on races to be held in the United Kingdom. This information includes the name, place, date of race, distance to be covered, criteria for eligibility to enter in the race, the date by which entries to be received, entry fee payable, prize money. This database contains essential information for not only those who directly involved in horse racing but also for radio and television broadcaster, bookmakers and their clients. The cost of running BHB database is £ 4 million per year. The BHB database is accessible on the Internet site jointly operated by BHB and Weatherbys Group Ltd. Some of the contents of database are also made available to Racing Pages Ltd. who then forwards data to its subscribers in the form of 'Declaration Feed' on the day before the race. Satellite Information Services Ltd. is authorized by Racing Pages Ltd. to transmit data to its own subscribers in the form of Raw Data Feed. This Raw Data Feed includes a large amount of information as name of the horses running the race, name of the jockeys.

[98]Colston, supra note 72.

[99]In the year 2000, BHB and others brought proceeding against William Hill in the High Court of Justice of England and Wales, Chancery division for infringing *sui generis* right. BHB contended that use of racing data from newspaper and Raw Data Feed by William Hill in day today basis amounted extraction or re-utilization of substantial part of the content of BHB database and even if it was not use of substantial part, it amounted to repeated systematic extraction and/or re-utilization of insubstantial part which conflict with normal exploitation of the database or which unreasonably prejudice the legitimate interest of the maker of the database. The High Court of Justice ruled that the action of BHB and others were well founded. William Hill appealed and the Court of Appeal referred some questions to European Court of Justice.

The referred questions were 1. Whether substantial part or insubstantial part of the contents of the database including works, data or other materials derived from the database did not have same systematic arrangement as found in the database, 2. What is the meaning of 'obtaining', 3. Whether 'verification' means ensuring from time to time that information contained in a database remained correct, 4. What is the meaning of 'substantial part evaluated qualitatively or quantitatively', 5. What is the meaning of 'insubstantial part of the database', 6. Does 'extraction' of content directly from the database and transfer to another medium include transfer of work or data which are derived indirectly from the database, 7. What is the meaning of 'substantial part of the database', 8. Does 'reutilization' means making available to public, 9. What is the meaning of 'act which conflict with normal exploitation of the database or unreasonably prejudice legitimate interest of the maker of the database', 10. What is the meaning of 'substantial change'? Both 2nd and 3rd questions are for the explanation of investment in obtaining and verification of the contents of the database.

Copying selection or structure of the database will lead to infringement of copyright in database. For the purpose of database, the term 'adaptation' has been redefined to include altered version of database and translation of database in order to offer better protection to databases.[100] Using database for the purpose of research and private use have been considered as fair dealing and will not amount to infringement and any research for commercial purpose has been excluded from fair dealing.[101] A legitimate user is allowed to use the content of database and this access cannot be restricted by agreement.[102]

In the First Instance, Judge Laddie observed, 'as one would expect, effort put into creating the actual data which is subsequently collected together in the database is irrelevant. This is confirmed by Article 7(4), which draws a distinction between right in the database and right in the data within the database. For this reason, the cost and the effort involved in BHB fixing the date of a racing fixture does not count towards the relevant investment to which database right is directed'. The Advocate General in her opinion pointed out that the interpretation for 'obtaining' excludes creation of materials contained in a database. 'Verification' refers to resources used for ensuring reliability of information of database.[103]

The Directive allows extraction and reutilization of the substantial part of the database for three purposes—extraction for private purpose in case of non-electronic databases, extraction for teaching and research, extraction and reutilization for public security. The information displayed in William Hill's website has come from newspaper and Raw Data Feed which eventually originated

[100]Section 21(3) Copyright Designs and Patent Act 1988.
[101]Section 29(1A) Copyright Designs and Patent Act 1988.
[102]Section 50D Copyright Designs and Patent Act 1988.
[103]British Horseracing Board Ltd. and others v. William Hill Organization Ltd., C-203/02.

from BHB database.[104] The data of BHB database thus have been made accessible to public for the purpose of consultation with the authorization of BHB. William Hill is a lawful user of the database but it conducts act of extraction and reutilization which is not an authorized act. It extracts data by transferring them into its own electronic system and it reutilizes by making those data available to public on its site to use it for betting. This extraction and reutilization is done without authorization and thus if they are related to substantial portion of the database then the *sui generis* right can be invoked.

As information displayed in William Hill's site represents a very small portion of the whole database, so they do not constitute substantial part evaluating quantitatively. The information displayed in William Hill's site contains date, time and name of the race, name of the racecourse etc. Now the issue is whether human, technical and financial efforts required by the maker of database in obtaining, verifying and presenting those data constitute substantial investment. BHB argued that these data represent significant investment as it requires 30 operators to be recruited by the call centre to develop the list. The intrinsic value of data affected by act of extraction does not decide question of substantiality.

The fact that data extracted by William Hill are vital to BHB is irrelevant to decide whether act of William Hill deals with substantial part of the content of BHB database. Moreover resources used for creation of such material included in a database cannot be considered in assessing whether investment in creation of database was substantial. So the information displayed in William Hill's site does not represent substantial part in qualitative term of the content of the BHB database. Thus substantial part evaluated quantitatively refers to volume of data extracted from the database in comparison with the total volume of data of the database.

The substantial part evaluated qualitatively refers to scale of investment in obtaining, verification and presentation of the content the database, regardless of the fact whether it represents quantitatively substantial part of general contents of the database. Justice Laddie observed that if the defendant used the database in such a way that extracted data were transmitted or made available to the public by putting it on the website, then it amounted to reutilization of data.[105] Most of the uses can be interpreted as substantial uses if they are beneficial to the user as observed by Judge Laddie in British Horseracing Board Ltd. and others v. William Hill Organization Ltd.[106]

In other words, an action for reconstitution through cumulative act of extraction can seriously prejudice the investment and thus should be treated as unauthorized act. Although information extracted by William Hill constitute a small portion of

[104]Information published in newspaper is supplied to press by Weatherbys Group who maintains BHB database. Satellite Information Services Ltd. is authorized by Racing Pages Ltd. to offer Raw Data Feed and the Racing Pages Ltd. is controlled by Weatherbys Group Ltd.

[105]British Horseracing Board Ltd. and others v. William Hill Organization Ltd., C-203/02.

[106]Supra note 72.

the BHB database but it has been extracted repeatedly and systematically on the occasion of each race. But as there is no possibility of reconstituting the BHB database by William Hill through the cumulative effect of extraction, investment made by BHB has not been seriously prejudiced and thus William Hill has not violated the *sui generis* right of BHB. The point remains that if the cumulative effect of extraction is to reconstitute a database, then it prejudices the investment and it becomes unauthorized act and thus can be prohibited. The database right presents inherent danger of granting monopoly right over major sources of information and that right will be owned by single right holder.[107]

Justice Laddie observed that estimated total of 8,000,000 new records or changes added to the database annually and annual cost of 4 million, 25 % of BHB's yearly expenditure. This estimate pushes for the argument on eternal protection. Although William Hill was the licensed user of the BHB database but action in the BHB litigation involved use of BHB database for new venture—online betting. Justice Laddie held that by purposive construction of the Directive, information used by William Hill amounted extraction of a substantial part of database and repeated extraction of insubstantial part of database. Although the extraction was indirect i.e., via SIS and RDF, it amounted to be infringement.

It was also pointed out that though the database could get a fresh term of protection due to substantial change, still the argument on repeated act of extraction of database continued to be valid. Justice Laddie was of the opinion that as the prime objective of the Directive was to protect investment in generating database, such investment would jeopardize if infringement was limited to rival database manufacturer. It has also been argued that *sui generis* right should not restrict information and it should cease to apply in case of re-expressed information.[108]

This argument takes a new form when is applied for individual element of database. If individual item constitutes substantial part and enjoys *sui generis* right, it starts enjoying a separate right from databases. This raises the question whether protection is given to database as collection or to its constituent information? Whether information derived from a database and re-expressed in a different form would qualify as a database or would constitute infringement? The BHB decision points out that there can be a protection in perpetuity if the database is a dynamic one. This argument does not match with the concept of incremental innovation.[109] Should the protection of databases be more flexible so that it can absorb technological changes? If the protection given to database tends to protect the underlying information in a database, then there has to be a detailed list of exceptions to infringement to ensure access to information.[110]

---

[107]Torremans P (2004) Holyoak and Torremans Intellectual Property Law. Oxford, p 538.

[108]*See* Rees, Chalton, supra note 1. In: Colston, supra note 72.

[109]Reichman and Samuelson, Intellectual Property Rights in Data? http://www.eon.law.harvard.edu/h2o/property/alternatives/reichman.html as cited by Cathrine Colston, Sui Generis Database Right: Ripe for Review, JILT, 2001, 3. http://www.elj.warwick.ac.uk/jilt/01-3/colston.html.

[110]Matthias Leistner, The Legal Protection of Telephone Directories Relating to the New Database Maker's Right, 2000, 31 IIC 950.

Chapter 5
Aborted American Attempts

The fundamental objective with which the journey of Intellectual Property Law in the United States has started is to advance the goal of promoting the progress of science and the useful arts through the granting of exclusive rights. To put it in the context of database debate, use of legal exclusivity is to promote creation of more and more databases. Along with this it has also to be remembered that exclusivity must be employed in a limited way, giving away no more of public domain than is necessary to achieve the desired promotional effect.[1]

To create this perfect utilitarian balance between incentive for knowledge producers and access for knowledge consumers has always been the most difficult job of the intellectual property law. Sometimes the problem aggravates due to lack of clear distinction of producers and consumers. For any producer who starts from scratch, he first undertakes the role of consumer before he starts producing. He consumes what has already been produced and then only comes to a position to produce. The database industry often likes to forget this logic and argues for 'I may have stood on the shoulders of those who came before but no one is going to stand on mine'.[2]

The Information Industry Association supported a model based on *sui generis* right. They felt that investment in data collation needed more protection in digitized world. As Feist diluted the protection otherwise available to databases, the Directive placed the United States database industry at a competitive disadvantage.[3] Thus the legislative initiatives to offer protection to databases in the United States came into picture.

The aborted legislative initiatives regarding database protection in the United States were the Collection of Information Anti-piracy Bill 1999, Consumer and Investor Access to Information Bill 1999 and the Database Investment and

[1]Conley J M, Brown M M, Bryan R M (2000) Database Protection in a Digital World: Why the United States Should Decline to Follow the European Model. Info & Comm Tech L9(1):49.
[2]Id.
[3]Colston, supra note 72.

A. Mazumder, *Database Law*, DOI 10.1007/978-981-10-2200-5_5

Intellectual Property Piracy Bill 1996. These Bills were dropped due to criticism from scientific and education communities for lack of fair use and public interest exception.

These Bills will be discussed on different headings like definition of database, unauthorized use, investment, infringement, permitted use, penalty, duration etc. These Bills will be compared inter se and also with the European Database Directive and Digital Millennium Copyright Act.

5.1 Definition of Database

The Collection of Information Anti-Piracy Bill 1999 defined 'collection of information' as 'information that has been collected and has been organized for the purpose of bringing discrete items of information together in one place or through one source so that users may access them'.[4] The definition of database given in the Directive is much wider as it includes all sorts of electronic and non-electronic collection.

5.2 Unauthorised Use

The Collection of Information Anti-Piracy Bill 1999 (H.R. 354) was not clear about the extent of 'making available' and did not specify whether it would give rise to action only when it causes material harm to primary market or a related market of the database proprietor.[5] The Consumer and Investor Access to Information Bill 1999 made distribution of duplicate database unlawful as Section 102 provided that it would be unlawful for any person to sell or distribute to public a database that was a duplicate of another and sold or distributed in competition with the original database. Though no express proprietary right is created here but arguably an implied proprietary right or quasi-proprietary right has been created. The underlying assumption here is that when a competitor wrongly misappropriates the property of database maker, the competitor should compensate the database maker for the economic loss suffered by the maker of the database.

The prohibition to sale or distribution of duplicate databases in competition with original database indicates *sui generis* law is confined to reasonable commercial activities. More over duplication per se has not been prohibited; it is prohibited only when it is distributed in competition with original database. Here it differs from copyright law where the very act of reproduction is prohibited unless exempted for specific reason.

[4] S. 1401.

[5] S. 1402 (a).

5.3 Investment

The Collection of Information Anti-Piracy Bill 1999 provided right to collection of information gathered, organized or maintained by another person through the investment of substantial monetary or other resources. The Directive provides a right for the maker of the database which shows that there has been qualitatively and/or quantitatively substantial investment in obtaining, verification or presentation of the contents.[6] The investment can be of financial, human or other resources. This is indirectly adopting 'skill and labour' or 'sweat of the brow'.[7] The investment may also include investment of time, energy and effort.

5.4 Infringement

The Collection of Information Anti-Piracy Bill 1999 created a situation where infringement would occur if whole or substantial part of database was made available or extracted in terms of an economic test—market harm. The infringement would occur if the extraction or making available of database cause harm to the actual or potential market. Potential market would be the market where person claiming protection had current or demonstrable plan to exploit and which was commonly exploited by offering similar products.[8] Actual market is the market in which the database is offered for sale and there is reasonable expectation to derive revenue directly or indirectly but potential market is the market in which proprietor is yet to enter. Interpretation of market will decide the ambit of the provision. Extending protection to qualitatively substantial part of database, which is not quantitatively substantial, would lead to protection of individual data or fact.[9] The Consumer and Investor Access to Information Bill 1999 looked at market and liability from a narrower sense. Here the liability would occur if one offered a duplicate in competition with protected database.[10]

The Collection of Information Anti-piracy Bill 1999 pointed out 'an individual item of information, including a work of authorship, shall not itself be considered a substantial part of collection of information'.[11] So a single but valuable item contained in a collection cannot be interpreted as qualitatively substantial part of collection of information.[12] But it was not allowed to repeatedly or systematically

---

[6]Article 7(1).

[7]Suthersanen, supra note 336.

[8]S. 1401.

[9]Phelps CE (1999) before Sub Committee on Courts and Intellectual Property of the House Comm. on the Judiciary. http://www.house.gov/judiciary/106-ct18htm. In: Suthersanen, supra note 336.

[10]S. 102.

[11]S. 1403 (b).

[12]Suthersanen, supra note 336.

make available or extract individual items or insubstantial part of database.[13] The Consumer and Investor Access to Information Bill 1999 prescribed 'any person who obtains directly or indirectly from a market information processor real-time market information and directly or indirectly sells, distributes or redistributes or otherwise disseminates such real-time market information without the authorization of the market information processor, shall be liable to that market information processor'.[14]

As per Section 4 of the Database Investment and Intellectual Property Piracy Bill 1996, no person would without authorization of the owner, extract, use or reuse all or substantial part qualitatively or quantitatively, of the contents of database in a manner that conflicts with the database owner's normal exploitation of the database or adversely affects the actual or potential market of the database.

5.5 Permitted Use

The Collection of Information Anti-piracy Bill 1999 prescribed that an individual act of use or extraction of information done for the purpose of illustration, explanation, example, comment, criticism, teaching, research, or analysis not a violation if it was reasonable. The reasonability was measured by 1. Extent of use, 2. Good faith of person making extraction, 3. The degree of difference between the collection from which extraction is made and the independent work of collection, 4. The effect of extraction on the market.[15]

The Collection of Information Anti-piracy Bill 1999 allowed non-profit educational, scientific and research uses of content of database without affecting actual market of the product.[16] There were no criteria for reasonable use in this case. The Collection of Information Anti-piracy Bill 1999 created an additional reasonable use which required satisfying the criteria for reasonable use. Any use which will lead to indirect, insubstantial and immaterial harm to the market will not be an infringement and thus liability of non-profit, public interest users will be limited as it will not cause any serious threat to the investment of the producers.[17] The question still remains whether these exceptions can still allow not only transformative use but also substitutive use which does not affect the market. The Consumer and Investor Access to Information Bill 1999 created exceptions like collection of information created by

[13]S. 1403 (b) The Collection of Information Anti-piracy Bill 1999.

[14]S. 201.

[15]S. 1403.

[16]S. 1403.

[17]Suthersanen, supra note 336.

government,[18] computer program,[19] use of subscriber list information,[20]non-liability of ISP.[21] Along with these, other exceptions were in the line of copyright law, like independent collection of information, news reporting, law enforcement, scientific and educational research activities. The Collection of Information Anti-piracy Bill1999 created exceptions like news reporting exception,[22] use of database to verify accuracy of information.[23]

5.6 Penalty

The Collection of Information Anti-piracy Bill 1999 did not allow using criminal sanction against employees of non-profit educational, research and scientific institutions and offered discretion to the court to allow attorney's fee and reasonable costs in case of actions in bad faith.[24]

5.7 Duration

The duration of protection under the Database Investment Bill was 25 years from the 1st January following the date when it was first made available to public.[25] The Directive offers protection for 15 years from the year following the completion of the database but if the database is first made available to public within this term, protection will be extended for another 15 years from the year following the date on

[18]S. 104 (a).

[19]S. 104 (C).

[20]S. 104 (e).

[21]S. 106 (a) Database Directive does not offer any such exception to facilitate functioning of the Internet though; the Directive does allow exception for public security, judicial procedure and computer program.

[22]S. 1403 (e) F or time sensitive information, a separate protection can be curved out. In International News Service v. Associated Press, 248 US 215, the Supreme Court held that Associated Press had a quasi property right in new stories against its competitor International News Service but not against the public. In National Basketball Assoc. v. Motorola Inc, 105 F. 3d.841 the Second Circuit Court did not allow misappropriation action against pager services' transmission of real time scores from National Basketball Association and held that INS-type claim could sustain only if it involved plaintiff who generates information at cost, information is time sensitive, defendant's use of information amounts to free riding on plaintiff's effort, defendant is in direct competition with product or service offered by the plaintiff, ability of other party to free ride on the effort of plaintiff would reduce incentive to produce.

[23]S. 1403 (c).

[24]S. 1406 (d) and 1407.

[25]S. 6, Database Investment and Intellectual Property Piracy Bill 1996.

which it is made available to public.[26] The Collection of Information Anti-piracy Bill 1999 was also restricted the term of protection by 15 years.

5.8 Review

The Directive prescribes for a study to be made not later than by the end of third year to examine whether application of sui generis right has lead to abuse of dominant position, interference with free competition.[27] The Consumer and Investor Access to Information Bill 1999 required Federal Trade Commission to submit report to the Congress latest by 36 months from the enactment to indicate effect on electronic commerce, availability of databases, extent of competition, availability of information.[28]

5.9 Comparison

In Europe protection of database is modelled on the basis of proprietary system but in America, protection was proposed on the basis of misappropriation approach. The perspective of protection to database maker against misappropriation can be different if viewed from the side of academic and scientific communities. To claim exemption, a public institution needs to qualify as lawful user and it has to ensure that the market of the database maker is not affected. This makes the European model slightly inclined towards interest of database makers. The American model proposed for better exemption by creating provision for non-commercial use. Interpretation of market harm and exceptions can truly assess the nature of protection offered by both models.

The Database Directive defines the term 'database' in a much broader way than the Consumer and Investor Access to Information Act. The US Act refers to 'items of information' to describe content of database but the Directive refers to 'work, data or other material' for the same expression.

The Collection of Information Anti-piracy Bill 1999 stipulated that no civil or criminal action would be available for any act occurring after 15 years from the year when that portion of the database was first offered in commerce.[29] This definitive period of protection was less confusing than the Directive as it made sure that maintenance of database would not result in renewal or extension of the term of protection of database.

---

[26]Article 10.

[27]Article 16(3).

[28]S. 108.

[29]Article 1408(c).

A comparative analysis among the legislative attempts made in the United States would be as follows—The Database Investment and Intellectual Property Anti-piracy Bill 1996 followed strongly the proprietary model of EU but offered a longer period of protection, i.e., 25 years and a broader right of exclusion to database makers. The Collection of Information Anti-piracy Bill 1997 also followed EU model but had no time limit for protection and offered limited permitted acts. This Bill was again introduced in 1999 with 15 years protection and some additional fair use exceptions. The Consumer and Investor Access to Information Bill 1999 did not create any proprietary right but prohibited duplication and commercial sale of database in competition with original database and also offered a list of permitted acts. The Anti-piracy Bill followed proprietary model like the Directive whereas the Consumer and Investor Access Bill followed misappropriation model. But even if the Consumer and Investor Access Bill was based on misappropriation model, the exception clause of it was more in the line of copyright law which created vagueness regarding the true extent of the Bill. The Consumer and Investor Access Bill limits extent to certain commercial activities but its broad definition of database and wide exceptions bring the uncertainty regarding the scope back to square one.

5.10 Comments

Reichman and Uhlir observed that the effect of The Collection of Information Anti-piracy Bill 1999 would be to prevent a second researcher from using protected information or data not allowed by site license. Where the data is based on one-time event that could not be regenerated, no subsequent research can fall within the permitted act of independent creation. They also opined that where regeneration might be physically possible, the cost would be so high that second comers would be likely to reproduce the data. Thus sole source database creator would remain a dominant player in the market and in the absence of competition, would perpetuate in creating barrier to entry.[30]

Reichman and Uhlir also felt that the long-term effect of this legislation would be very damaging for science and technology in the age of digitization.[31] Both in Europe and in United States, the concern is to secure effective balance between protection and access as the fear for consequences of protecting information looms large with the pressure from database industry.[32] The *sui generis* right has the

---

[30]Reichman, Uhlir (1999) Database Protection at the Crossroads: Recent Developments and Their Impact on Science and Technology. http://www.eon.law.harvard.edu/h20/property/alternatives/reichman.html. In: Colston, supra note 72.

[31]Id.

[32]Oram. The Sap and the Syrup of the Informaion Age: Coping with Database Protection Laws. Computer Law Reporter, Internet Law and Business 1(5). http://www.oreilly.com/people/staff/andyo/professional/collection_law.html. In: Colston, supra note 72.

potential to over protect sole source database unless compulsory license[33]and competition laws intervene. Competitive significance provokes reluctance in granting license as found in IMS litigation.[34] Adoption of the *sui generis* right has to be counterbalanced by a broad right of private non-commercial use. Any optimal solution regarding protection vis-à-vis access can be found only by combining effort of economist, intellectual property lawyer and competition lawyer. Another alternative can be a hybrid structure between copyright and unfair competition, with a remedy against misappropriation.

5.11 Effects

In the United States, the Database Investment and Intellectual Property Antipiracy Bill[35] proposed *sui generis* database right on EU model which offered protection for 25 years (10 years more than EU Directive) and broader right of exclusion. It limited certain uses of insubstantial portion of protected database which might affect proprietor's market or conflict with owner's normal exploitation of data. It lacked fair use or public interest exception because of which it was attacked by scientific and academic communities as it had the effect of monopolizing pure knowledge. Information Technology Association of America argued for a legislation based on law of misappropriation.[36] It created a cause of action in favour of a database producer against a person who made unauthorized use of information generated by a substantial investment of time or money, if the use competed directly with the producer's authorized products and served as disincentive to the creation of such product.

The Collection of Information Antipiracy Bill[37] also followed EU model and prohibited use of all or substantial part of collection of information gathered, organized, or maintained by another person through the investment of substantial monetary or other resources, so as to harm that other person's actual or potential market for a product or service. It did not prescribe any time limit on protection but offered some permitted acts like extraction or use of individual items of information

[33]It has been argued that compulsory license constitutes a form of price control and allows competitors to exploit only the most profitable database substituting externally determined rates for those secured by voluntary negotiations. Reasonable compensation shall always be a controversial issue. Tyson, Sherry, Statutory Protection for Databases: Economic and Public Policy Issues. House Judiciary Committee Hearing, 23 Oct 1997. http://wwwhouse.gov/judiciary/41118.htm. In:Colston, supra note 72.

[34]IMS Health GmbH & Co. v. NDC Health GmbH & Co., (C-418/01). IMS Health, a world leader in data collection in pharmaceuticals refused to license structure of their collection. The Commission ordered to grant the license.

[35]HR 3531.

[36]Conley, Brown, Bryan, supra note 566, at 47.

[37]HR 2652.

or insubstantial part of a protected collection or using protected information for purposes of verifying independently gathered data, conducting non-profit research without hurting actual or potential market for database or reporting news etc.

It was subject of protracted lobbying between database industry and the academic and scientific communities. Although it was drafted entirely from the proprietor's point of view, they were dissatisfied as any injection of information into the public domain was viewed as a threat to the market for proprietary database.[38] The Consumer and Investor Access to Information Bill took unfair competition approach and made it unlawful to sell or distribute in interstate or foreign commerce a duplicate of another database that was collected and organized by another person if the duplicate is sold in competition with that other database.[39] It offered exception for news reporting (but not for time sensitive information) and for scientific, educational and research purposes. It satisfied concerns of academic and scientific communities for taking unfair economic competition approach and offering much needed exceptions but at the cost of attack from database industry.

Under Digital Millennium Copyright Act 1998, it is a copyright offence to circumvent a technological measure that effectively controls access to a work or manufacture, sell or traffic in product whose only significant purpose is circumvention.[40] This can have significant effect on databases. So regardless of scope of copyright or other existing protection, proprietor of database can achieve fool proof protection by creating technical measure against unauthorized access. If this technical barrier works, then there will be no unauthorized access and if one wants to break it, then Digital Millennium Copyright Protection will come into effect. All the countries desirous of protecting database need to come out with similar legal provision. The expression 'a work protected under this title' in Digital Millennium Copyright Act has to be interpreted as a work falling generally within the subject matter of copyright, so that circumventing measure designed to protect database and compilation would be illegal, regardless of how thin protection of copyright might be.

5.12 Concluding Remarks

The English and EU laws create broad *sui generis* right in database which has many similarities with copyright protection though it goes beyond the reasonable need of commercial database producers. This type of protection is not popular across the world as appropriate mode of protecting commercial value of electronic databases but at the same time scholars are not unsympathetic to them. This protection may encourage production of databases but it may also affect the development. The problem of grey market can be handled by incorporating DMCA like legislation in

---

[38]Conley, Brown, Bryan, supra note 566, at 48.

[39]HR 1858.

[40]Section 17 USC.

all countries and by offering reciprocal national treatment to authors from other countries.[41] More over there should be provision forbidding importation of copies made under circumstances that would have constituted infringement under the law of the said country.[42] It is often felt by the proprietors of information systems that current level of protection for database is inadequate.[43] Post—Feist copyright protection is too thin. The standard set by the Feist is so low that it is eliminating many databases which are product of substantial investment or sweat. In case where copyright exists theoretically, it is nominal in application. For database proprietor, it may be difficult to obtain assent to restrictive contracts. There may be doubts regarding enforceability of contract. The remedies in the form of unfair competition and misappropriation can be pre-empted too easily. In these cases, issues like time sensitive data and free riding have to be dealt with specifically. The contractual protection may not turn out to be feasible both practically and legally.

[41]Article 3 WIPO Copyright Treaty.

[42]Like 17 USC Section 602 (b).

[43]The industry concerns were concisely articulated by Sen. Orrin Hatch (R-Utah), Chairman of the Senate Judiciary Committee, Lucas (1998) Database Protection Could be at Forefront of the 106th Congress's Legislative Effort. US Law Week 67:2355. In Conley, Brown, Bryan, supra note 566, at 27.

Chapter 6
Indian Database Industry and Its Aspirations and Existing Legal Regime

6.1 Indian Database Industry

The Govt. of India produces almost 80 % of databases in India.[1] Only a small portion of it is available to public as most of them are either held by different departments of the Govt. or they have been classified as sensitive as they are related to atomic research, space research or defence research. The private database industry in India is not organized and thus documented data about this industry is not available. Databases relating to legal information, banking and financial information, stock market information and market research information and travel information have tremendous commercial potential in India.

The Govt. of India has undertaken a program called Traditional Knowledge Digital Library (TKDL), which involves documentation of traditional knowledge existing in India and preparation of a database of traditional knowledge. India being a hotspot of biodiversity, it is a potentially rich source of animal, plant microbial genomic data and databases of these genomic data are expected to generate a positive commercial interest.

The exponential growth of information technology in India has also helped in creating different types of databases and has offered good support to database industry.

Dr. Mashelkar has described India as "ancient", "diverse" and "mathematical" where "ancient" denotes India's wealth of traditional knowledge, "diverse" qualifies India's rich pool of genomic data and "mathematical" indicates India's information technology capability. In this context if India wants to attract more investment to database industry then there should be a legal regime in place which will protect unoriginal databases.

---

[1]A Study on the Impact of Protection of Unoriginal Databases on Developing Countries: Indian Experience, World Intellectual Property Organization, Standing Committee on Copyright and Related Rights, Seventh Session, Geneva, May 13 to 17 2002.

A. Mazumder, *Database Law*, DOI 10.1007/978-981-10-2200-5_6

The growth of digital computing and telecommunications technology has contributed exponential growth in the information industry which has positively influenced not only compilation of information but also dissemination of it as well. This has also helped in the emergence of various commercial activities involving different types of databases. Although the database industry in India is a fragmented one but there is no doubt in its potential for growth. The private database industry though relies heavily on data generated by government agencies but government databases are not well accessible to public. Government databases in India have mainly been contributed by Council of Scientific and Industrial Research, National Institute of Oceanography, National Botanical Research Institute, Indian Institute of Petroleum, Geographical Society of India, National Informatics Centre, National Remote Sensing Agency, and Indian Space Research Organization. So there is a need to restructure the existing policy influencing the database industry in India.

The database created under the Traditional Knowledge Digital Library Project, a project which attempts to document traditional knowledge in India to prevent frivolous patent applications filed in different foreign patent offices, can claim copyright protection on the basis of its originality. The Human Genome Project has also generated huge amount of data having commercial significance and which may be analyzed to extract functional information. To protect these data existing copyright law which protects only original databases needs to be supplemented by sui generis law protecting unoriginal database.

India having one fifth of world's population, is expected to have the most diverse genomic data. India being a biodiversity hotspot, it is expected to have rich resource of animal, plant, microbial genomic data. India's potential in information technology can put India into leading position in Bioinformatics sector. Indian genomic sector can create databases which can generate resources by taking support from the bioinformatics sector. A stronger protection regime will be of help in these situations.

The range of databases available in India can include databases containing banking and financial information, legal information, and stock market information, ticketing information, travel information, market research information, credit card information, entertainment information, yellow pages, health care information, and crime information. To name few noteworthy databases will include Centre for Monitoring the Indian Economy who created integrated database on the country's economic and business sector. The Tata Energy Research Institute created Energy-Environment database and Rural Energy Database. There are several internet based databases operating in the country. According to Market and Research India, approximately for every unit of data which it supplies per day, it costs around Rs. 130.[2]

The Indian IT-BPO industry was estimated to achieve revenues of USD 71.7 billion in FY2009, with the IT software and services industry accounting for USD 60 billion of revenues. During this period, direct employment was expected to reach

[2]Id.

nearly 2.23 million, an addition of 226,000 employees. Indirect job creation was estimated to touch 8 million. As a proportion of national GDP, the sector revenues grew from 1.2 % in FY1998 to an estimated 5.8 % in FY2009. The net value-added by this sector, to the economy, was estimated at 3.5–4.1 % for FY2009. The sector's share of total Indian exports (merchandise plus services) increased from less than 4 % in 1998 to almost 16 % in 2008. Information technology enabled services have yielded revenue of Rs. 6500 crores by 2008 and employed 100,000 people.[3] The Internet revolution also took off in a big way. The number of Internet users also increasing every day. More and more Internet Service Providers have been given license. The excessive competition has reduced the rate to stay in the competition. All these and many more have contributed in the computer, Internet and database industry in India.

Various bibliographic, textual, statistical databases and information, education and entertainment materials in electronic form and audio, video and multimedia material have contributed in creating the content industry. This content industry has a major say in the development of database industry as content development is an integral part of the information system. Govt. offers lot of these materials to public like budget materials, customs rules, railways time tables, telephone directories, maps etc. India's rich cultural heritage and traditional knowledge also will contribute to this content industry.

The Information Technology Act 2000 has defined terms like data and computer database widely which enables extended protection for electronic databases. This protection under Information Technology Act 2000 does not require proving originality and it is also not subjected to fair use exception clause. It also offers protection to extraction of insubstantial portion of data. Proposed amendment of Copyright Act will offer protection against circumvention of technological measures. Section 81 of the Information Technology Act provides that nothing in this statute shall restrict any person from exercising any right conferred under Copyright Act 1957. So owner of a database can very well enforce his rights under Copyright Act while being operating under Information Technology Act.

6.2 Response of Indian Database Industry

Research on protection of databases in India shall not be complete if it does not take into account the aspiration of the database industry in India. To get a feedback from the industry regarding the type of protection they are looking for from the legislators, a structured questionnaire was prepared and circulated amongst database creators in India like Eastern Book Company, Microsoft, Google and Adobe. These responses were carefully studied; analyzed and following inferences were drawn:

[3]NASSCOM (2009) Strategic Reform. http://blog.nasscom.in/nasscomnewsline/2009/03/nasscom-launches-strategic-review-2009-at-the-india-leadership-forum/. Accessed 30 May 2006.

1. Non-original database require protection to continue to be in the market.
2. Existing copyright law regime is not efficient in protecting the interest of the proprietors of non-original databases.
3. Non-original database also require protection for regular updating of these databases.
4. These databases cater to a small but significant group of peoples who are looking for changes in every 3 months.
5. Fair use relating to personal use and commercial use need to be dealt with much more clarity.
6. Although database industry is not organized sector but it is essentially looking for protection for their investment in creating and maintaining databases.
7. The duration of protection should be 15 years.
8. The legal protection needs to be supported by technological protection like hardware locks.
9. Remedies should be available through a civil suit in a court of law

These inferences arising out of the feedback given by the industry will continue to influence the features of the law which will be proposed in the next part of the thesis.

6.3 Existing Legal Regime in India

It is well settled that in order to obtain copyright protection for literary, dramatic, musical and artistic work, the subject dealt with need not be original nor the ideas expressed be something novel. What is required is the expenditure of original skill or labour in execution and not originality of thought.

It is well recognized that all these books are capable of copyright in them. In these books amount of originality will be very small but that small amount is protected by law. To use common source plea one needs to go to the common source from which he has borrowed by employing his own skill and labour and not by copying from other's work. A man is not allowed to appropriate for himself the arrangement, sequences, order, idiom etc. employed by another, using his brain, skill and labour. In modern complex society, provisions have to be made for protecting everyman's copyright whether big or small, whether involving high degree of originality or originality at the vanishing point.

Copinger observed "In the case of compilations such as dictionaries, gazetteers, grammars, maps, and arithmetic, almanacs, and encyclopaedia and guide books, publications dealing with similar subject matter must of necessity resemble existing publications and the defense of common source is frequently made where the new publication is alleged to constitute an infringement of an earlier one".[4]

[4]Copinger and James, Law of Copyright, 8th Edition, p. 124.

The Indian Copyright Act 1957 protects databases through compilation which has been included in the definition of literary work provided it satisfies the criteria of originality. Even the Copyright Act 1911 used to protect compilation as literary work. Which work can be treated as compilation and when does it satisfy originality criteria have been evolved through cases over the years.

6.3.1 Nineteenth Century

Mr. Justice Wilson in Macmillan and another v. Suresh Chunder Deb[5] observed in the case of work not original in the proper sense of the term but composed of or compiled or prepared from materials which are open to all, the fact that one man has produced such a work does not take away from anyone else the right to produce another work of the same kind and in doing so to use all the material open to him. Justice Wilson opined that poems were selected and compiled with great care, time and judgment and were outcome of a large expenditure of learning, time and trouble and thus these selections were entitled to be protected from infringement and piracy.

The principle used in these cases is the defendant is not at liberty to use or avail himself of the labour which the plaintiff has been at for the purpose of producing his work, that is, in fact merely to take away the result of another man's labour or in other words his property. This principle has been applied to maps, to road books, to guide books, to street directories, to dictionaries, to compilations on scientific and other subjects. It is open to anyone who pleases to go through a like course of reading and by the exercise of his own taste and judgment to make a selection for him but if he spares himself this trouble and adopts other's selection, he offends against this principle. Two men might perhaps make the same selection from various authors but that must be by resorting to the original authors, not by taking advantage of the selection already made by another. Interestingly it was decide by House of Lords that there were two kinds of selection from official railway time table, one of which consisted in omission of smaller stations and indicating mileage,

[5]Macmillan and Co. was the proprietor of copyright of a selection of songs and poems, composed by numerous well known authors. The compilation was prepared by Palgrave. These poems were arranged not in chronological order of their production but in gradation f feelings and subjects and at the end of the book some critical and explanatory notes were given. Suresh Chunder Deb published a book containing same selection of poems and songs but the arrangement was different as poems of each author were placed together in order of their composition. The plaintiff contended that although copyright in the works of original authors had long lapsed but they were entitled to copyright in the selection and complained that defendant's book constituted breach of their copyright and prayed for relief by way of injunction and damages. It was held that defendant's book constituted piracy of plaintiff's book and had infringed their copyright. 1890 ILR 17 Cal 952.

the other one consisted in timetable for convenient tours round about a place. The later was protected but former was not.[6]

In Jarrold v. Houlston[7] a question was raised as to whether the author of a school book—Brewer's Guide to Science—was entitled to copyright. That was a book containing, in the form of question and answer, explanations collected from various scientific works of certain simple scientific doctrines. The Vice Chancellor observed "That an author has a copyright in a work of this description is beyond all doubt. If anyone by pains and labour collects and reduces into the form of a systematic course of instruction those questions which he may find ordinary persons asking in reference to the common phenomena of life, with answers to those questions and explanations of those phenomena, whether such explanations and answers are furnished by his own collection of his formal general reading or out of works consulted by him for the express purpose, the reduction of questions so collected, with such answers under certain heads and in a scientific form is amply sufficient to constitute an original work which the copyright will be protected. Therefore I can have no hesitation in coming to the conclusion that the book now in question is in that sense an original work and entitled to protection." This principle was used in Gangavishnu Shrikisondas v. Moreshvar Bapuji Hegishte and others[8] to decide that plaintiff's work was such a new arrangement of old matters as to be an original work and entitled to protection.

6.3.2 Twentieth Century

Justice Panchapkesa Ayyar observed in Govindan v. Gopalkrishnan[9] "I cannot agree that no originality can be claimed in dictionaries compilations, guide books, maps etc. as they involve no brains, skills and labour and the compilation by one

[6] Lesile v. Young, (1894) AC 335.

[7] (1857) 3 K & J 708.

[8] (1889) I.L.R. 13 Bom. 358—The plaintiff, a book seller brought out a new and annotated edition of a certain well known Sanskrit work on religious observances entitled "Vrtraj", having for that purpose obtained the assistance Pandits who recast and rearranged the work, introduced various passages from other old Sanskrit books on the same subject and added footnotes. The defendant printed and published an edition of the same work, the text of which was identical with that of the plaintiff's work, which moreover contained the same additional passages and the same footnote at the same places with slight differences.

[9] AIR 1955 Mad 392. The plaintiff Gopalkrishna, a publisher of Madurai published English—English Tamil dictionary in 1932. The defendant Govindan, the proprietor of Sakti Karyalayam of Madras published English—English Tamil Dictionary in 1947. It was alleged that the defendant infringed plaintiff's copyright. The lower court decided that the defendant's book was a piratical reproduction of plaintiff's reproduction as it was found that pages after pages, word after word slavishly copied including errors. It was also found that sequence, meaning, arrangements and everything else practically the same except for some deliberate differences introduced here and there in order to cover up piracy.

man will be exactly the same as the compilation by any other man. Many men have not got the brains, skill and labour to compile dictionaries, gazetteers, grammar, maps, almanac, and encyclopaedias and guide books. All of such compilations are not of the same nature. Then it will be obvious that only one dictionary, gazetteer, grammar, map, almanac, encyclopaedia or guidebook will sell and not the rest. Any man who refers to the Oxford Dictionary, Webster Dictionary and Chambers Dictionary can easily find out the difference between these dictionaries. There is considerable difference in dealing with the subject matter. That will be specially so when the dictionary is not at all the words in the language but some select words considered suitable for high school".

Mr. N.K. Anand argued in Rai Toys Industries and others v. Munir Printing Press[10] that there was no copyright in the Plaintiff's book on Tambola Ticket as it consisted of filling up numbers in the tickets which was not a matter in which copyright could exist. The court observed that tambola ticket book would require quite a deal of skill and awareness of placing numbers correctly. Each ticket must have different arrangement of numbers so as not to be confusing and mixed up with others. If tickets contain the same number it will all get mixed up and spoil the fun of the game. Preparation of 1500 tickets and placing them in one book would require good deal of skill and labour and would thus satisfy the test of being original literary work as compilation. Tambola ticket book cannot be called some easily available information which is bodily lifted and put in the compilation which does not require skill. Thus there is no doubt that Tambola ticket book qualifies as compilation and deserves protection as original literary work. The House of Lords observed in G.A. Gramp & Sons Limited v. Frank Smythson Limited[11] that pocket diary contained usual pages and were accompanied by pages containing information of the kind usually found in diary ie calendar for year, postal information, selection of days and dates for year, tables of weights and measures, comparative time tables etc. and decided that they were common place matters and left no room for taste, selection and judgment and thus were not original literary work.

The arrangement of numbers in tickets is an individualized contribution and bears his individuality and long hours of labour and the compilation satisfies the test of being original literary work. It is not information which could be picked up by all and sundry. The labour and skill employed in selecting and arranging existing subject matter demands copyright protection to the resulting work. Works like arrangement of broadcasting programs, school text books, list of railway stations,

[10]1982 PTC 85. Tambola Ticket book used in a game is called by different names like Tambola, Housie etc. Broadly there are three horizontal rows of 9 spaces in each row ie total 27 spaces. Of 9 spaces five in each row have numbers. Numbers are called out and whosoever is first able to score out of fifteen numbers is declared the winner. Tambola Ticket book of the plaintiff contained 1500 different tickets which were in the form of tables for which the skill ability and originality were necessary. The defendant brought out Tambola ticket book containing 600 different tickets in the forms of tables which have been copied identically from 600 tickets of the plaintiff.

[11]1944 A.C. 329.

columns of birth and death announcements in news paper, sheet of election result get copyright protection in the similar fashion.

The Judge in Brewer's Guide to Science opined "I take the illegitimate use as opposed to legitimate use of another's man's work on subject matters of this description to be this: if knowing that a person whose work is protected by copyright has with considerable labour compiled from various sources a work in itself not original but which he has digested and arranged, you being minded to compile a work of like description, instead of taking the pains of searching into all the common source and obtaining your subject matter from them avail yourself of the labour of your predecessor, adopt his arrangement, adopt moreover, the very questions he has asked or adopt them with but a slight degree of colourable variation and thus save yourself pain and labour by availing yourself of the pain and labour which he has employed, that I take to be an illegitimate use".[12] Justice Bennet and Justice Ganga Nath used this principle to decide in Gopal Das v. Jagannath Prasad[13] that defendant by reproducing substantial part of the plaintiff's book has committed infringement of the plaintiff's work. The Court observed that in copyright it is always possible to arrive at the same result from independent source and the fact that defendant produces something like the plaintiff's earlier work does not necessarily create an infringement. Published compilations are intended not merely to be read but to be used and the question is how far they may be used in the preparation of a subsequent compilation. The rule appears to be settled that the compiler of a work in which absolute originality is of necessity excluded is entitled, without exposing himself to a charge of piracy, to make use of preceding work upon the subject. The Court thus held that plaintiffs compiled their book with considerable labour from various sources and the defendant could not be allowed to copy plaintiff's work without taking pain of searching into all the common sources. "No man is entitled to avail himself of the previous labour of another for the purpose of conveying to the public the same information although he may append additional information to that already published".

The court also referred to Shyam Lal v. Gaya Prasad[14] where the court formulated few principles regarding compilation—1. A compilation which may be

[12](1857) 3 K & J 708.

[13]AIR 1938 All 266. The plaintiffs were publishers of "Sachitra Bara Kok Shastra" and the defendant published "Asli Sachitra Kok Shastra". The plaintiff alleged that the defendant's book was a colourable imitation of their book and had infringed plaintiff's copyright. The defendant admitted plaintiff's copyright in its book but not in the passages and ideas which they had borrowed from previous works. The trial court found that the defendant infringed plaintiff's work. The Commissioner's report also went against the defendant. There was a great deal of similarity in both the books. The defendant attributed similarity to common source from which both the books must have been compiled and the common ideas dealt with in them. Some of the similarities might be attributed to the defendant's own labour but there were good many similarities which had evidently been copied from plaintiff's work with but a slight colourable variation or addition of some new material. Same mistakes were found in both the works which led to the position that the defendant copied plaintiff's work which amounted to infringement.

[14]AIR 1971 All 192.

derived from a common source falls within the ambit of literary work. 2. A work of compilation of a nature similar to that of another will not by itself constitute an infringement of the copyright of another person's work written on the same pattern. 3. The question whether an impugned work is a colourable imitation of another person's work is always a question of fact and has to be determined from the circumstances in each case. 4. The determining factor in finding whether another person's copyright has been infringed is to see whether the impugned work is a slavish imitation and copy of another person's work or it bears the impression of the author's own labour and exertions. In the present case it was found by comparing data available from the defendant, that substantial number of entries is comparable word by word with plaintiff's clientele. In some entries, location of punctuations was comparable and spelling mistakes were comparable. It gave irrefutable circumstantial evidence that the defendant indulged into slavish imitation of the plaintiff's compilation. The court observed that if the defendant was allowed to use plaintiff's clientele, it would have caused an injury to the plaintiff and thus the defendant was restrained from carrying on business by utilizing the impugned clientele.

In Burlington Home Shopping Pvt. Ltd. v. Rajnish Chibber & Another[15] plaintiff is a mail order service company which publishes mail order catalogue dealing with several consumer items. It invests in making compilation of clientele which is of essential importance and consequence. The defendant was at one time employee of the plaintiff but his job had nothing to do with clientele or making database. After severing relation with the plaintiff, the defendant entered into mail order shopping business. Somehow the defendant managed to get a copy of the clientele of the plaintiff which was a secret thing for the plaintiff and started contacting plaintiff's customers. It was argued that the plaintiff was the owner of copyright of the clientele and the defendant infringed the same. The defendant argued that the plaintiff did not have copyright in the clientele; moreover defendant developed its own database. The issue was whether database consisting of mailing address can be subject of copyright and whether the defendant infringed it. Database containing customer detail can be protected both under copyright law as literary work and under trade secret law. The plaintiff has argued that he has developed this database over a period of 3 years by investing considerable amount of money and time. He has also argued that the said database is an expensive and gradual process of compilation. The defendant claims that he has developed his own database. The court formed its decision on the basis of the report of the court appointed commissioner who could notice striking similarities between the databases, indicating a prima facie evidence for substantial copy of the plaintiff's database and thereby held that the temporary injunction be granted to the plaintiff to restrain the defendant from using the list of clients. The court did not address the issue of originality of the plaintiff's database and thereby did not examine whether plaintiff's database is eligible to enjoy copyright protection. As the court accepted the

---

[15] 1995 PTC (15) 278.

argument that the plaintiff's database is an original one so it indicates that the court is recognizing the sweat of the brow doctrine as justification for copyright protection. This judgment does not offer much help as a precedent for standard of originality in case of copyright protection in India. In this case, the court referred to Waterlow Directories Ltd. v. Reed Information Service Ltd[16] where names and addresses appearing in plaintiff's directory was copied on to a data processor for the purpose of using it and it was held that a person could not copy entries from a directory and use such copies to compile its own directory and it amounted to reproduction.

6.3.3 *Twenty First Century*

In Eastern Book Company v. D.B. Modak,[17] the apex court has raised issue of copyrighting derivative work produced from pre existing material in the public domain. Through this case the court rejected the test of originality as laid down through sweat of the brow doctrine and American creativity doctrine and the court evolved a new Indo-Canandian test of skill and judgment with flavour of creativity. The court held that to claim copyright in a derivative work, the author must produce the material with the exercise of his skill and judgment with a flavour of creativity which may not be in the sense that it is novel or non obvious but at the same time it is not a product of merely labour and capital. The Supreme Court considered copy-edited judgment as a derivative work and examined the standard of originality for derivative work to be considered for copyright protection and opined "The originality requirement in derivative work is that it should originate from the author by application of substantial degree of skill, industry or experience. Precondition to copyright is that work must be produced independently and not copied from another person. Where a compilation is produced from the original work, the compilation is produced from the original work; the compilation is more than simply a rearranged copyright of original which is often referred to as skill, judgment and or labour or capital. The copyright has nothing to do with originality or literary merit. Copyrighted material is that what is created by the author by his skill, labour and investment of capital, maybe it is derivative work. The courts need not to go into evaluation of literary merit of derivative work or creativity aspect of the same."

The Court also relied on Feist and CCH to observe "The sweat of the brow approach to originality is too low a standard which shifts the balance of copyright protection too far in favour of the owner's right and fails to allow copyright to protect the public's interest in maximizing the production and dissemination of intellectual work. On the other hand, the creativity standard of originality is too high. A creative standard implies that something must be novel or non obvious—

[16]1992 FSR 409.

[17](2008) 1 SCC 1.

concepts more properly associated with patent law than copyright law. By way of contrast, a standard requiring the exercise of skill and judgment in the protection of a work avoids these difficulties and provides a workable and appropriate standard for copyright protection that is consistent with the policy of the objectives of the Copyright Act." The Court has not formulated norms for finding out workable and appropriate standard but observed "To claim copyright in a compilation, the author must produce the material with exercise of his skill and judgment which may not be creativity in the sense that it is novel or non obvious but at the same time it is not a product of merely labour and capital. The derivative work[18] produced by the author must have some distinguishable features." Though the court considered reported judgment as derivative work but for all practical purposes the court treated it as compilation for determining its originality standard. Thus, our law mandates that not every effort or industry, or expending of skill, results in copyrightable work, but only those which create works that are somewhat different in character, involve some intellectual effort, and involve a minimum degreevof creativity.[19]

> Creating property (or quasi-property) rights in *information*—which is what the plaintiffs (Star and BCCI) request the Court to do in this case—stands to upset the statutory balance carefully created by the legislature through the Copyright Act.[20]

6.4 Principles for New Legislation

- The labour and skill employed in selecting and arranging existing subject matter demands copyright protection to the resulting work.
- To use common source plea one needs to go to the common source from which he has borrowed by employing his own skill and labour and not by copying from other's work.
- All compilations are not of the same nature. Then it will be obvious that only one dictionary, gazetteer, grammar, map, almanac, encyclopedia or guidebook will sell and not the rest. Any man who refers to the Oxford Dictionary, Webster Dictionary and Chambers Dictionary can easily find out the difference between these dictionaries.

---

[18]Article 2(3), Berne Convention—a derivative work means translations, adaptations arrangement s of music and other alterations of a literary work that shall be protected as original work without prejudice to the copyright in the original work. S. 101 US Copyright Law—A work based upon one or more pre existing work such as a translation, fictionalization, motion picture version, condensation or any other form in which a work may be recast, transformed or adapted. A work consisting of editorial version, annotation, elaboration or other modifications which as a whole, represent an original work of authorship is a derivative work.

[19]Emergent Genetics Pvt Ltd. v. Shailendra Shivam and Others, I.A No. 388/2004.

[20]Akuate Internet Services Pvt. Ltd. v. Star India Pvt. Ltd., FAO(OS) 153/2013, CM APPL. 4665/2013.

- In copyright it is always possible to arrive at the same result from independent source and the fact that defendant produces something like the plaintiff's earlier work does not necessarily create an infringement.
- One is not at liberty to use or avail him of the labour which the plaintiff has been at for the purpose of producing his work, that is, in fact merely to take away the result of another man's labour or in other words his property.
- To claim copyright in a derivative work, the author must produce the material with the exercise of his skill and judgment with a flavour of creativity which may not be in the sense that it is novel or non obvious but at the same time it is not a product of merely labour and capital.
- A compilation which may be derived from a common source falls within the ambit of literary work. A work of compilation of a nature similar to that of another will not by itself constitute an infringement of the copyright of another person's work written on the same pattern. The question whether an impugned work is a colourable imitation of another person's work is always a question of fact and has to be determined from the circumstances in each case. The determining factor in finding whether another person's copyright has been infringed is to see whether the impugned work is a slavish imitation and copy of another person's work or it bears the impression of the author's own labour and exertions.

There exists a line of argument that believes that increased legal protection of databases is necessary because in absence of it, there will be less incentive for investment although there is no clear evidence that well-designed legal protection will encourage database protection as it was observed in the United States that after Feist, database industry flourished.[21] In India there exists admirable knowledge society and a booming information technology industry which go on to indicate that there is no reason why India will not a have a flourishing database industry.[22]

[21]It is believed that existing legal, contractual and technological protections are sufficient incentive for investment. Yen A C (1991) The Legacy of Feist: Consequences of the Weak Connection Between Copyright and the Economics of Public Goods. Ohio State LJ52: 1343.

[22]These are databases which contains more than 60,000 complete details of Companies/ Industries including Exporters all over India. Details include Company Name, Product Profile, Full Postal Address, Phone No., Fax No., Email Address (about 21,000), website Address (wherever available). Along with Over 9000 Records with full details viz Name, Address, Phone, Fax, E-mail, Website, Product, Year of establishment, no. of employees, Capital, Turnover, Banker, Key Person, Membership of Association. http://www.books-directory-projectreports.com/database.html. Accessed 18 Oct 2008.

Conclusion

Establishing property right over information product by extending concept of property will not inevitably create information monopoly. Rather legislature can use property right to balance between private and public interest. The structure and content of database law should indicate the purpose that is to support the commerce by offering a lead time to database producer for investing time, energy and capital in producing database.[1] Model adopted by European Union is overprotective and model based on copyright law creates vague exception which generates uncertainty.[2]

Guideline 1: The purpose of New Database Law should be to support commerce by offering a lead time to database producer for investing time, energy and capital.

Guideline 2: New Database Law should offer *sui generis* right to non original databasse and copyright to original databases.

In the United States, there exist tort/misappropriation model which takes interest in unfair conduct in commerce. A model has been proposed which is based on registration of database right where a governmental authority will oversee a register of database right, grant compulsory license, work as repository and resolve dispute.[3] Lawrence Lessig observed that market would be better regulator of resources than government and indicated that certain resources should not be regulated at all.[4] The idea of State-run management can take inspiration from the patent and trade mark system. The competing public and private interest in information product can offer argument in favour of overseeing by government as somebody must take responsibility of balancing the private interest of database producer by making a property right and public interest of gaining access to information product. Market will not be able to strike this balance properly as the database producers will make lobby for

---

[1]Supra note 44, at 773.
[2]Fair use defense for criticism, comment, news reporting, teaching, research—17 USC Section 107.
[3]Supra note 44, at 773.
[4]*See generally* Lessig L (2001) The Future Of Ideas: The Fate of The Commons in a Connected World. Random House, New York.

A. Mazumder, *Database Law*, DOI 10.1007/978-981-10-2200-5

protecting their interest. While striking the balance, government entity must ensure that public domain and fair use concept has been preserved.

Guideline 3: New Database Law should offer a mandatory system of registration of database right under a governmental authority who will oversee commercial exploitation of database right.

Some type of property or quasi property right in information product will emerge if the product has commercial value and creator of these products will any way use contract and technology to control the use of these products. The governmental authority must ensure that this control will not affect the quality and quantity of public domain. In information age, information products have gained importance. Products like customer list, catalogues have undeniable commercial value. Today information products have become valuable as information can be collected, collated and represented. The chance of copy by competitors has also increased. Often selection and arrangement of these information products are original enough to claim copyright protection. Protection through trade secret law requires confidentiality agreement with all users which makes it impracticable.

Guideline 4: Governmental authority under New Database Law should ensure that the quality and quantity of the public domain shall not be affected. Fair use exception should be same as available under copyright law.

Technological protection can reduce the scope for unauthorized access to the product. Technological protection needs always to be upgraded and also support of anti-circumvention law. Not having database protection legislation will encourage using contractual provision coupled with technological protection and having a database protection legislation will restrict public domain. Protection through shrinkwrap or clickwrap license or encryption technology and wide spread use of digital rights management will further restrict access to information. New database protection law must use property right in such a way that database producer cannot create a market monopoly. The new law should concentrate on need for commerce and public policy rather than follow the copyright tradition. It must also focus on freedom of information, scientific and educational communities' need and cultural differences etc. It is to be remembered that focus of law should be more on progress of commerce rather than expression of ideas.

Guideline 5: New Database Law should use property right in such a way that database producer cannot create market monopoly. Spin off databases should not get *sui generis* protection.

Guideline 6: New Database Law should pay attention to the need of scientific & educational community. Scientific & educational institutions should not be precluded from access to databases.

According to Raymond Shih Ray Ku, broad property right with vague exception clause is not suited for access to the content of database.[5] The existing little governmental oversight in copyright law may adversely affect the vulnerable class of users. The term 'database' should be defined in a restricted manner to limit commercial activities coming within the ambit of the legislation.[6] Carsten has defined database as 'simply a set of data stored and accessed by electronic means. No limit is put on the amount of data involved or on its arrangement. It may be a collection of full text materials or a compilation of extracts of works. It may be a collection of material in the public domain, such as list of names, addresses, prices or references numbers. Lastly it may consist of the electronic publishing of a single but voluminous work, such as encyclopaedia. The common thread is that a database requires effort to complete and arrange. A computer program aids the compilation and retrieval process by allowing the user to create or manipulate the database in variety of ways'.[7] According to Jacqueline Lipton, 'the protected rights under the Consumer and Investor Access to Information Act are much more limited than those under various iterations of the Collections of Information Anti-piracy Act. However I would still strongly argue that the Consumer and Investor Access to Information Act is overly broad in its definition of database and overly vague in terms of its fair use exception to be particularly effective'.[8]

Guideline 7: New Database Law should offer protection only to those databases which are created for commercial purposes. Private databases, non-electronic databases, government databases and scientific & educational databases should not be covered under this New Law.

The new legislation must differentiate between different types of databases and offer protection to database created for exploitation in commercial markets. Initially the Directive proposed to cover only electronic databases but as they could not find a pragmatic reason to differentiate, the protection was also offered to non-electronic databases. Although they enjoy similar protection under the Directive, electronic database is more user-friendly, comprehensive and easy to update and more

---

[5]Ku R S R (2002) The Creative Destruction of Copyright: Napster and the New Economics of Digital Technology. Univ Chicago L Rev 69:263.

[6]17 USC Section 101—compilation is a work formed by the collection and assembling of pre-existing materials or of data that are selected, coordinated or arranged in such a way that the resulting work as a whole constitutes an original work of authorship. Copyright, Designs and Patents Act 1977 Section 3A(1)—database is a collection of independent works, data, or other materials which are arranged in a systematic or methodical way and individually accessible by electronic or other means. The Consumer and Investor Access Bill, H.R. 1858 Section 101(1)—database is a collection of discrete items of information that have been collected and organized in a single place, or in such a way as to be accessible through a single source, through the investment of substantial monetary or other resources for the purpose of providing access to those discrete items of information by users of database.

[7]Castens D W (1994) Legal Protection of Computer Software: Patents, Copyrights and Trade Secrets. J Contemp L 20:13.

[8]Supra note 44, at 773.

vulnerable to copy due to digital technology. The electronic world has brought huge amount of comprehensiveness, mutability and functionality to electronic database which has increased its commercial value and attempts to suggest a better protection to electronic databases that non electronic databases. Private or personal database may have less chance of commercial exploitation which furthers an argument that private databases should be kept out of the purview of new legislation. Any unauthorized interference to a private database needs to be addressed through privacy law and not through intellectual property law. Regarding scientific databases two avenues are open, one is to remove them from the definition of database so that they cannot be commodified and the other is to include them within the definition of databases but with detailed permitted use. If databases created for scientific, educational and technical purposes are kept out of new legislation, it has to be remembered that a database created from the content of these database also should not be covered under this legislation. If necessary there should be contractual arrangement to prohibit further commercial exploitation of the content of these databases made for scientific, educational and technical purpose. The same can be applied in case of government databases were also further commercialization using content of databases needs to be prevented. Whereas database created for commercial purposes should come within the definition of database in the new legislation.

Guideline 8: There should be contractual arrangement to prohibit further commercial exploitation of the content of databases created for scientific and educational purposes.

For commercial database, there should be provision for fair use and compulsory licensing for protecting public interest and dilute monopolistic behaviour. Thus the definition of database in the new law should look as follows—database is collection of information, fact or works developed for commercial exploitation, created by substantial investment in selection, arrangement and presentation and can be accessed its content individually but does not include private databases, paper based database, database made for education, scientific and technical purposes. Creators of database made for commercial exploitation should be allowed to commercially exploit their product and prevent unauthorized access and utilization. They should be allowed to use both contractual and technological measure to achieve the desired goal. Generally the objectives of creator of database are to permit authorized user to use database, to prevent unauthorized person from using it and to prevent competitors from copying it.

Guideline 9: There should be compulsory licensing for sole source databases.

Commercial use needs to be interpreted carefully. It includes not only commercial licensing but also creator's own use in commerce. To achieve the desired objectives of creator of database, only contractual terms are not enough as the unauthorized person trying to have access is not bound by any contractual terms and thus contractual terms should be supplemented by intellectual property instrument. A proprietary or quasi-proprietary remedy will be very useful in case of unauthorized access to the databases. Technological protection like encryption, water marks, and time-limited software will be useful for controlling unauthorized access. Sometimes technological measures turn out to be more effective than legal measures. It is also true every technological protection can be crossed by another superior technology. For best possible protection law and technology must work together. This techno-legal protection should be encouraged so long it does not interfere with the public domain and once it gains a tendency of monopolizing information to the detriment of public domain, law must strike it down. Time limit to be prescribed for the new legislation can be based on either by calculating time, effort and cost invested in creating the database, or by giving database creator a commercial head start over his competitor, or by an arbitrary number of years.

Guideline 10: New Legislation should offer protection for a short and limited period to offer commercial head start over competitors.

To conclude any database debate must point out which database is to be protected and on what basis and it must also address the need for governmental supervision in commercial exploitation of databases so that promotion of commercial activity does not take place at the cost of public interest. The new legislation must balance between private interest and public right while ensuring commercial need of database producers, access to information and prevention of unfair competition.

Bibliography

Statutes and Reports

Arrow K J (1962) Economic welfare and the allocation of resources for invention, the rate and direction of inventive activity: economic and social factors. A report of the National Bureau of Economic Research, p 609. In: Hilty, supra note 264, at 130
Berne Convention
Collection of Information Antipiracy Act, HR 354,
Consumer and Investor Access to Information Act HR 1858
Convention of Council of Europe on Trans-frontier Television, 1989
Copyright Act (1957)
Copyright Act (1911) (UK)
Copyright Act (1956) (UK)
Dingley B (2005) US periodical prices. http://www.ala.org/ala/alctscontent/alctspubsbucket/alctsresources/general/periodicalsindex/05USPPI.pdf. Accessed 15 April 2009
EU Directive (96/9/EC)
First Evaluation of Directive 96/9/EC on Legal Protection of Databases, Commission of the European Communities, Brussels, 12th Dec 2005
German Copyright Act
Hugenholtz B (2004) Abuse of database right—sole source information bank under the EU database directive. In: Conference on 'antitrust, patent and copyright', Paris
Maurer M (1999) Raw knowledge: protecting technical databases for science and industry. In: Workshop on promoting access to scientific and technical data for the public interest: an assessment of policy options, National Academy of Sciences, January 1999
OECD Report on the Scientific Publishing Industry, Digital Broadband Content: Scientific Publishing, September, 2005
Report of the Registrar of Copyright on the General Revision of the U.S Copyright Law, 87th Congress, 1st Session, p. 9
The Database Investment and Intellectual property Piracy Act. HR 3531,
The Impact of Protection of Non-Original Databases on the Countries of Latin America and the Caribbean, WIPO, Standing Committee on Copyright and Related Rights, Eights Sessions, Geneva, 2002
U.K. Commission on Intellectual Property Rights, Integrating Intellectual Property Rights and Development Policy. http://www.iprcommission.org/graphic/documents/final_report.htm. Accessed 13 April 2009, p 107
US Copyright Office, Report on legal protection of databases, 1997
World Information Technology and Services Alliance, The Global Economy, www.witsa.org/press/degitalplanetpressrelease_rev.doc

A. Mazumder, *Database Law*, DOI 10.1007/978-981-10-2200-5

Workshop on Promoting Access to Scientific and Technical Data for the Public Interest: An Assessment of Policy Options, National Academy of Sciences, January, 1999

WIPO Standing Committee on Copyright and Related Rights (2002) The impact of protection of non-original databases on the countries of Latin America and the Caribbean, Eights Sessions, Geneva, p 5

Articles

Aplin T (2001) Case comment Australia: infringement—yellow and white pages. EIPR

Baron P (2001) Back to future: learning from the past in the database debate. Ohio State L J 62:880

Baron P (2001) Back to the future: learning from the past in the database debate. Ohio State L J 62:912

Band J, Gowdy JS (2006) Sui Generis database protection, has its time come? www.tjdl.cn/Dlib/June97/06band.html (Visited On 28.08.06)

Belleflamme P (2003) Pricing information goods in the presence of copying. In: Gordon WJ, Watt R (eds) The economics of copyright, Edward Elgar, U.K., p 26

Book Review of Christophe Geiger (2006) E.I.P.R. 357

Boyarski JR (1999) The highest of feist: protections for collections of information and the possible federalization of hot news. Cardozo L Rev 21:871

Breyer S (1970) The uneasy case for copyright: a study of copyright in books, photocopies and computer programs. Harv L Rev 84:281

Brown MM, Bryan RM, Conley JM (1999) Database protection in digital world. Rich JL Tech Symp 6(1)

Casamiquela RJ (2002) Contractual assent and enforceability in cyberspace. Berk Tech L J 17:475

Castens DW (1994) Legal protection of computer software: patents, copyrights and trade secrets. J Contemp L 20:13

Chafee (1940) Unfair competition. Harv L R 53:1289

Chen Y, Puttitanun T (2002) Intellectual property rights and innovation in developing countries. Center For Economic Analysis, Department Of Economics, University Of Colorado

Cohen JE (1998) Copyright and jurisprudence of self help. Berk Tech L J 13:1089

Colston C (2001) Sui Generis Database Right : Ripe for Review, JILT 3. http://www.elj.warwick.ac.uk/jilt/01-3/colston.html

Conley JM, Bemelmans K (1997) Intellectual property implications of multimedia products: a case study. Info Comm Tech L 6:3

Conley JM, Brown MM, Bryan RM (2000) Database protection in a digital world: why the united states should decline to follow the European model. Info Comm Tech L9(1):27

Conley JM, Brown MM, Bryan RM (2000) Database protection in a digital world: why the united states should decline to follow the European model. Info Comm Tech L 9(1):49

Davies S (1998) Computer program claims. EIPR 11:429

Davison M, Hugenholtz P (2005) Football fixtures, horserace, and spin-offs. EIPR p 114

Denicola RC (1981) Copyright in collection of facts: a theory for the protection of non fiction literary work. Colum L Rev 81:516

Derclaye E (2002) What is a database. J World Intell Property 5:986

Devid PA (2000) A tragedy of the public knowledge 'commons'? global science, intellectual property and the digital technology boomerang. Oxford Ip Research Center, Working Paper No, 04/00, 2000. P4

Djavaherian D (1998) Hot news and no cold facts: NBA V. motorola and the protection of database contents. Rich JL Tech

Fisher W (1988) Reconstructing the fair use doctrine. Harv L Rev 101:1661

Francione (1986) Facing the nation: the standard for copyright infringement and fair use of factual works. Univ PAL Rev 134:519

Forrai G (1971) Confidential information—A general survey. Syd L R 6:382

Garrigues C (1997) Database: a subject matter for copyright or for a neighbouring right regime. EIPR3
Geiger C (2006) Copyright and free access to information: for a fair balance of interest in a globalize world. E.I.P.R. 366
Ginsburg A (1990) A tale of two copyrights: literary property in revolutionary France and America. Tul L Rev 64:991
Ginsburg JC (1990) Creation and commercial value: copyright protection of works of information. Colum L Rev 90:1903
Ginsburg J (1997) Copyright, common law and *Sui Generis* Protection of databases in the united states and abroad. Univ Cin L Rev 66:151
Ginsburg J (2001) Copyright and control over new technologies of dissemination. Colum L Rev 101:1613
Gorman (1963) Copyright protection for the collection and representation of facts. Harv L Rev 76:1569
Gorman (1982) Fact or fancy? The implication for copyright. J Copy Soc 560
Gordon (1989) an inquiry into the merit of copyright: the challenges of consistency, consent and encouragement theory. Stan L Rev 41:1343
Greenbaum DS (2003) The database debate: in support of an inequitable solution. Alb L J Sci Tech 13:431
Haungs M J (1990) Copyright of factual compilations: public policy and the first amendment. Colum J L Soc Prob 23:347
Heller MA (1998) The tragedy of anti commons. Harv L Rev 111(3):621–688
Hilty RM (2006) Five lessons about copyright in the information society. J Copy Soc USA 53:103
Hohfeld (1913) Some fundamental legal conceptions as applied in judicial reasoning. Yale L J 23:16
Hughes (1989) The philosophy of intellectual property. Geo L J 77:287
Hugenholtz B (2004) Abuse of database right—sole source information bank under the EU database directive, conference on antitrust, patent and copyright, Paris, 2004
Hunsucker GM (1997) The European database directive: regional stepping stone to an international model? Fordham Intell Prop Media Ent L J 7:697
Hurt RM, Schuman RM (1966) The economic rationale of the copyright. AM Eco Rev 56:435
Jones G (1970) Restitution of benefits obtained in breach of author's confidence. LQR 86:463
Kitch (1980) The law and economics of rights in valuable information. J Legal Stud 9:683
Kreiss RA (1995) Accessibility and commercialization in copyright theory UCLA L Rev 43:1
Ku RSR (2002) The creative destruction of copyright: napster and the new economics of digital technology. Univ Chicago L Rev 69:263
Ladd (1983) The harm of the concept of harm in copyright. J Copy Soc 30:421
Landes WM, Posner RA (1989) An Economic analysis of copyright law. J Legal Stud 18:325
Leistner M (2000) The legal protection of telephone directories relating to the new database maker's right. 31 IIC 950
Leistner M (2003) Creating cyberspace—intellectual property law and competition law protection of the web designer, Iic. 34(2): 138
Leistner (2005) Comment To Bhb V. Hill, 36 Iic 592, p 593
Libling (1978) The concept of property: property in intangibles. LQR 94:103
Liebowitz (1985) Copying and indirect appropriability: photocopying of journals. J Pol Econ 93:945
Laddie H (1996) Copyright: over-strength, over-regulated, over-rated? EIPR 5:253
Lipton J (2002) The E.U database right and university teaching material. J Info L Tech 1
Lipton J (2003) Balancing private right and public policies: reconceptualising property in databases. Berk Tech L J 18:773
Litman J (1990) The public domain. Emory L Rev 39:965
Lunney G S (1996) Reexamining copyright's incentive-access paradigm. V and L Rev 49:483

Maurer SM, Scotchmer S (1999) Intellectual property rights: database protection: is it broken and should we fix it? Science 284:789

Maurer SM, Hugenholtz PB, Onsrud HJ (2001) Europe's database experiment. Sci 294:789

Menell (1989) An analysis of the scope of copyright protection for application programs. Stan L Rev 41:1045

Monnotti A (1992) Copyright protection of computerized databases. Austl Intell Prop J 3:135

Nimmer D, Menell P, Mc Gimsey D (2003) Pre-existing confusion in copyright's work for hire doctrine. J Copy Soc 50:399

Oram A (2000) The sap and the syrup of the informaion age: coping with database protection laws. Comput L R Internet L Bus 1(5)

Patterson L, Joyce C (1969) Monopolizing the law: the scope of copyright protection for law reports and statutory compilations. UCLA L Rev 36:719

Plotkin M (1999) The times they are changin'. Vend J Int L Pract 1:46

Polivy DR (1998) Feist applied: imagination protects but perspiration persists—the bases of copyright protection for factual compilations. Fordham Intell Prop Media Ent L J 8:773

Position Paper By The Max Planck Institute For Intellectual Property, Competition And Tax Law On First Evaluation Of Directive 96/9/Ec On The Legal Protection Of Databases.P.1

Reichman JH (1992) Electronic information tools—the outer edge of world intellectual property law. Univ Dayton L Rev 17:797

Reichman JH (1995) Charting the collapse of the patent—copyright dichotomy: premises for a restructured international property system. Cardozo Arts Ent L J 13:475

Reichman JH, Samuelson P (1997) Intellectual property rights in data? V L Rev 50:51

Reichman JH, Samuelson P (1997) Intellectual property rights in data? http://www.eon.law.harvard.edu/H2o/Property/Alternatives/Reichman.html

Response To The European Commission On The Evaluation Of Eu Rules On Database, European Bureau Of Library, Information And Document Association,www.eblida.org/Position/Database_Response_March06.htm (Dated. 15.5.06)

Riis T (2002) Economic impact of the protection of non-original databases in developing countries and countries in transition, standing committee on copyright and related rights, seventh session, Geneva

Samuelson (1986) Allocating ownership right in computer—generated works. Univ Pitt L Rev 47:1185

Simon C V (1995) Feist or famine: American database copyright as an economic model for the European union. Brook J Int L 20:729

Stuckey JE (1981) The equitable action for breach of confidence: is information ever property? Syd L R 9:402

Suthersanen U (2000–2001) A comparative review of database protection in the European Union and United States. The ATRIP Papers 2000–2001

Swanson (1988) The role of disclosure in modern copyright law. J Pat Tra Off Soc 70:217

Thakur (2001) Database protection in the European Union and the United States. IPQ 100

Tyson L, Sherry E (1997) Statutory protection for databases: economic and public policy issues', House Judiciary Committee Hearing, 23rd October, 1997. http://wwwhouse.gov/Judiciary/41118.htm

Vandervelde (1980) The new property of the nineteenth century : the development of the modern concept of property. Buff L R 29:325

Warren SD, Brandeis LD (1890) The right to privacy. Harv L R 4:193

Weinrib A S (1988) Information and property. Toronto L J 38:121

Wolken JC (1998) Just the facts, ma'am: a case for uniform federal regulation of database in the new information age. Syrac L Rev 48:1263

Yen AC (1990) Restoring natural law: copyright as labour and possession. Ohio St L J 51:517

Zimmerman DL (1994) Copyright in cyberspace: don't throw out the public interest with the bath water. Ann Surv Am L 403

Books

Birrell A (1971) Seven lectures on the law and history of copyright in books, vol 195. Kelley, New York
Bainbridge D (2002) Intellectual property. Peasrson Education Ltd. 5th edn
Bentley L, Sherman B (2001) Intellectual property law. Oxford University Press
Clarke L (1990) Confidentiality and the law. Lloyd's Of London Press Ltd.
Cornish (1999) Intellectual property: patents, copyright, trade marks and allied rights. Sweet & Maxwell
Cornish W, Llewelyn GID (2003) Intellectual property. Sweet & Maxwell
Curtis GT (2005) Treatise on the law of copyright in books; dramatic and musical compositions; letter and other manuscripts, engravings and sculptures; as enacted and administered in England And America. Little Brown & Co, Boston
Drahos P, Braitwaite J (2002) Information feudalism. Earthscan publications, London
Drone ES (1879) A treatise on the law of property in intellectual productions in Great Britain And The United States. Little Brown & Co, Boston
Epstein MA (1999) Epstein on intellectual property. Aspen Law & Business
Eric Stastic, Patent Or Perish. Althos Publishing
Feather J (2004) The information society. Facet Publishing
Goldstein P (2000) Copyright. Aspen Law & Business, 2nd edn
Griffiths J, Suthersanan U (2005) Copyright and free speech. Oxford University Press
Halpern SW (2002) Copyright law. Carolina Academic Press
Hugenholtz P (1996) Adapting copyright to the information superhighway', the future of copyright in a digital era. Kluwer
Kaplan B (2005) An unhurried view of copyright. Lexis Nexis Matthew Bender
Leaffer M (1999) Understanding copyright law, 3rd edn. p 428
Lessig L (2001) The future of ideas: the fate of the commons in a connected world
Lloyd I (2000) Information technology law. Butterworths, London
Locke J (1690) Two treaties of government, Book Ii, Ch. V
Mercuro N, Medema S (1997) Economics and the law: from posner to post-modernism, p 96
Nimmer MB, Nimmer D (1987) Nimmer on copyright: a treatise on the law of literary; musical and artistic property and the protection of ideas. Mathew Bender, New York
Patterson LR (1968) Copyright in historical perspective
Rees C, Chalton S (1998) Database law. Jordans
Ricketson S (1987) The berne convention for the protection of literary and artistic works. Kluwer
Shapiro C, Varian H (1999) Information rules: strategic guide to the network economy. Harvard Business School Press, Boston
Sherman B, Bently L (1999) The making of modern intellectual property law: the British experience (1760–1911)
Suthersanen U (2000–2001) A comparative review of database protection in the European Union And United States. The Atrip Papers 2000–2001
The Concise Oxford Dictionary Of Current English, 294 (8th edn) 1997
Torremans P (2004) Holyoak And Torremans intellectual property law. Oxford, p 538
Walterscheid E (2000) The nature of the intellectual property clause in the historical perspective
Williams ME (1999) The state of databases today

Cases

Autocaps Pvt Ltd. v. Pro-Kit Pvt. Ltd. (1996) 46 IPR 339
Baker v. Selden, (1880) 101 US 99
Banks v. McDivitt, 2F Cas. 759 (1875)
Barfield v. Nicholson (1824) 57 ER 245

BBC v. Wireless League Gazette Publishing Co. (1926) Ch.433
Bell House Ltd.v City Wall Properties Ltd (1966) 2 W.L.R. 1323
Blacklock v. Pearson (1915) 2 Ch. 376
Bleistein v. Donaldson Lithographing Co, 188 U.S 239 (1903)
Boardman v. Phipps (1967) 2 A.C. 46
British Horseracing Board Ltd. v. William Hill Organisation Ltd. [C-203/02]
Callaghan v. Myers, 128 US 617 (1888)
Campbell v. Acuff Rose Music Inc. 510 US 569
Cary v. Kearsley, 170 Eng. Rep. 679 (1802)
CCH v. Law Society of Upper Canada (2004) SCC 13
Cramp v. Smythson (1944) AC 329
Data Access Corporation v. Powerflex Services Pvt Ltd (1999) 73 ALJR 1435
Deta Nominees Pct. Ltd. v. Viscount Plastics Pvt. Ltd, (1979) V.R 167
Dun & Bradstreet Ltd. v. Typesetting Facilities Ltd (1992) FSR 320
Eastern Book Company and others v. Navin J. Desai and Another (2002) (25) PTC 641 Del
Eldred v. Ashcroft 537 US 186
E.I. Du Pont de Nemours v. Masland (1917) 244 U.S 100
Elanco Product Ltd v. Mandops Ltd 1980 RPC 213
Emerson v. Davies. 8 F. Cas 615 (C. C. D. 1845) (No. 4436)
Exchange Telegraph Co. Ltd. v. Central News Ltd. (1897) 2 Ch. 48
Exchange Telegraph Co. Ltd. v. Gregory & Co. (1896) 1 QB 147
Exchange Telegraph v. Howard (1906) 22 T.L.R. 375
Faccenda Chicken Ltd. v. Fowler (1986) 1 All E.R. 617
Falsom v. Mars, 9 F. Cas. at 345
Federal Commissioner of Taxation v. United Aircraft Corporation, 68 C.L.R 525
Feist v. Rural (1991) 111 S.Ct 1282
Financial Information Inc. v. Moody's Investors Serv. Inc. 808 F 2d. 204 (2nd Cir.1986)
Fixtures Marketing Ltd. v. Svenska Spel AB C-338/02
Franklin v. Giddins (1978) Qd. R. 72
Football League v. Littlewoods (1959) Ch. 637
F.W. Dodge Co. v. Construction Information Co. 66 N.E. 204 (1903)
Govindan v. Gopalakrishnan, AIR 1955 Mad 391
Greyhound Services Ltd. v. Wilf Gilbert Ltd (1994) FSR 723
Gyles v. Wilcox 26 Eng. Rep. 489 (1740)
Harper & Row Publishers Inc. v. Nation Enterprises, 471 US 539 (1985)
Hartfield v. Peterson, 91 F.ed 998 (2nd Cir. 1937)
Health GmbH & Co. v. NDC Health GmbH & Co. (C-418/01)
Herbert Morris Ltd v. Saxelby (1916) 1 A.C. 688
Hoehling v. Universal City Studios Inc. 618 F.2d 972 (2d Cir. 1980)
Hogg v. Scott (1874) L.R. 18 Eq 444
Hotten v. Arthur, 1 H& M 603
Huie v. National Broadcasting Co., 184 F. Supp 198
Ichard v. Frangoulis (1971) 2 All E.R 461
IMS Health GmbH & Co. OHG v. NDC Health GmbH & Co.KG; ECJ C-418/01
Independent Television Publications v. Time Out—[1984] FSR 64
International News Service v. Associated Press, 248 US 215 (1918)
Jeffrey v. Rolls-Royce Ltd, (1960) 40 Tax Cas 443
Jeffery v. Boosey 10 Eng. Rep. 703
Jeweler's Circular Publishing Co. v. Keystone Publishing Co. 281 F.83 (2d Cir. 1922)
J.L.Mott Iron Works v. Clow, 82 F. 316(7th Cir. 1897)
Kargos v. Associated Press, 937 F.2d. 700 (2nd Circuit 1991)
Kelly v. Morris, L.R. 1 Eq. 696

Key Publications Inc. v. Chinatown Today Publishing Enterprises Inc 945 F. 2d 509 (2nd Cir 1991)
Krouse v. Chrysler Canada Ltd (1972) 25 D. L. R. (3d) 49
Kuddle Toy Inc. v. Pussycat Toy Co. 183 U.S.P.Q. 642
L.Batlin & Sons v. Snyder, 536 F.2d 99 (2nd Cir.)
Ladbroke v. William Hills (1964) 1 WLR 273
Leon v. Pacific Telephon & Telegraph Co., 91 F.2d 484 (9th Cir. 1937)
Leslie v. Young (1894) AC 335
Longman v. Winchester, 16 Ves. 269, Eng Rep. 987 (1809)
Lotus Development Corporation v. Paperback Software International 740 F. Supp. 221
Macmillan & Co v. Cooper AIR 1924 PC 75
Macmillan v. Suresh Chander Deb, 1890 ILR 17 Cal 951
Mathew Bender & Co. v West Publishing Co158 F. 3d 693, 2nd Circuit, 1998
Mathewson v. Stockdale, 33 Eng. Rep. 103 (1806)
Mawman v.Tegg (1826) 38 ER 868
Mazer v. Stein, 347 US 201 (1954)
Millar v. Taylor, (1769) 98 E.R 201
Miller v. Universal City Studios Inc., 460 F. Supp. 984
N.T. Ragunathan v. All India Reporter, AIR 1971 Bom 78
National Business Lists Inc. v. Dun & Bradstreet Inc. 552 F.Supp. 89
Oxford v. Moss (1978) 68 Crim. App. Rep. 183
Printers & Finishers Ltd. v. Holloway, (1964) 3 All E.R. 731
Purefoy v. Sykes Boxall (1955) 72 RPC 89
R.G. Anand v. Delux Films AIR 1978 SC 1613
Radio Telefis Eireann (RTE) and Independent Television Publication (ITP) Ltd. v. Commission of Europe Communities, C-214/91 P, April 6, 1995
Rolls-Royce Ltd. v. Jeffrey (1962) 1 All E.R. 801
Roworth v. Wilkes, 170 Eng. Rep. 889 (1807)
R. v. Mc Ewen, (1947) 2 D. L. R. 62
R v. Offley, (1986) 45 Alta.L.R. (2d) 23
R v. Stewart, (1983) 149 D.L.R. (3d) 583
Rockford Map Publishers Inc. v. Directory Services Co. 768 F2d. 145 (7th Cir 1985)
S.K. Dutt v. Law Book Co., AIR 1954 All 570
Schroeder v. William Morrow & Co., 566 F.2d 3 (7th Cir. 1977)
Seager v. Copydex (1967) 1 W.L.R. 923
Sheldon v. Metro-Goldwyn Pictures Corp., 81 F.2d 49 (2nd Cir.)
Shyam Lal v. Gaya Prasad, AIR 1971 All 192
Sony Corp of America v. Universal City Studio Inc. 464 US 417
Story v. Halcombe, 23 F. Cas. 171(C.C.D. Ohio 1847) (No. 13,497)
Stowe v. Thomas, 23 F. Cas. 201 (C.C.E.D. Penn. 1853) (No. 13,514)
Tele-Direct (1997) 154 DLR 4th 328
Tele Direct (Publications) Inc. v. American Business Information Inc. (1996) 35 IPR 121
Telstra Corp Ltd. v. Desktop Mktg Sys Pvt. Ltd (2001) FCA612
The Trademark Cases, 100 US 82 (1879); 111 US 53 (1884)
Toksvig v. Bruce Publishing Co, 181 F.2d 664 (7th Cir. 1950)
Triangle Publications Inc. v. Sports Eye, Inc. 415 F. Supp. 682 (1976)
Twentieth Century Music Corp v. Aiken, 422 US 151 (1975)
University of London Press Ltd., v. University Tutorial Press Ltd., [1916] 2 Ch. 601
U.S. v. Bottone, 365 F. 2d 389(1966)
United States v. LaMacchia, 871 F. Supp 535 (1994)
Van dale v. Romme (1991) Ned.Jur.608

Victor Lalli Enters Inc. v. Big Red Apple Inc. 936 F 2d 671 (2nd Cir. 1991)
W.H. Anderson v. Baldwin Law Publishing Co., 27 F.2d 82 (6th Cir. 1928)
Walter v. Lane, [1900] AC 539
Waterlow v. Reed, [1992] FSR 409
Webb v. Powers 29 F. Cas at 517
Wheaton v. Peters 33 US 591
Yale Univ. Press v. Row, Peterson & Co. 40 F.2d 290 (S.D.N.Y. 1930)

MIX
Papier aus verantwortungsvollen Quellen
Paper from responsible sources
FSC® C105338

If you have any concerns about our products,
you can contact us on
ProductSafety@springernature.com

In case Publisher is established outside the EU,
the EU authorized representative is:
Springer Nature Customer Service Center GmbH
Europaplatz 3, 69115 Heidelberg, Germany

Printed by Libri Plureos GmbH
in Hamburg, Germany